FROM THE BOARDROOM TO THE BEDROOM...
FROM HIGH SOCIETY TO HOLLYWOOD ...
FROM CALL-GIRLS TO CONGRESSMEN ...
HERE'S ALL THE DIRT THAT'S FIT TO PRINT!

The terrifying account of Claudine Longet's shooting of
Spider Sabich in their Rocky Mountain hideaway ...
Why did she do it?

The shocking story of Elvis's manager, Colonel Tom Parker ...
How did he cheat the King out of millions of dollars?

The unknown facts behind the arrest of society doctor, Sam
Sheppard ...
Was he a murderer or a victim?

The titillating tale of Linda Lovelace ...
When she was finally ungagged, did the star of *Deep
Throat* tell the truth?

You'll find the answers and much, much more in

SCANDAL!

A wild, irreverent, and indecently witty look at the
headlines that rocked the worlds of business, politics,
show-biz, and high society — and kept millions of readers
gasping.

Janet Street-Porter

A DELL TRADE PAPERBACK

A DELL TRADE PAPERBACK

Published by
Dell Publishing Co., Inc.
1 Dag Hammarskjold Plaza
New York, New York 10017

A different version of this work was first published in
Great Britain by Penguin Books Ltd.

Dell ® TM 681510, Dell Publishing Co., Inc.

ISBN: 0–440–58260–1

Printed in the United States of America
First U.S.A. printing — August 1983

Designed by Philip Hall and David Grogan

For Frank

Contents

Acknowledgements

Research: Linda Sonntag. Picture research: Diana Korchien. Thanks to Tom Kelly of the *Daily Mail;* John Frost for his Historical Newspaper Service, and for his patience and enthusiasm; journalists and other friends who helped, including Christopher Finch, David May, Tony Elliott, Quentin Falk, Geoffrey Wansell, 'World in Action', Peter Murphy, London Weekend Television, Christopher Ward, Ed Victor, Chris Rees of the *Daily Mail,* Mike Molloy of the *Daily Mirror,* the *Daily Express,* and London Express News.

PHOTOGRAPHS

Thanks are due to the following: Associated Newspapers: p. 106; Associated Press: pp. 91, 96, 133, 134, 135, 152, 164, 166, 196; BBC: p. 61; BBC Hulton Library: pp. 42, 64, 68, 195; Camera 5: pp. 108, 124; Camera Press: pp. 136, 144, 167, 168; Mark Ellidge/*Sunday Times*: p. 109; Features Ltd: p. 176; John Kobal Collection: pp. 15, 18, 24, 30, 37, 41, 48, 57, 63, 74, 78; John Topham Picture Library: pp. 110, 114, 115, 126, 127, 194; Kemsley Pix: p. 174; Keystone Press: pp. 102, 111, 176, 180, 219; London Express News: p. 17; National Motor Museum: p. 94; Newspix: p. 138; Photopress: p. 206; Popperfoto: pp. 14–15, 18, 32, 59, 67, 79, 100, 114, 151, 153, 154, 165, 198; Press Association: pp. 144, 183; *Private Eye*: pp. 98, 138; Rex Features: p. 112; Ronald Grant Archive: pp. 29, 31, 34, 40, 54, 62, 87, 88; Scope Features: p. 46; *Sunday Pictorial*: p. 204; Syndication International: pp. 44, 142, 145, 162, 179, 184, 185, 191, 205, 215; United Press International: pp. 58, 89, 133, 134, 209, 216; Wide World Photos: pp. 19, 20, 21, 23, 26, 27, 28, 49, 50, 51, 70, 71, 72, 73, 80, 81, 82, 83, 84, 85, 86, 116, 117, 118, 119, 120, 121, 122, 130, 131, 132, 141, 155, 156, 157, 158, 169, 171, 186, 187, 188, 189, 202, 203, 208, 210, 211, 212, 213, 214, 218.

Introduction

SCANDAL: Noun. 1. A state or action which offends other people's idea of what is right and proper. 2. A public feeling or action caused by such behaviour. 3. True or false talk which brings harm, shame or disrespect to another.

Longman New Generation Dictionary (1981)

This book could be subtitled 'Prat-falls of the Famous', for what the definition doesn't let on is that a scandal is a very enjoyable object of interest. Why else would newspapers be filled day after day with stories that eager journalists hope (and the victims fear) will turn into a full-bodied vintage *scandal*? An incident which starts off as a run-of-the-mill piece of information becomes a scandal when the first denials take place. Scandals are the product of pyramids of lies that suddenly collapse, leaving businesses bust, the famous caught with their pants down in the company of someone else's husband or wife.

Although this book is split into four sections – Show-business, Politics, Finance and Hijinks – there are one or two common themes that run through the majority of the stories. The sections tend to apply to the victim's line of work or social position, but all scandals contain some of the following elements: bribery, sex, lies, power and fame. If a sanitation man takes $20 in cash for taking away your rubbish, then it's not a scandal. But if Spiro Agnew is accused of accepting up to $100,000 in bribes and he's the Vice-President of the United States, then Agnew, although an unattractive individual, will be the face on the front pages. Big people can be toppled by small things; in the case of Agnew, one charge of tax evasion. But you can guarantee that what was discussed in court was just the tip of the iceberg. So big sums of money don't always make big scandals – it's all relative to the individual's social position.

Likewise with sex: wife-swapping in Muncie or the activities of bored housewives with milkmen in Miami are not the stuff of scandal – even though tired copywriters may use it in their headlines and in ads for the *Sun* or *Daily Star* on television. However, when a Congressman (Wayne Hays) has on his payroll a 'secretary' who can't type, doesn't answer the phone, and who spends her time at 'work' between the sheets with her boss, then that's a scandal. Scandal alters your perception of people and events. When former Vice-President Nelson Rockefeller died in the company of a glamorous 'researcher', his respectable image as a senior politician and philanthropist suffered something of an instant rewrite, as his family tried (unsuccessfully) to hush up his long-running affair and the fact that he died with his mistress rather than his wife at his side. Another political name with an image problem is Kennedy. But in the Kennedys' case – from father Joe's fling with Gloria Swanson right through to John, Bobby and Marilyn Monroe – unfaithfulness was almost a family motto. The Kennedys liked to risk scandal by existing on a heady diet of sex and political power – and as much of both as possible.

Another interesting aspect of sexual scandals is how they belong to a particular period. After the Second World War homosexuals were hounded, as it was thought there had been an increase in offences during the 1940s. There was no major press campaign for a change in the law – not surprising, as it gave popular newspapers plenty to write about. Kiss-and-tell memoirs really took off in the late seventies. They had previously been rather tame affairs, the subjects often being famous stars past their prime and anxious to cushion their fading years with a few crispy notes. But the new breed of memoir-writer had been told by editors and their agents that the more sex they included, the more the copy would be worth. A new genre was discovered – Britt Ekland's particularly young ex-lover told readers that his paramour enjoyed making him wear her knickers and eye shadow ... *men* were starting to fight the tidal wave of actress-anecdotes and call-girl chronicles at last. At least, men who could remember the nasty details that hungry scandal-hooked readers crave ...

I've said that sex and power are linked in many scandals, and nowhere more so than in the worlds of showbusiness and politics. Many powerful people undoubtedly think that their position alone will deter any adversaries or slighted parties from actually challenging them or mud-slinging in public. The ones who do cause scandals.

Business men often wield power off the backs of thousands of small investors. What many people find scandalous is their attitude to their position. They often use the company's money as if it is their own. Another element in a business scandal is when the central figure, in order to minimize the collapse or failure he is connected with, bills his career as 'helping' others in some way, promoting some vital service that people cannot possibly manage without. In fact, they are helping themselves, and when the press find out, it becomes a full-blown scandal. As account books are peeled back to reveal what the 'help' has cost, they are stripped of their emperor's clothes.

What kind of behaviour constitutes a scandal depends on whether the characters sit on their bottoms in Congress or lounge by their pools in Beverly Hills, and whether they are married to members of high society or living with rock-and-roll singers. It takes a lot more on the Richter scale of ludicrous behaviour to constitute a rock-and-roll scandal – so jaded are the participants that only a lifetime devoted to outrageous posturing culminating in a nasty death seems to qualify. Step forward Sid Vicious, the winner of the prize! In political circles the hint of an ill-judged affair (for example, Wilbur Mills and Fanne Foxe) can be considered more scandalous than in Hollywood. A Canadian Prime Minister's wife with a penchant for the jet-set life is nowadays not even considered a scandal, just a figure of fun. A royal friendship can be scandalous, just because it is considered inappropriate.

As a profession, politicians seem to pick the most scandalous friends – and indulge in the most bizarre behaviour under stress. Reagan's National Security Adviser, Richard Allen, seems to have ruined his career for a paltry $1,000. Billy Carter, when told his associations weren't helping his brother, more or less said he couldn't care less and opened another can of beer. Oscar Levant once wrote, 'Strip away the phoney tinsel of Hollywood and you find real tinsel underneath.' That applies to Hollywood *scandal* too. No matter how bizarre the circumstances seem at first sight, the more you read, the more filth and muck will lie beneath. The tinsel in Hollywood fills volumes of 'confidential' magazines and reams of gossip papers, and is finally rounded off with the selective books the stars have ghosted about themselves. Only in the last ten years have books started to be written about Hollywood from the inside, stripping away the second layer of tinsel and starting to get to grips with what lies beneath. When Christina Crawford wrote *Mommie Dearest*, the scandal it caused in Hollywood revealed how anxious the film industry is to preserve a false history of itself, a history based on retouched photos and vacuous studio handouts.

The same stripping away of myth has being going on in the rock world too. We haven't expected our rock stars to be private saints for many a decade now, but somehow the name Presley seemed to stand above all that was cheap and tawdry in the pop music scene. Elvis had been elevated – by his publicists, by journalists, and by fans eager to latch on to a white male stud (they thought) who seemed to epitomize the American dream of achievable success beyond one's wildest imaginings – on to a pedestal from which it seemed impossible to dislodge him. Then along came a writer, Albert Goldman, with nerves of steel, no preconceptions about his subject, and an insatiable appetite for interviews. Three and a half years after he started work, Goldman's *Elvis* hit the bookstands and the King's image was never the same again. His *scandalous* revelation – that Elvis rarely made it with girls normally, was in fact a voyeur and constant masturbator, a man who sexually never even got out of short pants – sold a lot of books, enraged a lot of people, but most of all tarred Mr Presley with the brush of scandal that means that when you hear an Elvis song, he'll just never seem the same again.

The scandals in this book are simply my personal favourites. Some stories have not been included because they have been dealt with at length elsewhere and are too complex to be told in the space available. Perhaps Watergate is the most obvious of these. Medical subjects have been omitted, because I felt that they constituted grounds for moral concern and did not sit easily amongst the subject-matter dealt with here. Examples would be thalidomide and the fight for damages, the Seveso poison-gas disaster in Italy, Rely Tampons and toxic shock, and price-fixing and Hoffman La Roche. Sporting scandals have not been dealt with except in a business context; there are many, and books have appeared specifically on the subject. Likewise spies – I am aware of omissions, partly through lack of space and partly because any book like this has to be selective.

Murders have not been included unless they involved famous people and scandalous circumstances. Violence doesn't come within the scope of the book. Silly, sensuous, and sensational behaviour does.

Showbiz

Showbiz Affairs and Marriages

The affairs and marriages described here don't have much in common. What is surprising, however, is that within the fickle environment of show business people marry and divorce with consummate ease, and yet affairs keep burning on a slow fuse for many years. The press is always ready to seize on such stories, although William Randolph Hearst and Marion Davies, who spent over thirty years together, made sure it never got mentioned in *his* papers. George Formby expected the press to believe a story as tall as one of his songs: the three-day courtship of his long-standing secret girlfriend, Pat. Whether it's for the long-haul, the short-term, on paper or on the sly, they pursue it with the utmost enthusiasm.

Daddy and Marion

WILLIAM RANDOLPH HEARST was already immensely rich and successful when he met Marion Davies, chorus girl, in New York in 1915. She was just eighteen and had danced her way through several Broadway shows without ever playing a part of any note, while W.R. owned a huge chain of newspapers and had been thwarted only in his attempt to become a politician. With Marion, however, he was to create a new project that would keep him happily occupied for many years: he decided to make her a star. But there was a price, and from the moment he gave her his first present, a Tiffany watch, Marion was under no illusions what the man in his early fifties wanted from *her*.

SUGAR DADDY

Hearst set up Cosmopolitan Pictures for Marion, put her through intensive acting classes and speech therapy, set her up in houses, and saw to it that she was well read and surrounded by antiques. Hearst, married with five sons, hardly saw his family from the early 1920s, although he and his wife, who always referred to Marion as 'that woman', never got round to a divorce. Marion's first pictures were serials, but within two years she was accomplished enough to star in her first full-length feature, *Cecilia of the Pink Roses*. Naturally enough, Hearst used his papers to drum up publicity for his star and lover, and she made a whole string of mostly undistinguished efforts for him. But W.R. was captivated by Marion, and she brought to his later years all the fun and gay living that made his life less gloomy. According to legend, Marion was the only person allowed to call him by his Christian name, although she often referred to him as 'Daddy'. At her house in Santa Monica and his spectacular retreat further up the coast at San Simeon Marion tirelessly organized costume parties, picnics, and lavish balls attended by everyone who mattered in Hollywood. Behind his back, she didn't work too seriously, turning up late and fooling around on the set with pranks that cost his company thousands of dollars. But Hearst didn't mind as long as she was by his side when he required. She also had several affairs, some more public than others, and naturally a number of abortions.

The worst scandal that Hearst and Marion got involved in occurred in November 1924, when they decided to throw a party on Hearst's yacht, the *Oneida*, for the birthday of director Thomas Ince. They sailed down to San Diego, where Ince joined in the fun. What happened next is a source of speculation; the

body of Ince was the hard fact. The first newspaper headlines read MOVIE PRODUCER SHOT ON HEARST YACHT, but they were quickly changed in Hearst's papers to read SPECIAL CAR RUSHES STRICKEN MAN HOME. At the inquest it was decided that Ince had died from acute indigestion. During the hearing many of the people who had been on board changed their stories and gave the usual amount of conflicting evidence. The *New York Daily News* decided to print their version, that Ince had been shot by Hearst because W.R. had found out that Marion and the director were having an affair. Whatever the truth, it terrified Hearst, and he returned to his wife for six months until the scandal had died down. Then his affair with Marion resumed, and in 1937, when his empire was in great financial difficulties, Marion lent him a million dollars and, after selling her jewellery and begging around her friends, provided a second million to bale him out.

FRANTIC DISPUTE

Thereafter W.R. and Marion were very close. They lived together in Beverly Hills, and in business matters he relied increasingly on her opinions, especially after the mid forties when his health declined. In 1950 he wrote a will ensuring that after his death Marion would be able to virtually control his empire through shares. When he died on 14 August 1951, his newspapers ran the death as banner headlines, declaring LOSS SADDENS ALL WALKS OF LIFE, which was slightly over the top. Marion and the family entered into a frantic private dispute over the will. They produced an earlier version in which she had been left property and antiques, with many of his assets bequeathed to charity. Millicent was determined that the case should not reach court, where W.R.'s affair with 'that woman' would be gone over for all to read about. A settlement was finally announced on 30 October 1951: Marion remained a rich woman, but the Hearst family retained control over their empire.

Reds Demand U.N. Yield on Truce Line **RACE RESULTS**

Los Angeles Examiner

W.R. HEARST DEATH MOURNED BY NATION

'U.N. Plan Fantastic' d Delegate Storms | LOSS SADDENS LEADERS IN ALL | A Great American | Publisher-P

15

MANAGER 'DIED AFTER SLAPPING SARAH MILES'

Death riddle in Sarah Miles's flat

THE AGONY of Robert Bolt

AND THE MAGIC of Sarah Miles

Man Dies of Love

SARAH MILES, who was then married to Robert Bolt, playwright and script-writer of *Lawrence of Arabia* and *A Man for All Seasons,* had a nasty shock when she returned to her motel room in Gila Bend, Arizona, at noon on 11 February 1973. Her business manager David Whiting lay dead on the floor, with blood on his face and on the bed.

At the inquest a strange story unfolded. Sarah and her husband had met David Whiting a couple of years before. He was a former journalist on *Time* magazine and had become infatuated with Rosie Ryan, the character Sarah played in the film *Ryan's Daughter.* The Bolts had employed him and found the fellow pleasant enough company at first, and he came to live in their house as a secretary-cum-business-manager. He had accompanied Sarah on her travels but became something of an embarrassment to her and her husband, and so they asked him to leave. He had always threatened to commit suicide if he was forced to leave Sarah, and in March 1972 was admitted to hospital after taking an overdose. They reluctantly kept him on, and he went with Sarah to America, where she started work on the film *The Man Who Loved Cat Dancing* with co-stars Lee J. Cobb and Burt Reynolds. Bolt stayed behind in England.

CHEESED OFF

Sarah and the film crew stayed at the Travel Lodge Motel in Gila Bend, and she brought a nanny to look after her children. Whiting had his own room, and became increasingly resentful of the time she spent with the other actors. She and Whiting had rows, she told journalists later, 'It was not my business to be nanny to my business-manager.' On 10 February she went out to dinner with Lee J. Cobb. When they returned to the hotel, they drank some more and she danced a little. Then she went to Reynolds's room 'to explain why she had returned from dinner with Cobb' – apparently Big Burt was rather cheesed off that Sarah had not dined with him, even though a Japanese lady was giving him a massage in his room.

Sarah watched TV and fell asleep, returning to her own room at 3 a.m. There Whiting was waiting for her, and demanded to know where she had been. There was a fight and he hit her about the face, all of which was witnessed by Sarah's nanny, who heard the noise from her adjoining room. Sarah ran out of the room back to Burt Reynolds and spent the rest of the night in his room.

'LIBERATED'

When she returned to her own room at noon the next day, she found Whiting dead from an overdose. At the inquest MGM obtained an injunction preventing Sarah and Burt Reynolds from giving evidence, claiming that they were needed to work on the film. Newspapers rose to the occasion with wonderful headlines like THE AGONY OF ROBERT BOLT AND THE MAGIC OF SARAH MILES, which accompanied a piece sympathizing with Mr Bolt's predicament. The man who had let his wife lead a 'liberated' life was now placed in a somewhat embarrassing position, though Sarah angrily denied that there had been any sexual relationship between her and Reynolds. Sarah told the press that David Whiting had told her, 'Nobody but me knows how to die of love', and it transpired that her life had already been blighted by the suicides of two people close to her. The first was her flatmate Thelma who, having less success than Sarah at acting, threw herself off a block of flats. The second was John Windeatt, Sarah's ex-gardener. Owing her £2,000 he had gassed himself and left her his white Pyrenean dog. Pictures accompanied most of the articles featuring Sarah in the title role of the film her husband had written for her, *Lady Caroline Lamb*. Her nipples may have photographed well, but the picture flopped.

Sarah Miles tells of drug man's own epitaph

NOBODY BUT ME KNOWS HOW TO DIE OF LOVE

The husband
Playwright Robert Bolt, 18 years Sarah's senior.

Gentleman Prefers Blonde but Marries Brunette

HARRY COHN, head of Columbia pictures, had spent a fortune on Kim Novak, grooming the girl from Chicago into the Lavender Lady, his answer to Marilyn Monroe. Kim's first picture was *Pushover*, and it was clear that the lady could act as well as look terrific. When Harry found out in 1957 that Kim was seeing Sammy Davis Jnr, he went berserk. Items kept popping up in the gossip columns implying a romance, and the last thing Big H wanted was his blonde love-goddess seen out with a negro. Even if Sammy was a top cabaret star earning a million dollars a year, this was before the black power revolution of the sixties, and Hollywood was a conservative place. Kim refused to comply with Harry's request to stop seeing Sammy and took off for Chicago, where he was doing a benefit concert. She saw her family and introduced Sammy to all the relatives. According to Hedda Hopper, Cohn got somebody in the Chicago Mafia to lean on Sammy when he returned to Las Vegas. They told him, 'You have one eye left – want to try for none?'

NEGOTIATIONS

Cohn had been furious that Kim had disobeyed him. At one stage there were phone negotiations between Sammy's agent, Cohn, and Frank Sinatra to try to sort out the mess. Sinatra had been friendly with Sammy for ten years, and was even rumoured to fancy the beauteous blonde for himself. Kim denied everything in Chicago when she boarded the train for Los Angeles, saying, 'Sammy Davis and I have been discussing making a movie together, but I doubt if my studio would give me permission.' Reporters really thought that Mr Davis had asked Kim's parents if he could marry her, but no one was talking. Sammy joined Kim's train in Las Vegas, but got off before it reached Los Angeles. She was met by studio executives who denied any marriage was in the offing. By the end of the week Sammy had married a black dancer, Loray White, in Las Vegas, announcing his plans in the middle of his show to a startled Loray – they had never even dated. Loray later told reporter Jim Bacon that Sammy gave her a cheque for $25,000, and that they never slept together during the marriage, which ended in divorce after a respectable time.

Debbie and Eddie
and Liz and Richard

DEBBIE REYNOLDS, star of musicals like *Singing in the Rain* and the 'girl next door' of Hollywood, was the perfect and cutest wife of teen idol and so-smooth crooner, Mr Clean-cut Eddie Fisher. Their romance had been chronicled by the fan mags from the minute they became an 'item'. Eddie had courted Debbie (who still lived at home with mom in spite of being in her twenties) under the eyes of an adoring public, and they were nicknamed 'America's sweethearts'. According to Eddie, by the time they had married in September 1956 they were both cool to the idea and were beginning to fight – but he went through the ceremony because everyone else seemed to expect it of them.

Eddie had started off as a short Jewish kid from Philadelphia who won talent contests, progressed through the borscht belt to his own twice-weekly TV show 'Coke Time' on NBC, and was a smash hit with the bobby-sox generation. Debbie's image was so wholesome that press reports claimed that when she was at high school her mother had embroidered N.N. – for 'No Necking' – on her sweaters. In spite of his juvenile appearance, Eddie had had a number of affairs (including one with Marlene Dietrich) before he arrived in Hollywood to do a stint at the Coconut Grove night spot in June 1954. Eddie met Debbie on a film set and was immediately attracted to her. On their first date they did nothing but kiss; but although Eddie had thousands of adoring women fans, Debbie's mother was not one of them. Debbie wore frocks made by mom and seemed 'sweet and unspoiled'.

Although Coke wasn't too thrilled about it, an engagement was soon announced – the pair of teen idols seemed destined for the kind of marriage dreamt of by publicity agents. By March 1955 Eddie was getting cold feet and stalled the wedding day. The press blamed his entourage for keeping them apart. So in September they tied the knot at Grossingers resort hotel in the Catskills, where Eddie had had some of his first successful club dates. Now the press expected them to live happily ever after...

However, Hollywood is a small town, and Debbie and Eddie, the wonderful twosome, soon made some friends who were to have a most surprising effect on their lives: Liz Taylor and her new husband, showman Mike Todd. Todd was Liz's number three. They had met in 1956 when she was still married to actor Michael Wilding. Before long a divorce had been obtained, and Liz and Mike wed in Acapulco in

February 1957. Todd had staged flops as well as successes, and his current project was producing a wide-screen epic entitled *Around the World in 80 Days*. Liz got pregnant, and the Todds and the Fishers were often seen out together; they even toured Europe in a foursome. Todd was somewhat dumpy (like Liz and Eddie), and constantly chewed on a cigar. Nevertheless she found him enchanting, and was totally distraught when he was killed in a plane crash in March 1958. At the age of twenty-six she was widowed with three children. Debbie was exactly the same age, also with a baby daughter – Carrie. In spite of her grief, Liz finished shooting *Cat on a Hot Tin Roof*. Eddie Fisher accompanied Liz to Mike's funeral, and he and Debbie did their best to comfort their shattered friend.

According to Eddie, Liz and Debbie weren't exactly compatible. 'Coke Time' had come to the end of its run by now, and he had another TV show, this time sponsored by a cigarette company. In May 1958 Liz turned up at Eddie's opening at the Tropicana, and the three were all photographed together. But by this time Eddie and Debbie had a son – Todd – and were not getting on at all. Eddie was sleeping in another bedroom and discussing a separation. Liz was virtually

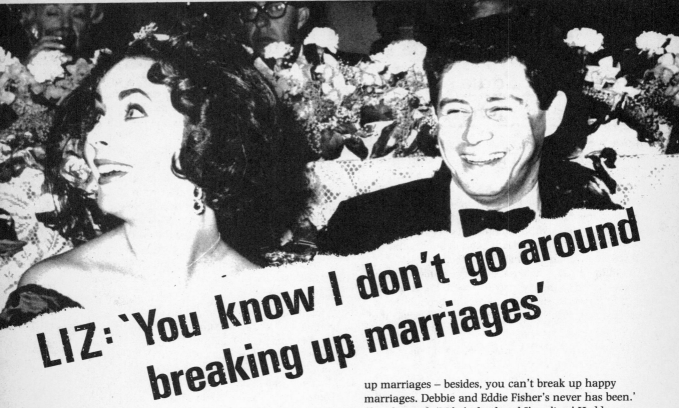

LIZ: 'You know I don't go around breaking up marriages'

in seclusion, trying to cope with her grief. After Eddie's thirtieth birthday in August 1958, he and Liz realized they were falling in love. They met in New York in September when Liz was supposed to be going to Europe with Mike Todd's secretary, but she changed her mind and started dating Eddie instead. Within a week it was all being acted out on the front pages of the world's trashier papers, with headlines like HOW CAN SHE BEHAVE LIKE THIS? The press, who had absolutely no inkling that anything was wrong with the 'dream' marriage of Eddie and Debbie, were outraged.

Liz and Eddie called up Debbie from New York and told her of their romance. They all decided to discuss it when they were back in Los Angeles. Debbie went to the airport to meet him on his return to Los Angeles – the only trouble was, Eddie hadn't gotten on the plane. Liz went into hiding as Eddie and Debbie proceeded to fight in front of reporters. Within a week the model marriage had undergone a 'misunderstanding' which had then become 'a separation', and finally 'divorce' was on the cards.

On Eddie's return to Los Angeles, Debbie cooked his favourite lima beans as she tried to win back her man. She wore diaper pins in her sweater as she told journalists that it seemed unbelievable to have been living happily with a man who didn't love her. Liz was interviewed by Hedda Hopper, the Grande Dame of Hollywood gossip, and was asked what was going on. Liz remarked, 'You know I don't go around breaking

up marriages – besides, you can't break up happy marriages. Debbie and Eddie Fisher's never has been.' She also said, 'Mike's dead and I'm alive.' Hedda was shocked and sided with Debbie, writing her up as the innocent victim. When Eddie and Liz appeared together in public, placards announced she was 'the biggest slut in town', and Eddie got boxes of hate mail as his clean-cut image went down the drain. When he did a show in Las Vegas and Liz joined him, there were placards outside the hotel telling her to 'go home'. Other people accused him of taking advantage of a widow. By December 1958 Debbie was firmly cast in the role of marytr, and public feeling was so strongly against the Taylor–Fisher affair that they dared not be seen in public together.

Divorce Agreed

Would they have cared so much if it all hadn't been so wicked? According to Liz, they were fighting the world. But first they had to persuade Debbie to agree to a divorce. In March 1959 Liz converted to Judaism and, with Eddie still married, they announced their engagement on 1 April. He, of course, gave her a fifty-diamond bracelet as a small token of his affection. Debbie finally gave in and said she was exhausted by the whole episode. After getting a Nevada divorce, Eddie married Liz on 12 May 1959. She announced she was going to give up her career after three more pictures and devote her life to her husband and her family.

Eddie's Chesterfield TV show had been scrapped in January 1959, and now that he was married to Liz he realized he was going to play a new role – that of comforter and protector to his hugely successful new wife. When she went to Spain to do the exteriors for *Suddenly Last Summer* Eddie was reduced to hanging round the set. When they returned to America in the autumn and he performed in Las Vegas, it was the first time he had sung in public for months. Eddie had read the script of *Cleopatra* which had been sent to Liz, and he told her about it. Liz wasn't keen, and when Fox called she said she'd do it for a million dollars – almost as a joke. To everyone's amazement they came up with the money. First she did *Butterfield 8* to complete her contract with MGM, and at her request Eddie was given a small part. He was a disaster, and was voted 'worst actor of the year' by the *National Lampoon*.

In August 1960 Eddie and Liz came to London to start the shooting of *Cleopatra*, with Peter Finch cast as Caesar. After three months of production and endless bickering, only six minutes of the action was on film. In the spring of 1961 Liz became ill and underwent a tracheotomy. Production of the film was then completely shut down while Liz made a slow recovery. Finch was paid off and the completed bit of film was junked. During the time that Eddie and Liz spent in London, he had begun to tire of his role as nurse and nannie to his demanding wife. He returned to Hollywood for a spell to try and set himself up as a film producer, but nothing materialized. He was beginning to realize that he needed to establish his own career away from her.

Cleopatra was being resurrected when (according to Eddie) he suggested Richard Burton for the part of Caesar this time around. When filming started in Rome, Eddie was once again reduced to hanging

around waiting for his wife to come home from work. She turned up at their rented villa later and later, and after a party where Richard Burton and Liz were engrossed in each other Eddie began to get the message: Liz had fallen for her leading man. By January 1962 it was all over the papers, and Eddie was now cast in the Debbie Reynolds role. She seemed unable to make up her mind between the two men, but finally Eddie left for New York and didn't see Liz again for two years.

As Eddie relied increasingly on 'wonder' injections from his doctor to help to put his career back together, rumours spread that he had spent some time in a psychiatric hospital. *Cleopatra* opened to lousy reviews in June 1962, but that didn't undermine the great Burton–Taylor romance. Eddie started gambling heavily, and dated a succession of glamorous ladies: Ann-Margaret, Juliet Prowse, and even Judy Garland. In 1963 *Esquire* nominated him 'bachelor of the year', even though technically he was still married to Liz. Their break-up had affected him deeply, and they continued to bicker through lawyers over the terms of their divorce and settlement. One of the biggest disputes was over Liza, Liz's daughter by Mike Todd, and Maria, the little girl they had adopted together.

In January 1964 Liz and Richard were together in Mexico. Richard had obtained a divorce from his long-suffering wife, Sybil, the previous December. Liz claimed that Eddie was holding out for a pay-off of a million dollars, to which Fisher retorted, 'I'm not objecting to giving up anything ... the one thing I'd like to give up is my marriage certificate.' While Eddie was performing at the Desert Inn in January, he was told that Liz had obtained a divorce from him on the grounds of abandonment. His attorneys disputed the validity of a Mexican divorce, but two months later Liz and Richard were married in Montreal.

Liz and Eddie, however, were still linked by business, if not by love. They had formed a company together, and they sued Fox over what they claimed was the poor distribution of *Cleopatra*, claiming that it had cut their share of the profits. Fox counter-sued, claiming that the couple's antics had cost the film a lot of money and that Liz personally had added $5 million to the cost of making *Cleopatra*. Eddie never recovered either the fame or the income he had enjoyed during his period with Liz. Eventually they met each other in New York and sorted out their settlement. Burton was appearing on Broadway, and it seemed to Eddie that already Richard was slipping into the role that he had played for a time – taking care of Liz and succumbing to her whims. Debbie had by now remarried a much older man, a millionaire, and eventually Eddie married actress Connie Stevens in 1967.

GABOR HANDS OVER HER ROMANCE

Zsa Zsa Has the Last Laugh

ZSA ZSA GABOR has been married so many times that I stopped counting after the seventh.

After her first marriage to a Turkish newspaper magnate flopped, she married Conrad Hilton, millionaire hotel-owner, and had a daughter. When the ex-Miss Hungary tired of 59-year-old Hilton's charms, she claimed that at one stage of their relationship she had been 'doped into continuous slumber for six months' and that she was hoping for settlement of £2,500,000. She ended up with £58,000 and was then robbed of jewellery worth £187,000, according to the press. A year later she announced she was to marry George Sanders, the actor, and they tied the knot in the spring of 1949. On 6 November 1951 Sanders said he was moving out. 'I have been discarded like a squeezed lemon,' he told journalists.

By now Zsa Zsa was doing well on American TV panel games and quiz shows, where her outrageous remarks were highly entertaining. She told one viewer who complained that her husband kept running off with other women to 'shoot him in the leg'. Luckily Sanders decided not to apply this philosophy to his own marriage. He and Zsa Zsa fell out while doing a radio show together which was supposed to be a satiric look at a couple like them. Sanders said, 'We have been married a couple of years and I haven't spoken a word to Zsa Zsa since she said yes.' Taking great offence at this, Zsa Zsa told reporters, 'My marriage to George won't end in divorce, it'll end in murder. We fight all the time.'

MILLIONAIRE PLAYBOY

Then in May 1953 she was photographed in Paris with playboy and millionaire Porfirio Rubirosa, who was the representative in Paris for the Dominican Republic. Rubirosa was much sought after as an escort, and he and Zsa Zsa had one thing in common – they had both been married three times. Like her relationship with her husband, Zsa Zsa's affair with

Rubirosa was one long battle and even though George Sanders found them in bed together in December, directly after Christmas Zsa Zsa said, 'It's all over,' and reports appeared stating that Rubirosa was to marry the exceedingly rich Barbara Hutton, the Woolworth heiress. One headline read ZSA ZSA HANDS OVER HER ROMANCE as Zsa Zsa told journalists that she was 'more than happy' that Rubirosa was to be the fifth husband for Barbara. A few days before, Rubirosa had flown from New York to see Zsa Zsa in Las Vegas, going on to Los Angeles to announce his forthcoming marriage before flying back to Barbara in New York. Zsa Zsa told journalists that lover boy had asked *her* to marry him, but she turned him down in favour of her career. Zsa Zsa was then photographed with an eye-patch covering what she said was a black eye given to her by Rubirosa on 26 December when she declined his offer of marriage.

DENIAL

In New York on the 30 December Rubirosa denied the whole story, although Zsa Zsa told the press that he phoned her three times to ask her to change her mind. Barbara Hutton was quoted as saying 'I am delirious with joy' at the prospect of marrying Rubirosa.

The next day the ceremony took place, and Barbara looked distinctly fraught in the photographs. You can't blame her. Rubirosa, when asked how it felt to have married one of the richest women in the world, replied, 'Money is nothing, Barbara has brought

something new into my life. She is so ...' **At this** point he ran out of adjectives, and Barbara suggested 'sincere', to which he agreed, 'Yes, sincere.' Meanwhile back in Las Vegas Zsa Zsa claimed 'he would have left her at the altar for me' and, still wearing her eye-patch, was photographed holding up the photo of the miserable newly-weds and crowing 'See how unhappy they look.' On the honeymoon Rubirosa left Barbara and disappeared to see Zsa Zsa. Barbara sent out search parties and he turned up the next day. SOMETHING TO LAUGH ABOUT was the headline when Zsa Zsa and Rubirosa were photographed going off to Paris for a holiday together on 27 March 1954. The marriage had lasted just seventy-seven days. Rubirosa commented, 'Barbara did nothing but lie in bed all day,' and said of his relationship with Zsa Zsa, 'We have sworn love and fidelity for life.' In April 1954 Zsa Zsa got her divorce from George Sanders. By then she and Rubirosa had split up again.

SEVENTH KNOT FOR ZSA ZSA

Showbiz
Exotic Behaviour

This section is devoted to a handful of examples of what was regarded – in one case, many years later – by the people who run film studios and record companies, and by pious newspaper reporters, as indecent behaviour. In the cases of Errol Flynn and Elvis Presley, their alleged sexual practices in no way detract from their artistry and performances. As for Jerry Lee Lewis, it is incredible to think that only twenty years ago audiences booed him because he was married to a girl the same age as juvenile film stars like Judy Garland whom grown men had ogled at in the legitimate confines of the matinée performance. The press will always treat exotic behaviour by the famous in the same way: if there's no other news, they slap it on the front page.

THE AMAZING TRUTH ABOUT ERROL FLYNN

Nazi Spy and Gay Lover?

ERROL FLYNN, for twenty-five years cast by Hollywood as the most virile, athletic, clean-cut, and heroic of the idols they created on the screen, died on 14 October 1959. Although he had been involved in many scandals during his lifetime (see Embarrassing Court Cases), they always tended to reinforce the screen stereotype that he played so well. Everyone knew he drank, took drugs, liked young girls, and kept a wide circle of friends. But a book appeared in 1980 which effectively shattered the image of Errol Flynn, matinée idol. Whether the conclusions the author, Charles Higham, drew were correct or not, it is certain that nobody will ever gaze up at Errol Flynn on a cinema screen again without viewing him differently: he is no longer the smooth super-hero the studios of the thirties and forties went to such lengths to manufacture.

FLYNN BETRAYED HIS FANS TO THE GESTAPO

SECRET FILES

In *Errol Flynn: The Untold Story*, Higham alleged that Flynn had worked actively in Hollywood as a Nazi agent throughout the Second World War, although by the end of his life he no longer had any sympathy with the Nazi cause. Under the American Freedom of Information Act, the author gained access to previously secret FBI files which had been kept on Flynn by J. Edgar Hoover. Flynn's close friend, Doctor Hermann Friedrich Erben (whom he had known from his early twenties), was a known Nazi agent, and according to Higham Errol passed Erben information about American harbours and naval installations which he photographed from his yacht. Flynn also sought out the company of known Nazis in South America and Mexico and went to enormous lengths to help Erben stay in America, asking President Roosevelt's wife to help iron out problems that Erben was having with his passport. When a warrant was eventually issued for Erben's arrest, Flynn smuggled him across the border to Mexico. Ironically enough, in 1942 Errol Flynn made a film entitled *Desperate Journey*, a war epic about an American bomber crew downed behind Nazi lines. His co-star was none other than Ronald Reagan.

ERROL AND TYRONE

Fury over claim that they had a love affair

Another allegation made in Charles Higham's book, which made headlines around the world, was that Errol Flynn was gay; or to be more precise, that from his teens he had been bisexual. Higham was told by Johnny Meyer (a pimp and ex-nightclub owner, who was later mysteriously killed in a car accident) that Meyer had been paid by Flynn to find girls for him, and that in the course of his demanding duties he discovered that in 1939 Flynn had had an affair with another matinée idol, Tyrone Power. According to Meyer, Tyrone Power had also been bisexual from his teenage years. Then Meyer went on to make even more astounding claims involving Flynn and Howard Hughes, for whom he also worked. Apparently he had set up a date for Hughes (whom Meyer claimed was bisexual) and Flynn, but never found out what had taken place.

REBUTTAL

The book aroused much hostility: Flynn's second wife, Nora Eddington, telephoned Higham and is quoted as saying, 'Errol would have flattened any man who dared to call him a queer. I wish I could punch your nose instead.' The *Daily Telegraph* in London carried a report rebutting the charges that Flynn was a Nazi agent, based on a conversation with a friend of Sir William Stephenson, Canadian director of Allied wartime intelligence. According to this report, Flynn was not working for the Nazis at all. David Niven derided the book, saying that if Flynn were alive he would have laughed at the allegation that he was an enemy agent. Since Sir William Stephenson has stated publicly that he will never talk about anyone who worked for him, the speculation will go on. Was J. Edgar Hoover just being unnecessarily nosey when he started keeping files on Flynn after the actor was charged with raping two under-age girls in 1942 and 1943, or was the star of *The Adventures of Don Juan* not quite what he portrayed? On his death the press followed the line put out by the studios, and the *Daily Mirror* reported ERROL FLYNN DIED LAUGHING – 'I INTEND TO DEVOTE MY LIFE TO WOMEN.' His companion when he died was actress Beverly Aadland, whom he had started dating almost two years before when she was fifteen. Flynn left the bulk of his money to his third wife, Patrice Wymore, and to his four children by various marriages.

Errol Flynn died laughing 'I INTEND TO DEVOTE MY LIFE TO WOMEN'

THE KING WAS NAUGHTY!

'Little Elvis' Got Hot for White Panties

WHEN ELVIS PRESLEY DIED on 16 August 1977, two things started to happen. First, literally hundreds of thousands of women around the world went into shock and started mourning the loss of one of the most potent sex symbols of the twentieth century: regardless of his music, his love for B-movie parts and his grotesquely swollen physique, Elvis in his prime, both on record and on stage, represented the ultimate white male stud. The second thing that happened, even before his coffin was carried out of Graceland, his palatial home in Memphis, was that many writers set about investigating just how much truth the Presley legend contained: as the man who'd sold more records than any other, who'd never performed outside the United States, and who inspired more fan worship than anything else in trousers, Elvis had been the subject of endless columns in the press about his girls, his marriage, his divorce, and his manager, Colonel Tom Parker.

One man who set about dissecting the macho image of Presley was writer Albert Goldman, who had formerly taught English at Columbia University in New York. He'd already written a well-received biography of the controversial comedian Lenny Bruce, and was able to negotiate a $300,000 advance for promising to come up with never-before-revealed material about The King. After 600 interviews and three and a half years' work Goldman produced a massive book, which was published at the end of 1981. It immediately hit the best-seller list – although as far as Elvis fans were concerned it was disgusting. The book sold over 150,000 copies in hardback, and the paperback rights were sold for $1 million.

For any book to get that kind of money it had to be controversial, and Goldman's certainly was. He totally tore apart the image of Presley as a healthy heterosexual male. In interviews Goldman was unrepentant. He'd thought that reviewers would look upon his efforts as an attempt to portray the reality behind the make-believe, but all the critics turned roundly on him. Elvis seemed to be a sacred subject, particularly in the rock press, where the book was condemned as 'ugly'. One man wrote: 'Goldman works hard to convey . . . his disgust for his subject.' Another said: 'The torrents of hate that drive this book are unrelieved.' According to Goldman, Elvis was 'an outrageous repulsive character . . . it was all down to drugs and comic-book macho'. He claimed that Elvis died 'of an excess of himself' and was living in a fantasy world where he had completely lost any concept of reality.

What made so many people so mad at Goldman, and made others rush out and buy the book? The primary reason was the description of Elvis's weird sexual preferences, which Goldman thought may have stemmed from the fact that the singer had a split personality and a twin brother who had died at birth. Throughout his life Elvis worshipped his mother, and when she died he never related to the opposite sex in a normal way, failing to ever establish real long-term relationships.

After his mother's death in 1958, Elvis surrounded himself with a gang of men who carried out his every whim, serviced his every need, and agreed with everything he said or did. When he was in the army in Germany in 1959, he got a few days off and went to Paris with the 'Guys'. They established a pattern of going to the Lido for the first show, taking all the Bluebell Girls back to their hotel for a party, returning them for the late show, and then going back to the hotel to continue the party. This same routine went on every night – and, in one form or another, the rest of Presley's life.

ELVIS'S TURN-ON

By the time Elvis returned to the United States he and the Guys had established a reputation for being thrown out of hotels because of their endless parties and pranks. They all moved into a house in Bel Air found by Colonel Parker, where they could hold parties as long and as loud as they liked. The Guys had to find girls for Elvis, and he had very specific requirements. He was only interested in asses and legs; the girls had to be tiny, not look older than eighteen, be (or pretend to be) virgins, and wear white cotton panties. These were Elvis's total turn-on and, according to Goldman, it was thought to have evolved from an incident when Elvis was at school and had seen up a girl's skirt. Having got several girls in white panties, the Guys had to get the message across to them that the King liked to watch them wrestle on the floor and pretend to fight with each other. Every night the Guys would invite scores of young hopefuls up to the house, while others would just wait outside and plead to be let in. Elvis would spend most of the evening ignoring them, watching the TV with the sound off and the jukebox on. In the early hours he would retire to his room with two or three girls that had taken his fancy, and the Guys would then be able to have their pick. Once in the privacy of his room, however, Elvis rarely engaged in normal sexual intercourse – and it's thought this is one of the reasons that he never suffered from VD. Perhaps it was because he was frightened of catching the disease or of having a paternity suit slapped on him. Most of these girls never saw Elvis nude – and he didn't want to see them naked either. After they had aroused him by wrestling with each other, he would usually either masturbate or go down on them. He also like girls to masturbate him – and if he ever did stray from the usual and actually have normal sex with a girl, he took great care never to ejaculate inside her. He was deeply embarrassed about the fact his penis was uncircumcised, and called it 'Little Elvis'.

Elvis, according to Goldman, was the ultimate voyeur. In one house he installed a huge two-way mirror so that he could watch the Guys screwing girls in another bedroom while masturbating to his heart's content. There was another two-way mirror which overlooked the dressing room at the pool in a house he owned in Bel Air.

Elvis's whole attitude to girls had never really progressed beyond that of an immature twelve-year-old. He once owned a badly behaved horny chimp called Scatter, and loved it when the animal played with itself in front of women or ran into a bedroom where a couple were in bed together. Elvis took his voyeuristic tendencies to the limit when he bought

video equipment and made his own porno-movies of girls wrestling and of lesbian sex. In some his penis appeared in the frame as he masturbated. No one was allowed to view these tapes except Elvis, and although it was thought he had destroyed nearly all of them, some copies are now being sold in Los Angeles.

He was totally uninterested in women who had babies, and after his wife, Priscilla, gave birth to their daughter Lisa Marie, he never slept with her again, even though, physically, Priscilla had satisfied all his requirements when he had first seen the shy teenager while serving in the army in Germany.

Goldman claims that Elvis's growing preoccupation with drugs wasn't surprising, given his lack of interest in the world outside the bizarre and distorted one he inhabited. He was uncommunicative, couldn't hold a decent conversation with a girl, and lapsed into broad Memphis slang with his buddies.

So although Elvis typified the wholesome all-American boy in his movies, the truth was very different. He was just a country kid who'd never grown up and whose mother had died leaving a lot of things unexplained to him, and a man whose sex life was simply tragic.

IS NEW BOOK ON ELVIS TRUE ?

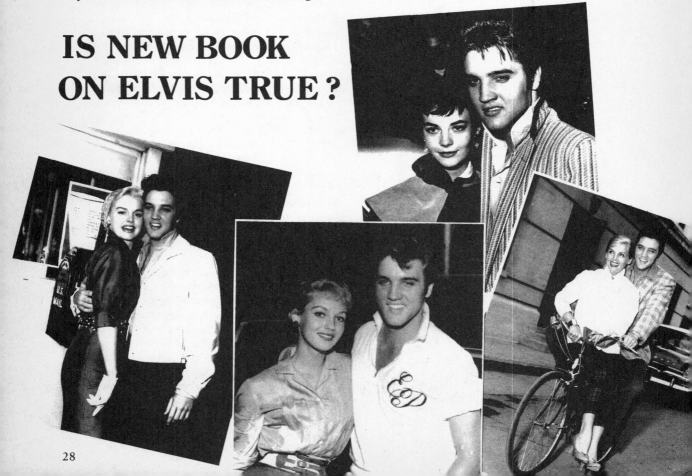

Don't Take Your Top Off If You're Going To Regret It Later

IN THE FIRST film she ever made – at sixteen – Hedy Lamarr, the daughter of a wealthy Viennese banker, created an image she could never erase. As this story unfolds, you will see to just what lengths someone went to pretend that Hedy had never done certain things in front of a film camera.

Ecstasy, the film she signed to make her screen début in, brought Hedy instant fame – and notoriety. She didn't bother to read the contract, and the script was just a five-page outline. When she did get down to the small print, she found herself having to play several scenes stark naked, or else refund the full cost of the picture to the producers. In her book *Ecstasy and Me: My Life as a Woman*, she explains that a compromise was reached: she would take off her clothes, run into the water, and swim a few strokes; the cameras would record it all from a tasteful distance. According to Hedy, to get her to react more passionately in the nude love scenes which were shot indoors, the director Gustav Machatý stood out of camera range and stuck a safety pin into her backside from time to time to produce suitable contortions of passion. When the camera caught her face exploding with pain as the safety pin struck home, the director shouted 'Cut', delighted with the result. It is not recorded whether Miss Lamarr could sit down that evening or not. Hedy was either incredibly naive or just more desperate for stardom than she would later own up to, for when she took her parents to the première in 1932, they were outraged and stormed out of the cinema.

ECSTATIC

A few months later, Hedy was appearing in a stage play in Vienna when she met Fritz Mandl, a millionaire munitions-manufacturer. They were married in 1933, and shortly afterwards the storm about *Ecstasy* reached its peak. Mandl went berserk when he finally saw the picture, and ordered his associates to buy every copy of the film that they could lay their hands on. He spent around £60,000 trying to prevent the public having the pleasure of seeing his glamorous wife in the nude, but he never managed to lay his hands on the negative. The result was that more and more prints were made, different versions were screened, and Mandl paid higher and higher prices in a hopeless effort to stem the attention that the film had aroused. He jealously kept his teenage bride locked up at home, a prisoner watched by his servants, until in 1937 she escaped to America,

signing a film contract with producer Louis Mayer whom she met on the journey over.

She spent the next fourteen years in Hollywood as a successful actress, although her private life didn't run quite so smoothly. She married six times and, saddest of all, appeared in court in Los Angeles on a shoplifting charge in 1966, but was acquitted. Shortly after, she wrote her autobiography. In 1980 she announced she was filing a five million pound libel suit over a story and photograph of a two-headed goat named Hedy Lamarr. She claimed it intended to destroy her reputation and 'her image as the very personification, essence and epitome of beauty'.

Fran Farmer Gets 6 Mos. in Jail, Hits Matron, Fells a Cop

Frances Farmer Freaks Out

FRANCES FARMER's experiences make depressing reading, for it is obvious that the star needed some kind of professional help as she continued to hit the headlines with her spectacularly bizarre behaviour, and yet none was forthcoming. Hollywood only liked its stars to misbehave in private, and the studio bosses found Frances an embarrassment they could do without. The newspapers, on the other hand, found her lively copy because her performances in court were as entertaining as those they were paying to see at the cinema.

Frances was a cinema usherette in Seattle in 1935 when she won a popularity contest. The first prize was a trip to Russia, and on the boat back she was screen-tested and signed by Paramount. Frances accepted the contract because she hoped to further her ambition to be a serious actress. That was mistake number one. She starred in *Come and Get It* in 1936 and then worked steadily for the next few years. But Frances said loudly that she hated California, and she refused to conform to all the unwritten rules about how film stars should behave. The first signs that all was not well came in 1942 with the headlines PUBLICITY STUNT, SAYS FRANCES FARMER'S MOTHER, after

she had been sentenced to 180 days' jail and put on probation for a drunken driving offence. Apparently Mrs Farmer thought that her daughter might have got herself arrested in preparation for a film involving prison scenes. She expected Frances had wanted to experience jail at first hand.

ASYLUM HELL OF FALLEN FILM STAR

The next headlines said ACTRESS HEARS VOICES. She claimed to hear 'voices' night and day, and had to be taken to hospital when she insisted that her food was being tampered with, making her ill. A few months after this she failed to report to her probation officer, and the police pursued the distraught actress across town – an escapade during which she streaked through a hotel topless, and hit a hairdresser so hard that she dislocated the lady's jaw. When Frances was signed in at the police headquarters, she gave her occupation as 'cock-sucker', which didn't please the studios too much. The court case made headlines like FRAN FARMER GETS SIX MONTHS JAIL, HITS MATRON, FELLS COP and FILM STAR IS JAILED. As she was dragged screaming and kicking from the court, she shouted at the judge, 'Have you ever had a broken heart?' It transpired that the previous autumn her husband, Leif Erikson, had divorced her and she had fallen in love in New York with the director of a play she had worked in. He totally ignored her, however, and sad Frances turned to drink.

LOCKED UP

The jail sentence imposed by the court was later revoked and Frances was placed in a sanatorium. Taken from there by her mother, Frances failed to respond much and returned soon after. Three weeks after her release she was arrested for vagrancy and fined ten dollars, which the judge himself paid. He then took her to lunch and gave her a ticket home to her parents, although her father rang up to ask that she be kept in jail until he arrived to collect her.

Fourteen years after her nervous breakdown, in 1957, the ex-star was working as a hotel clerk in San Francisco. Between her remarriage in 1958 and her death from cancer in 1970, she never really made a comeback, even though her talents had been admired by many directors including Howard Hawks, who once said of her, 'The girl is different. She thinks.' At one point, she was even rumoured to be the next Garbo. The *Sunday Mirror* serialized her autobiography with the headline ASYLUM HELL OF FALLEN FILM STAR, and in it she told of her experiences in the sanatorium. Frances claimed she was attacked, raped, and locked up in a cage. Once, after being beaten, she was placed in a straitjacket. When the nurse removed it, she asked Frances for her autograph.

Sweet Little Thirteen

JERRY LEE LEWIS was at the peak of his career as a rock-and-roll performer when he arrived in Britain to tour in 1958. Ensuing events brought Lewis's bid to rival Elvis Presley to an abrupt end, and he never again enjoyed the same degree of success artistically or financially. So why did Elvis make it and where did Jerry Lee go wrong?

The story started in the early fifties in Memphis, where Lewis had been playing piano professionally from the age of fifteen. At one point he even studied to become a preacher, but changed his mind. Lewis knew that Sun Records had been responsible for Elvis Presley's early hits, and so he turned up at their studios seeking a recording deal. His first record was 'Crazy Arms', which sold well locally but made no impact nationally. From then on, though, Lewis started to produce his own brand of piano boogie which can be heard on 'Whole Lotta Shakin' Going On', and he became an international rock-and-roll star. The follow-up, 'Great Balls of Fire', confirmed that Lewis was a truly original and talented performer. Lewis appeared all set to topple Elvis Presley.

Then in mid 1958 he married Myra Brown, who turned out to be his third cousin.

She also turned out to be only thirteen years old. The word went out in the business that it was incest, and TV shows refused to book him, radio stations declined to play his records, and he didn't get any more movie offers. When he arrived to tour England, he met the full force of hypocrisy that the media reserve for singers, actors, and the like. The tour was cancelled after scenes at the Granada cinema in Tooting, South London, where the audience had shouted, 'Go home, baby-snatcher' and 'Go home, you crumb'. The Home Office investigated the fact that Lewis had arrived with his 'wife' Myra before his divorce from his previous wife had become final. His manager asked the US Embassy in London to find an official to remarry Lewis and Myra, but they refused, saying that she was below marriageable age under British law. Jerry Lee and Myra left England when two of the theatre chains that had booked his tour refused to let him perform.

After this his career hit a low period. Although he toured clubs in America for ten years, he didn't really break the taboo that surrounded his work until the late sixties, when he combined country material with the rest of his rock act. He got back into the charts and his early work was re-released. So Jerry Lee Lewis finally regained some of his earlier success, after spending ten years paying for that wedding ring he placed on little Myra's finger. Trouble was, unlike the record, she wasn't even 'Sweet Little Sixteen'.

Showbiz
Happy Families

Growing up as the child of a star couldn't have been much fun in Hollywood. One day you were being spoilt silly, the next disciplined when mommie thought she wasn't bringing you up properly. It seems as if many film stars' children led lives that went up and down according to their parents' whims. It is not surprising, therefore, that some of the wounds inflicted by famous mums went so deep that their daughters later decided to tell all. Or could it be that the kids grew up and found out that it was the only way to cash in on the family name? And finally, having those kids in the first place would have cost a female star like Jayne Mansfield a lot of money in time and lost work. No wonder they felt screwed up about them.

Whatever Happened to Mommy Joan?

WHEN *Mommie Dearest* went on sale in America in the autumn of 1978, it caused a sensation. For the first time, the image the public had of a top film star was ruthlessly picked apart and the sordid reality of their life portrayed – not by the usual gossip magazines, but by their 'nearest and dearest'.

Christina Crawford had been adopted by Joan Crawford in 1940 when she was only a few weeks old. When the star died in 1977 aged seventy-one, a lonely, cranky old lady in New York, her version of the story died with her. Christina says that she and her mother always tried to love each other, and that as both got older it seemed easier. But when Joan's will was read, it was obvious that mommie and daughter had never really made up. Christina and her brother Christopher (adopted by Joan in 1943) were

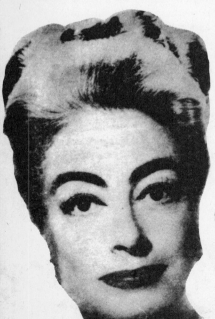

The fiend who lopped off her daughter's hair

The tyrant who locked her son in a cupboard

Bitch mother, or thankless child?

Mommie the Monster

Movie star Joan Crawford was adored by millions. But behind the glamour lurked a Sadistic woman, hated by her children

cut out – and the other two adopted children were left some money in a trust fund. Christina sat down and wrote *Mommie Dearest*, some would say as an act of final revenge, others to exorcize the pain of her childhood. *She* said it was to draw the world's attention to child abuse, and that those in Hollywood who criticized her were the very people who turned a blind eye to Joan's behaviour. Certainly *Mommie Dearest* made Christina more money than mommie ever picked up for a single project in her lifetime: she got around $250,000 for the hardback rights, $750,000 for the paperback rights, $300,000 for the film rights, and $200,000 to write the screenplay. It was rumoured that nine top actresses had turned down the part of Joan because of the fear of causing offence to those from Joan's era who were still in power in the film business. Finally Joan was played by Faye Dunaway, who looked uncannily like her. It was rather ironic that *Time* magazine recalled Crawford's remark: 'Of all the actresses . . . only Faye Dunaway has the talent and class and courage it takes to make a real star.'

So what was between the covers of *Mommie Dearest* that made it so explosive? Readers, used to portraits of her mother written by journalists who saw the kids all dressed in matching outfits, happy in the spotless living room of their home, and lovingly cared for by their devoted and beautiful mother, saw what happened after the front door had shut and the last guest had gone home. Mommie, it turned out, was a tyrant who made the kids scrub the floors endlessly, wear the same torn clothes for a week when they misbehaved, washed their mouths out with soap when they swore, and tied them to the bed at night if they sucked their thumbs. If they refused to eat their food, it was continually served up at every meal until they did. She went into blind rages after drinking, and would indulge in night raids where she entered their rooms and smashed everything in sight. She employed professional photographers to record her 'happy family' for publicity purposes, and her daughter claims that Joan only adopted four children because it was good for her image; she wasn't interested in the problems of bringing up four youngsters at all. Christopher ran away four times and was sent to approved school; Christina was sent away to a remote convent and didn't see her mother for more than a year. They learned of one of her marriages over the radio – she only told them afterwards. The one group of people she *was* devoted to were her fans, and she employed two secretaries to make sure every letter got a personal answer.

My evil mother, Joan Crawford

Her own daughter tells the tough truth about a great star.

To understand Joan's behaviour, you have only to look at her own childhood. She was illegitimate, and her father was rarely around. Her mother was poor, and Joan had to work for everything she wanted, going to iron shirts for cash at the age of eight. Discipline was strict and she was often whipped. At boarding school she was beaten, and she ran away. After a variety of jobs, she became a dancer and eventually a star. Joan believed that stars should live how their fans expected them to, and told *Photoplay* magazine, 'Everything I earn, I spend.' It was a star's duty to live in luxury, it seemed, even though the rest of the country was struggling through the Depression.

COSMETIC SURGERY

Joan was totally determined to succeed, to the extent of changing her date of birth, changing her name, having cosmetic surgery at regular intervals to fight off the wrinkles, and even having her back teeth out to give her face a better contour. Christina said of her, 'She learned to be a dancer ... an actress ... a star. She just never had any time over to learn how to be a human being.' By the time she was twenty-one she had made it. She was earning a lot of money and married Douglas Fairbanks Jnr. Later she had a three-year affair with Clark Gable, and then married actor Franchot Tone. Joan had plenty of admirers, although one of them said, 'To be Joan Crawford's boyfriend a man must be a combination of bull and butler.'

Joan Crawford: The ugly truth

Another book about Joan came out at the same time as Christina's, written by Bob Thomas. While it too showed the star to be not the person the public had believed her to be, it did reveal a more caring side of the tyrant. She had collaborated with a doctor in 1934 to help pay for hospital treatment for studio technicians, and was furious when the news leaked out – it was no publicity stunt; she gave lavish dinners for the film crews she worked with; she helped set up schools for the children of women working for the war effort. So how come Joan switched all this off once she stepped inside her own front door? Christina thought there was evidence that her mother had been sexually abused as a child and needed psychiatric help. Certainly the star behaved oddly – dressing her third and fourth adopted children identically and calling them twins, even though they were different ages, looked different, and came from different families.

DECLINE

Up to 1945 Joan seemed to be able to cope with her children, but then she started to drink heavily, her behaviour got more and more unpredictable, and in the early fifties she fell heavily into debt (partly from gambling). It was a film called *Queen Bee*, made in 1955, starring Joan as an evil woman trying to destroy all those around her, that enabled her to pay off her bills. But as she aged, she just couldn't stand the competition from her young family, and so her punishment of them grew. *Confidential* magazine wanted to run an article saying that she was strict with the kids at home, but Joan got her friend, columnist Jim Bacon, to call up the editor. The piece miraculously never appeared.

HEARTLESS

Before Christina's book came out, the cracks had already begun to open up in the carefully constructed picture of Joan Crawford Wonder-Mum. Writer Anita Loos said, 'I don't think she cared for her children at all.' Writer Helen Laurenson recalled a horrific visit to Joan's house, when the home help let her in on a few home truths, and an article in *Viva* magazine described her as a 'woman with no heart'.

THE SHOCKING SECRET LIFE OF JAYNE MANSFIELD

The Girl Can't Help It

AFTER Christina Crawford had dished out the dirt on mommie Joan, and Brooke Hayward revealed another tale of growing up in Hollywood in the best-selling *Haywire*, it seemed as though many aggrieved offspring of the famous would be rushing into print in the hope of earning the same kind of lolly as Brooke and Christina. Sometimes they had been typing fast enough to beat the biographies being written by non-blood relations, for it seemed at the end of the seventies that a new kind of star biography had surfaced: one in which warts – indeed nose-jobs, bosom-lifts, sex, and dope – and all were dished up for public consumption.

MY SEX-CRAZED MOMMA!

Jayne Mansfield's daughter Jayne announced that she too was writing a book about mom, but big Jayne's ex-press-agent and secretary, Raymond Strait, got there first. He revealed that although Jayne had been devoted to her kids (four by three marriages) when they were younger, the same old story occurred when Jayne's eldest daughter became a teenager. Mom resented it deeply, and told her last boyfriend, lawyer Sam Brody, to beat her kid up: 'If you love me, make her bleed.' (Nor was Brody averse to giving mommie a black eye or two.) Jayne too used to beat up her daughter, and the story eventually leaked out in the press, but this was nothing new for her: from the moment she appeared in films, Mansfield had received an incredible amount of publicity, some good, and most pretty outrageous.

She couldn't cope with life as a Hollywood sex goddess – so she turned to drugs, drink and countless lovers for consolation

Jayne Mansfield played a screen siren in the Broadway play *Will Success Spoil Rock Hunter*, and her life story could be suitably subtitled *Success Probably Ruined Jayne Mansfield*. From there she went to Hollywood and, although her first screen parts were nothing much, she quickly learnt how to attract attention when not actually working. When Sophia Loren, then a hot new star from Italy, made her first trip to Hollywood in 1957, she encountered Jayne at a party at Romanoff's restaurant. It was supposed to be in honour of Sophia, but every time the cameramen tried to take a picture of the Italian, Jayne stood behind her and bent over in a low-cut dress, revealing just about everything. Sophia later wrote, 'I became aware of someone looming over me.' The same year Jayne posed topless for *Playboy*, the first star of any note to

Jayne loved to love so many times each day

do so. It was typical of the girl who decorated her mansion on Sunset Boulevard in pink and made everything heart-shaped, from the swimming pool right down to the bed. Luckily someone talked her out of carrying the theme right through to the toilets, which could have been rather uncomfortable. Jayne drove a pink cadillac, kept so many small dogs and assorted pets that they stank the house out, and was the inventor of the strategically broken bikini strap in the middle of a publicity picture session. As *The Times* wrote, 'Her most obvious asset as a performer was the way she looked.' But Jayne was no dumb blonde: it was said she had an I.Q. of 164 and, although the studios were pushing her as a straight competitor to Marilyn Monroe, she was a good comedienne and, some critics thought, had a promising career ahead if she chose the right parts. Her most successful comic role was *The Girl Can't Help It*, but after that she all too often played the dumb blonde to end them all and appeared a ridiculous and pathetic figure.

Her daughter revealed that, while making *The Girl Can't Help It*, Jayne slept with Elvis Presley and got a pink motor bike in return. Baby Jayne also told of her mother's affair with Robert Kennedy and of the wild parties at home, where guests photographed each other naked. Jayne married Paul Mansfield, who was baby Jayne's father, then Mickey Hargitay, the ex-Mr Universe, and finally agent Matt Cimber. She had a son and second daughter by Hargitay and another son by Cimber. But although Mickey Hargitay was devoted to his family, life can't have been too easy at home. As Jayne's career went into decline, she worked more as a nightclub singer and made some pretty bad films in Europe. She toured Europe and then America in 1967 with a decidedly sleazy cabaret act, and by then was consuming a lot of pills and booze. She started seeing lawyer Sam Brody, who was rumoured to be involved with witchcraft and terrified her children, and a book came out recently which claimed that she even went so far as to attend meetings of a Satanist church.

WAS JAYNE MANSFIELD KILLED BY SATANISTS?

Jayne was killed when she was only thirty-three on 29 June 1967, when the car carrying her and Brody to a nightclub engagement hit a lorry. She was decapitated, and the press even ran pictures of her dead dog at the side of the road. At the height of her fame, in the early sixties, Jayne was getting £12,000 a week from Fox, and all her expenses paid. A few years later she was reduced to opening supermarkets for a couple of thousand dollars a time. Her daughter and her secretary attacked her in print, yet she remains a lovable, slightly absurd lady, who always realized she was pretty ridiculous. The *Times* obituary said, 'Show business will be decidedly less colourful without her.'

Showbiz

Embarrassing Court Cases

Court cases involving stars usually sold plenty of newspapers, boosted cinema and theatre ticket sales, and gave the public the rare pleasure of seeing the famous and self-confident sweat it out in the witness box, admitting to horrid little foibles like locking ladies out of the house, plying them with gin, or – even more bizarre – fighting off their attentions. Sixty reporters packed the court when Charlie Chaplin was accused of transporting Joan Barry to New York for immoral purposes. Mr Arbuckle met the men and women who had acquitted him at a small reception afterwards. These stars' lawyers all knew that once in the witness box their clients would have to give the performance of their lives.

Cockney Cad or Man of Morals?

CHARLIE CHAPLIN'S passion for teenage girls was as well known as his busy sex life. But the girl he probably always regretted getting between the sheets with was the one who forced him through two of the most unpleasant experiences of his life.

Chaplin had been married three times when he met Joan Barry in the spring of 1941. He signed up Joan on a $75-a-week contract, thinking that with a bit of improvement she might make a leading lady in a film he was planning called *Shadow and Substance*. Joan attended drama and singing lessons paid for by Charlie and, according to evidence given later in court, even 'had her teeth fixed at the expense of the Chaplin studios'. Between fillings Joan and Charlie did some out-of-hours tuition together, and their affair continued throughout 1942.

In the autumn of that year she went to New York, and he followed. By Christmas he had decided Joan wasn't leading lady material and reduced her salary. She came round to his house, made some threats, and took an overdose. The police removed her when she turned up a second time, and she got a month's jail sentence, abruptly terminated when everyone discovered that Joan was *very* pregnant. She rushed into the office of Hollywood columnist and keeper of the town's moral code, Hedda Hopper, and made the announcement. That night she dashed round to Charlie's again and was removed. In June 1943 she filed a paternity suit against Charlie, alleging that he

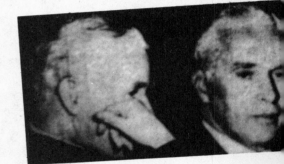

Police 'peek' at girl in panties

was the father of her child. Hedda Hopper had a field-day – she had never warmed to the fact that Chaplin had left-wing sympathies and hadn't taken out American citizenship. She used to write, 'I always get a kick out of Jim Tully's line on Chaplin. He praises the poor in the parlours of the rich.' Even before the paternity suit had been filed, Joan's lawyers were muckraking, alleging that the police had stared at the young lady naked in the police cells after they had taken her away from Chaplin's mansion. Headlines like POLICE PEEK AT GIRL IN PANTIES gave an expectant public a hint of what was to come. Hopper said it would be the greatest show since the Errol Flynn rape case.

Film Star's Tears In Court Duel

'I'M NO MONSTER' DENIAL OF GIRL'S LOVE STORY

Judge Instructs Jury

CHAPLIN AWAITS FATE

But before the paternity case reached court, the FBI slapped another charge on Chaplin. They accused him of offences under the Mann Act, of transporting Joan across state lines to New York for immoral purposes. Chaplin engaged top lawyer Jerry Geisler to deal with this latest example of Chaplin-bashing. When the hearing opened in New York, Geisler said in court, 'The Mann Act had been made law by Congress to stop commercialized vice. None of those who spoke on its behalf thought of it as aimed at private romance.' Newspapers carried dozens of photos of Chaplin at the trial, with the splash CHAPLIN AWAITS HIS FATE and 60 REPORTERS IN COURT. Geisler had implied in his questioning that Joan had sought to get money out of Chaplin for her baby and her mother, although she denied this. Fifty-four-year-old Chaplin wept while he gave evidence about his affair with young Joan, and said that 'sex was not important' to him. In spite of such hard-to-believe remarks it was obvious that the charge wouldn't stick, and Chaplin was acquitted. He said to the press, 'I believe in the American people. I have abiding faith in them. In their sense of fair play and justice their instincts are correct.'

That was April 1944. In December, when the paternity suit started in court, he was probably regretting those remarks. Joan's daughter had been born in October 1943 and she brought the little girl to court every day. Chaplin still denied he was the father, although he had been paying Joan money since she filed the suit. Blood tests proved he wasn't the father but, without the wily Geisler to defend him, he had a tough time. He got plenty of seedy publicity at the hands of Joan's lawyers: CHAPLIN CALLED A COCKNEY CAD, FILM STAR'S TEARS IN COURT DUEL – 'I'M NOT A MONSTER' DENIAL OF GIRL'S STORY, said the press. Chaplin was described in court as 'a master mechanic in the art of seduction'. Joan told of a bedroom scene where Chaplin had posed in front of a mirror and asked, 'Don't I look a little like Peter Pan?', and another when she had arrived at his house to discover him in the bedroom with a naked lady, whose toe 'he was tickling'. Chaplin's lawyers showed that Paul Getty had paid some of Joan's bills, and that she definitely had another lover during the time she and Chaplin had a relationship; but to no avail. After a mis-trial had been declared, the court ordered that he should pay a settlement to the child. Meanwhile his new wife Oona had already had another baby Chaplin.

Robin Hood
Charged with Rape

THAT WAS the headline when Robin Hood, alias Errol Flynn, appeared in court in Los Angeles in October 1942. The story started in August 1941. He had gone sailing for the weekend in his yacht *Sirocco* with some friends, and they had brought along a girl called Peggy Satterlee who had agreed to be photographed with Errol for a picture spread in *Life* magazine. On Saturday night the two of them danced at a nightclub on Catalina Island and later spent the night in the same cabin. His friend Buster dropped Peggy home after they docked on Sunday night. On Monday Errol called her up, only to be told that she had informed her mother they had had intercourse, and that she was only fifteen. Her mother took her down to the District Attorney's office, but no charges were pressed. Errol was told by his lawyers to be careful in future.

Errol Flynn Was Seduced, Jury (9 Women) Is Told

He completed filming *Desperate Journey* and *Gentleman Jim* and then went on a trip to Mexico, where he started an affair with the glamorous (and then unknown) Linda Christian. Flynn was depressed when he failed an army medical, and he didn't feel well when he started work on *Edge of Darkness*. He felt even worse a couple of weeks later when the police showed up at his house and accused him of having sex with another underage girl, Betty Hansen. He had met Betty at a tennis party a few days before. She had drunk herself sick and Flynn, being Gentleman Jim, had taken her upstairs to the bedroom and helped her undress – only trouble was, Betty happened to be just seventeen.

The District Attorney thought that by linking this with the case of Peggy Satterlee, which was still on his files, he could make the charges stick, but at the first hearing nobody's stories tallied. The jury announced a verdict of 'not guilty' and Flynn thought his troubles were over. To his horror, the District Attorney overruled the verdict and ordered a re-trial. At the second trial the jury was composed mainly of housewives, who looked rather embarrassed at some of the evidence. Reporters filed headlines like ERROL FLYNN WAS SEDUCED – JURY (9 WOMEN) TOLD, as Flynn's lawyer set about proving that his client had not had sexual intercourse with the girls at all, for sex with a minor, whether she consented or not,

constituted rape. The wily Jerry Geisler constructed a case which, according to reporters, 'set out to prove ... that, rather than have violated a teenage girl, the screen Lothario was actually seduced'.

Although this seems a laughable tack to take, Geisler managed to get the jury to see that the girls had a far from convent upbringing. Betty was described by the papers as 'a movie-struck waitress'. Peggy told the jury that Errol called her and her sister 'his little J.B. and his little S.Q.Q.' – meaning Jail Bait and San Quentin Quail. Betty testified that 'he had an act of intercourse with me'. She was asked, 'You mean by that that the private parts of Mr Flynn were inserted in your private parts?' Answer: 'Yes.' Betty remarked that she had kept her shoes on and Flynn his socks, at which point the court collapsed in laughter as his film *They Died with Their Boots On* was showing then.

After Flynn's Academy-Award-style performance under oath, the court broke into applause. He was acquitted, and girls gave him flowers. The two pictures he had finished between meeting the girls did very well, and his salary was raised. Linda Christian walked out of his life before the end of the trial, but Errol, being Errol, didn't wait long. He started dating and later married Nora Eddington, a redhead he had noticed working at the tobacco stall in the lobby of the courthouse.

FATTY ARRAIGNED AS SLAYER

Fatty Gets Rapped

EXACTLY WHAT went on in a hotel room in San Francisco on Monday 5 September 1921 between Fatty Arbuckle, comedian, and Virginia Rappe, ex-model and hopeful starlet, has never been fully pieced together. For a start, most of the fifty guests at Fatty's two-day party were so drunk that it's a wonder they could remember even their names in court a few days later. Whatever did happen behind the locked bedroom door, though, certainly brought his career to an abrupt end. The funny fat man could only ever find any kind of work again under a pseudonym, so vicious was the press campaign against him.

Fatty Arbuckle had been discovered by Mack Sennett in 1913, and by 1921 he had signed his second lucrative contract with Paramount. His only real rival was Charlie Chaplin. Arbuckle portrayed a gentle humour on screen, the kind of performance that made the events of 5 September seem unbelievable when recounted in court. Fatty had decided to celebrate his new deal with a party in San Francisco, driving up there in one of his many flashy cars and booking into the St Francis hotel on Saturday night. Two days later the party was still going strong, and he disappeared into a room with Virginia Rappe, a beautiful girl hoping to get her first big part in pictures. What

happened next has been told and re-told thousands of times in different versions, but the facts are that later a doctor was called and the girl placed in another room. She was admitted to hospital and sank into a coma, dying of a burst bladder on 10 September.

After receiving a phone call from the hospital, the District Attorney took a look at some of Virginia's remains in a jar and decided to start questioning the party guests. Having talked to a mutual friend of Fatty and Miss Rappe, Maude Delmont, the District Attorney arrested Fatty on charges of murder and rape. FATTY ARRAIGNED AS SLAYER was splashed across papers all over America. Rumours ran rife, dividing generally into two versions. The first was that Fatty, unable to perform sex normally because he was drunk, had raped the girl using a bottle; the second was that he

ARBUCKLE'S DEFENCE.
FIVE WOMEN ON JURY FOR THE TRIAL.
DOCTOR'S OPINION OF COLD BATH EPISODE
("News of the World" Special.)
Everybody connected with the cinema world is watching with growing interest the trial at San Fran-

ARBUCKLE INDICTED FOR MANSLAUGHTER IN ACTRESS' DEATH

Grand Jury Acts After Two Hearings—Mrs. Delmont Tells of Hotel Tragedy.

SAYS VICTIM ACCUSED HIM

Admits She Herself Had Ten Drinks of Whisky, Danced and Wore Man's Pajamas.

UNDUE INFLUENCE CHARGED

Prosecutor Says Witnesses Are Being Tampered With and Believes One Is Perjurer.

was so well endowed that his natural attributes had caused the same damage. Cinema audiences pelted the screen with objects when Fatty came into vision, and his films were hastily withdrawn. Women's vigilante groups were formed to press for a conviction. The newspapers seized on the affair as an example of all that was wrong with the Hollywood life-style. The head of Fatty's studio telephoned the San Francisco District Attorney, realizing that a trial could cost him plenty at the box office. He was accused of bribery and of trying to alter the course of justice.

At the first hearing the evidence was confused, to say the least. Witnesses disappeared, not wanting to lose work or suffer recriminations. They changed their stories every time they told them, and were threatened with perjury. Some witnesses were placed under police surveillance, either to protect them from bribery, or to prevent them from running away. Maude Delmont, the chief witness for the prosecution, didn't perform terribly well. She made the papers with headlines such as 'SHE HAD TEN DRINKS OF WHISKEY, DANCED AND WORE MEN'S PYJAMAS', and when a lawyer asked how she felt, she replied, 'I had a hypodermic this morning and I'm all right.' A friend of Fatty testified that he retrieved Virginia's torn underclothes from the wastebasket at the hotel because he thought 'they would make a good nice dustcloth for my machine'.

GRAVE INJUSTICE

Fatty was acquitted. But the District Attorney, perturbed by conflicting evidence, ordered a re-trial, this time on a manslaughter charge, and Fatty was convicted. Again a re-trial was ordered. By now Fatty was selling his possessions to pay for his defence. His

'Just Let Me Work'

lawyers tried hard to drag Virginia's reputation through the mud, saying that she had had plenty of lovers. As most of the witnesses had consumed gallons of home-made gin and orange juice as well as bootleg whisky, it's not surprising they could never agree as to what had happened. It transpired that Virginia had been placed in a cold bath to try to calm her down and soothe her, and this appeared in the press as ARBUCKLE'S DEFENCE . . . DOCTOR'S OPINION OF COLD BATH EPISODE. Finally, on 12 April *The New York Times* carried the headline ARBUCKLE ACQUITTED IN ONE MINUTE VERDICT: ONE OF HIS FILMS TO BE RELEASED IMMEDIATELY, and informed its readers that after the trial 'the jurors held an informal reception with Arbuckle while the photographers took pictures'. The jury announced in a statement, 'We feel a grave injustice has been done him.'

SCAPEGOAT

The feeling around the country was such, though, that Paramount cancelled the rest of Fatty's contract. The film industry, realizing that if they did not clean up their image the Government might step in and do it for them, set up the Hays Office as their own form of censorship. Hays immediately banned Fatty from acting for eight months, but the truth of the matter was that he was unable to get any kind of work for years. He became a scapegoat for every bit of sordid behaviour that had gone on before his trial, and only a few close pals like Buster Keaton stuck by him. For a very long time, the only way in which he could get a job as a director or gag writer was by using a different name. In *Photoplay* in March 1931 he begged, 'just let me work.' He took to drink, and when at last in 1933 he was offered his first acting role in a feature film since the case, he died of a heart attack the next day.

Illusions lost and hope fading, Roscoe Arbuckle just jogs along directing other people's comedies

But was Fatty's murder trial ever really justified, or was it simply a witch-hunt by the authorities of the day against what they saw as the excesses of Hollywood? The key part of Maude Delmont's story was that she saw Fatty Arbuckle come out of the room he had entered with Virginia wearing her hat, and with his pyjamas wet through. But in a recently published book entitled *The Day the Laughter Stopped*, author David Yallop says that at the time of the incident Maude herself was in another room with a man. He claims that Arbuckle and Virginia were only alone together for a few minutes and that at previous parties she had torn off her own clothes when drunk. She also had a long history of bladder complaints and had been told by doctors not to drink. So she may have died of natural causes, aggravated by the drink she had consumed and by the cold bath used to try to revive her.

Fatty told *Photoplay*, 'I've no resentment against anybody for what happened. My conscience is clear, my heart is clean.'

DEATH AT THE STAR SPANGLED ORGY

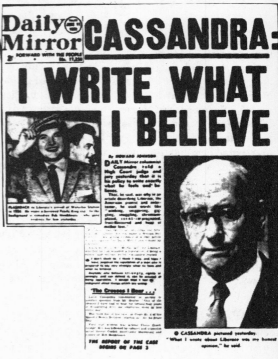

Piano-Player Preserves
Reputation

WILLIAM CONNORS joined the *Daily Mirror* before World War II; during it he wrote for the army newspaper, the *Union Jack*. Under the name of Cassandra he wrote punchy outspoken columns in the *Mirror*, and he didn't mince his words. But Cassandra met his match with his column about the man whose name was more usually linked with a candelabra than a member of the opposite sex, the pianist and 'entertainer' Liberace.

Cassandra was the man who had written tough stuff about Billy Graham and then met him over a pint in a pub appropriately named the Baptist's Head. But there was no question of meeting the diamond-adorned big L to make up over the strains of 'Cocktails for Two'. On 26 September 1956 Cassandra turned his attention to Liberace and made much of the performer's more extravagant mannerisms. Words like 'mincing' and 'sniggering' were employed, and Liberace was described as 'scent-impregnated' and 'fruit-flavoured'. But Liberace turned out to be no soft-centred jelly baby. He slapped a libel writ on Cassandra and the *Mirror*, and brought them the most widely publicized case of its kind for fifteen years. Stars like Bob Monkhouse and Mantovani stood in court as

character witnesses for Liberace, droning on about what a truly wonderful performer he was. Cassandra took the stand and the *Mirror* headlined the case I WRITE WHAT I BELIEVE. Some of the exchanges had the spectators in court in fits of laughter. Much was made of an incident at Waterloo Station when a young lady had kissed Liberace through a window – he had pressed his lips to the glass in reply. Cassandra was asked whether, if he'd been years younger and unmarried, he would have done the same, to which he replied; 'My passion, although it has always been strong, has never forced itself its way through plate-glass' – a reply which produced suppressed hysteria in court. Papers described the goings-on as 'The case of the year' and 'The Liberace Show', giving it massive day-by-day coverage. The *Daily Mirror* was called 'salacious and sensational' by the prosecution.

All this, of course, sold thousands more copies each day. But it was at some cost – £35,000 to be exact, according to Hugh Cudlipp in *At Your Peril*. They had to pay £8,000 in damages, £2,000 of which were awarded specifically because of the imputation that Liberace was a homosexual; the rest was in legal fees. What Cassandra had written was ruled as 'not fair comment', but the case certainly brought Liberace back into the public eye in Great Britain.

Showbiz Memoirs

As long as we spend our cash to smirk at the exploits of the famous, newspaper editors will still shell out large sums to actresses, ex-models, secretaries, and even domestics, for a bit of detail about what goes on behind the front doors of the stars. Over the last three years the genre has definitely got rather worn out. The same randy characters have started to reappear just too often: Ryan, Warren, and dear old Mick. Why, they are all well over thirty and must be getting a bit tired by now. This kind of memoir wouldn't harm a star's career as it did Clara Bow's in the twenties.

Exclusive today: Britt Ekland's sensational revelations

Britt's Boys

In August 1979 Swedish actress Britt Ekland sold her memoirs to the *News of the World* for a reported £110,000, certainly the highest price ever for kiss-and-tell tittle-tattle. For this kind of money Britt was going to have to name names and sling a lot of details in. And she certainly did. Before the publication of the first episode on 12 August 1979, her ex-husband Peter Sellers tried unsuccessfully to get a court injunction to prevent Britt from revealing details of their married life. This only spurred her on to even greater frankness: 'I don't like very hairy men, which my ex-husband Peter Sellers is,' she trilled to the delight of the *News of the World*. She was then aged thirty-six, and had two children: a daughter by her marriage to Sellers and a son by her four-year affair with film and record producer Lou Adler. Britt had always regarded herself as a glamorous film star, an international celebrity. She had sought out the right kind of escorts to be seen with, and had dated Michael Caine before Peter Sellers. When she married Peter

Sellers in 1964 her career was just starting, and after their divorce four years later she made a string of films, including *The Night They Raided Minsky's*. But then her career seemed to falter, and she went out with a string of desirable men: Patrick Lichfield, Warren Beatty (he crops up in every kiss-and-tell story somewhere along the line), George Hamilton, and Ryan O'Neal (another kiss-and-tell perennial). Finally she met Lou Adler and they lived together for four years, during which she didn't appear in any important films. When she split up with Adler she was very depressed, but when Joan Collins and her husband Ron Kass introduced her to rock star Rod Stewart, Britt had found the right kind of man again. She gushed to journalist Rod Gilchrist of the *Daily Mail*: 'Rod and I are really the Liz Taylor and Richard Burton of the seventies – but without the yuckiness. I mean, I think we have more class, more style. People say we are pop's most charismatic couple and it's true.' By 1976 she was telling the *Daily Express*: 'Rod will stay with me – for ever. I am an able woman, domineering and self-sufficient.' Rod had been telling the press that they would never marry, much to Britt's fury. By 1975 she had made twenty-two films, most of them instantly

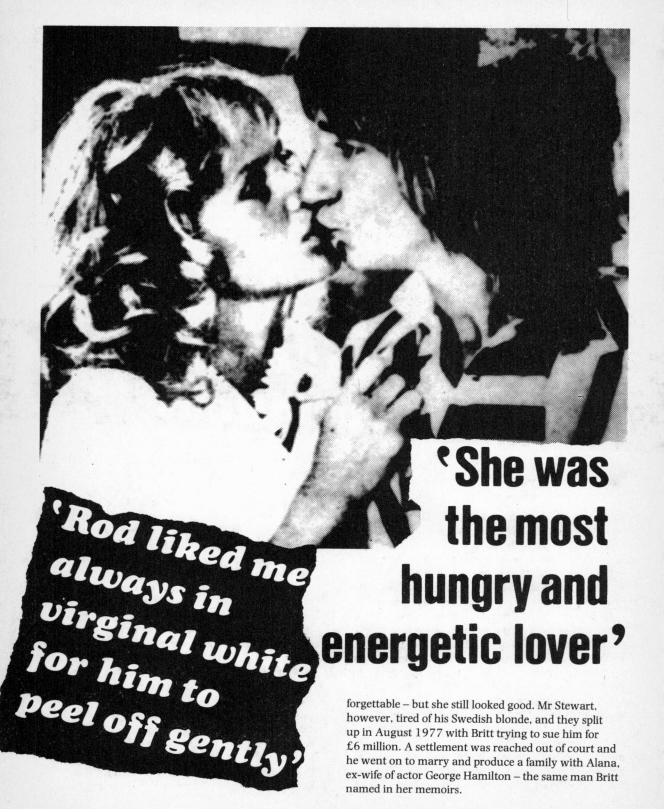

'She was the most hungry and energetic lover'

'Rod liked me always in virginal white for him to peel off gently'

forgettable – but she still looked good. Mr Stewart, however, tired of his Swedish blonde, and they split up in August 1977 with Britt trying to sue him for £6 million. A settlement was reached out of court and he went on to marry and produce a family with Alana, ex-wife of actor George Hamilton – the same man Britt named in her memoirs.

'We tried to set fresh records each day in bed'

Sounds sordid, doesn't it? Well, the story so far is nothing compared to what Britt revealed in the *News of the World*. It seemed to be an act of revenge as much as anything else. Journalistically Britt was no Shakespeare, but you can forgive a lady a lot when she starts an episode, 'If I could create the perfect man out of all those I have loved, I would start with Rod Stewart's backside.' She informed the readers that Rod was stingy with money, wouldn't pay bills, liked to wear her cotton panties on stage (more about clothes-swapping later), and while he called her 'poopy' she addressed him as 'soddy'. Although a wonderful lover etc. etc., Mr Stewart had some drawbacks: 'For me he was never particularly mentally stimulating,' she owned up. Of her other lovers, she said of Lord Lichfield, 'One would sneak down the corridor, do it, then sneak back to one's room again.'

STRAIGHT ACTOR

If Rod was gnashing his teeth, so was the the rest of Fleet Street. But the *Sunday Mirror* upstaged the lot of them, including the *News of the World*, by hitting back the next weekend with the memoirs of 'Britt's boy'.

Simon Turner was a twenty-three-year-old actor when he met Britt, just after she had split up with Rod. At a party she asked him, 'Simon, are you straight?' and, having got the answer she required, they then had an eight-month affair. Once again it transpired that there was much exchanging of clothes.

MAKE-UP

Britt required Simon to be fully turned out in items from her wardrobe during the whole time they were together. The only thing he could call his own were his shoes. She painted his face, powdered him, and even applied his nail varnish. She dyed his hair blonde to match hers; they looked like Pinky and Perky puppets. Simon, not unnaturally, got rather fed up with all this, although he claimed to love Britt, the 'Swedish housewife'. He said of Britt's insatiable desire for publicity that 'she made more entrances at Heathrow airport than she ever did on stage' and, commenting on her flop disco record, remarked that her voice was like 'a duck flying backwards'.

TOO OLD

Britt had told Simon that she would never date anyone over twenty-five. When he was twenty-four, she packed him in for someone younger and fresher. The *Sunday Mirror* had paid just £5,000 for two weeks' worth of Britt-baiting, and probably sold as many extra copies as the *News of the World*. Britt's book *True Britt* came out in 1980 and sold well. She is currently writing another, also of her memoirs. When asked how someone in their mid thirties could be writing their life story, her agent Don Short replied, 'They've probably packed more into a year than an ordinary person would do in a lifetime.'

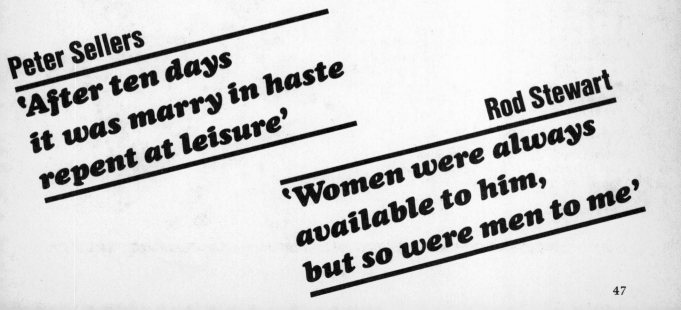

Peter Sellers
'After ten days it was marry in haste repent at leisure'

Rod Stewart
'Women were always available to him, but so were men to me'

Daisy Does It

CLARA BOW, forever known as the It Girl, just didn't know the meaning of the word discreet: for a start, she liked to drive around in a red sports car with her two dogs dyed red to match both the car and (naturally) the colour of her hair. The girl that seemed to personify the carefree spirit of the twenties was born into a poor family in New York. She worked as a typist and a receptionist, and at the age of seventeen won a 'fame and fortune' beauty contest in a fan magazine. From then on Hollywood moulded her into a star, and by the time she was twenty-three, Clara was up there with the most successful in Hollywood. In 1929 she didn't have a care in the world, but within three years she was forced into retirement after a series of nervous breakdowns.

BEAUX

Clara's love life wasn't much of a secret. She starred with Gary Cooper in *Children of Divorce* and, even though she told Hedda Hopper that 'when he puts his arms round me I feel like a horse', she had an affair with the ex-cowboy actor; perhaps he lassooed her. She also had an affair with actor Gilbert Roland, but trouble really began to brew when the star of *It* ran up a series of gambling debts in Nevada, claiming she didn't know the value of the chips she was playing with. She later repaid the money. She was named in a divorce case involving a Doctor Pearson, and ended up paying his wife a hefty sum for alienation of her husband's affections. But the bad publicity reached its peak when Clara fell out with her secretary and friend Daisy Devoe, who promptly sold her memoirs of four hectic years with Clara to the decidedly sleazy *New York Graphic*. Daisy compiled a rather embarrassingly long list of Clara's beaux, and even claimed that the *It* lady had done *it* with the entire football team of the University of California in Los Angeles. Daisy recalled wild parties and bootleg whisky, gambling and playing cards with the servants. The film colony was hypocritical as usual and put on shocked faces.

STOLEN LETTERS

It didn't matter that Clara wasn't unusual and that some of Daisy's claims were ludicrous – they didn't want their dirty washing done in public. Matters weren't helped by a court case in Los Angeles which Clara brought against Daisy alleging theft and the unauthorized writing of cheques. In evidence, some of Clara's love letters stolen by Daisy were read out in court, and they certainly made 'hot' reading. Daisy ended up with a jail sentence, and Clara then married one of her boyfriends, cowboy actor Rex Bell.

DECLINE

Soon after, she had a nervous breakdown. On leaving the sanatorium, she found her contract was about to expire, and Paramount didn't bother to renew it. She was just twenty-six. By then she had talkies to worry about too, and her first attempt was a flop. The public weren't expecting a Brooklyn accent to pop out of the deliciously heart-shaped lips of their *It* girl. Her comeback picture *Call Her Savage*, made in 1932, was more successful, but afterwards Clara had another nervous breakdown. It was the Depression and there wasn't much demand in films for the red-haired flapper of the twenties. She went into retirement, had two children, and was described by one of them as a chronic insomniac who painted and read a lot as she got older, but rarely went out. There is no doubt that Daisy's Memoirs had played a considerable part in her undoing.

LOVELACE GOES DOWN FIGHTING

Linda's 'Ordeal'

IN 1972 LINDA LOVELACE became the most ogled-at girl in any porno-movie this century when *Deep Throat* was released. Aged just twenty-three, Linda played the part of a girl whose clitoris was situated in her throat and so was 'desperate' for oral sex with men. The film, starring Linda's mind-boggling tonsil work, grossed about $18 million, a phenomenal amount for a low-budget venture. It was the first porno-movie that was considered OK to take your girlfriend to – if only to be astonished by Linda's swallowing techniques. It was also the first 'chic' dirty movie.

Linda had been taught how to relax her throat muscles so that she didn't gag when confronted with a large penis, and her mentor and master was her husband Chuck Traynor. In all the interviews she gave about the film, she seemed happy with the part she played and the reputation it saddled her with. She'd been discovered by Gerry Damiano, the director of the movie, and when he heard of Linda's unusual capabilities he built the idea of the film around her. The money to make it was supplied by Lou Peraino, who was subsequently arrested by the FBI for criminal activities in the porno-movie business. A female reporter who'd been upset by the movie telephoned Linda and was told: 'I totally enjoyed myself making the movie.' This was a pretty typical response.

'THROAT' STAR

Imagine the amazement, then, in 1980 when Linda (real name Linda Boreman, now married to her second husband, TV cable installer Larry Marchaino, with a small child) wrote her autobiography and called it *Ordeal*. She said she'd hated every minute of her time with Traynor and that he had totally dominated and humiliated her into total submission to his will. First time around, as the star of *Deep Throat*, she wasn't seen on prime-time television, but this time, as the wronged lady, she was on all the talk-shows plugging her harrowing story.

Against her will !

Ordeal was a lurid book. She was very specific about all the men with whom she said Chuck had forced her to have sex. She related how she had tried to escape him three times but had given herself up each time. The third occasion was after Chuck had forced her to star in a sex-film with a dog. She claimed that she hated exhibitionist sex, and that Chuck used to force her into it at gun-point. She alleged that he collected hand-grenades and had a machine-gun to intimidate her with. Chuck dictated the answers to all the questions that reporters ever asked her, and punished her if she didn't say the right thing. The second time she tried to escape, she was betrayed by her own mother. She said the intimidation consisted of such tricks as having a garden hose shoved up her rectum – with the threat of it being turned on if she didn't expose herself in restaurants and to truck-drivers. Linda claimed that she married Chuck because he wanted to make sure she wouldn't testify against him on drug charges. She was said to have to wear surgical stockings to protect the veins in her legs which had been damaged by severe beatings, and the silicone which she'd had injected into her breasts had shifted and would need surgery. Linda claimed she had been subjected to rapes and gang-bangs and had

to pay for services like the silicone job with her body. Countering this, Traynor dismissed Linda's story totally and said he had 'created' her.

Finally, she managed to escape from Traynor after he met another porno-movie star, Marilyn Chambers, in 1974, by which time Linda and her husband were living on partial welfare – hence the book. It did seem as if much of what she'd said about Traynor's behaviour had an element of truth in it when an interviewer went to talk to Marilyn Chambers. Traynor answered all the questions for her, and when she said she wanted to go to the bathroom he told her to sit still and shut up. He later told the reporter: 'I don't tell you how to write your column – don't tell me how to treat my broads.'

UNGAGGED!

SEX ON A TRAPEZE

Chambers had starred in *Behind the Green Door*, another 'fashionable' porno-movie, which had grossed $3 million. She had embarrassed Proctor and Gamble by her movie debut, because she had once modelled as the happy mother on the 'Ivory Snow' packets. Now she portrayed a sex-mad lady who managed to copulate with four acrobats on a trapeze – all at the same time. Traynor was trying to launch her as a nightclub act, but she was met with jeers and laughter. Her voice was said to be pretty feeble, and the reporters present at her debut were surprised when a porno-movie director approached them and said: 'I want to you to feel for that girl who's being exploited.' Chambers had been a high-school cheerleader, and had modelled in TV commercials for Pepsi and Clairol. Apart from *Behind the Green Door* she had made another X-film, *The Resurrection of Eve*. Her book *Marilyn Chambers – My Story* was said to have sold over 600,000 copies, and she had written another book with the 'Happy Hooker' Xaviera Hollander.

According to Chuck, 'Marilyn's got what Linda never had – talent,' but Linda's book had caused many people to wonder how on earth women got into this kind of life, and, once inside it, how difficult it was to emerge unscathed. Linda for one was pretty scarred, both physically and mentally. She said that she had been upset during a visit to the Cannes Film Festival that people had found *Deep Throat* fashionable when she found it merely disgusting.

Showbiz

Mafia Connections

Although it is well known that the Mafia runs Las Vegas and used to take a healthy interest in the unions in Hollywood, it is hard to know just how closely famous entertainers have been involved with the mob. Such connections have always been shrouded in mystery, and one can rarely have more than mere suspicions. Perhaps Mario and Thelma and Frank just didn't know how to choose friends.

GOLDEN-VOICED LANZA IS DEAD

Tenor Silenced

MARIO LANZA'S real name was Alfred Arnold Cocozza. It is not hard to see why he changed it in his twenties when he started to make a name for himself as a tenor. Alfred was born in Philadelphia and had been an enthusiastic weightlifter and piano-mover before he took voice-training lessons at the late age of twenty. It was obvious he had an extremely rare talent, and within nine years Alfred became Mario, the star of concerts and films. But Mario never learnt self-control; his appetite was legendary, consisting of six steaks for breakfast and sometimes a couple of dozen bits of fried chicken for dinner. His weight fluctuated between thirteen and twenty stone, which led him into terrible rows with film producers when he appeared on the set too fat to photograph. This happened with the film *The Student Prince* and Edmund Purdom took over the part, with Lanza's voice being dubbed in afterwards for the songs.

Lanza certainly was larger than life. After starring in *The Great Caruso*, he firmly believed that Caruso's ghost spoke to him at regular intervals; and once, when he was to give a concert at the opening of a casino in Las Vegas and could not perform because he had got a throat infection, got drunk, and taken too many sleeping pills, 'Caruso's ghost told me I should not perform in a gambling den.' Making him unconscious at the time he should have been on stage was the great Caruso's way of punishing Mario. Amazingly, even though all the seats had been sold,

WAS MARIO LANZA MURDERED?

His daughter says yes. And the Mafia may have ordered his execution

people thought he was dead at thirty-eight because of too many women, too much food, too many gallons of wine, and too many pills. Five months later his wife was dead from an overdose. She had been totally distraught at his death.

NEW THEORY

In 1976 this story of Lanza's death became open to question when one of his friends, Raymond Strait, wrote a book, *Star Babies*, in which he said that the singer had been killed on the orders of Mafia boss Lucky Luciano. Lanza had been ordered to sing at a charity concert in Italy which was to have been attended by visiting American Godfathers. He refused, claiming he was unwell, and checked into hospital to try to lose weight. His daughter, who was fourteen when he died, agreed with this theory. She told Strait that her father always had his chauffeur sleep at the bottom of the bed. When the man awoke, he found that the intravenous tube keeping Lanza alive had been tampered with and air was pumping into his veins. Lanza lay dead, murdered by persons unknown.

and the casino threatened damages, Lanza got away with it. He refunded his fee and was asked back again.

His fortunes fluctuated, just like his weight. He offended film bosses with his unreliability and was threatened with court actions of over half a million pounds through his habit of contract-breaking. He arrived in London to do a concert at the Albert Hall, but couldn't perform because he was so drunk. Nevertheless it was re-scheduled. He got away with all this simply because his voice was magic. His temper was something else. Hedda Hopper once characterized him as a man who would use his Cadillac to smash down the mailbox of a movie executive he thought had double-crossed him. But his luck couldn't hold for ever, and during the fifties he found himself unable to compete against either the appeal of Presley's rock-and-roll music or the reliability of performers like Perry Como.

SWAN SONG

Lanza was found dead in a hospital bed in Rome in October 1959, reportedly the result of a heart attack. The *Daily Mail* stated that a nurse said 'he died singing one of his songs' – a rather romantic story in keeping with the Lanza image, but probably untrue. Most

Mario was 'murdered by Mafia'

FILM star Mario Lanza was murdered by the Mafia because he refused to perform in an underworld "charity" concert.

That is the claim made in a book about Lanza's

Hot Toddy Found Cold

ON THE MORNING of Monday 16 December 1935, a maid opened a garage door in Malibu, the beach colony just outside Los Angeles, and found top comedienne Thelma Todd dead in her car. That maid also opened up a scandal which to this day has never been fully explained. Although the ignition was turned on in Miss Todd's car, the engine was not running. Her face was covered in blood which had spotted her evening dress and fur coat, and her lip was cut and a tooth dislodged.

VAMPING VENUS

It looked like suicide – as if she had left the engine running and slumped over the wheel when the fumes began to reach her. But why would the glamorous Thelma, star of films like the Marx Brothers' *Horse Feathers* and *Monkey Business*, have taken her own life? Thelma was known in the press as the Vamping Venus. Her friends called her Hot Toddy, which fan mags explained was 'for her lively participation in filmdom's gay revels'. She had worked with Bing Crosby and Buster Keaton, had no shortage of work offers, and plenty of friends. Although divorced, she wasn't lacking admirers. So why was Thelma dead?

GRAND JURY

Apart from working as an actress, Thelma was a partner in a successful restaurant in Malibu, Thelma's Café. She lived above it in a small apartment. Close by in the building lived her partner, Roland West. The garage was 500 yards down the road. At the first inquest the verdict was suicide. Apparently she had died at 7 a.m. on Monday morning. Her lawyers were dissatisfied with this, and dropped the name of a well-known Mafia figure as a reason why all was not well in Thelma's little world, with the result that a second inquest was called before a Grand Jury.

CAR MURDER OF FILM STAR

Victim of 'Pay or Die' Threat

By now it was clear that Thelma's friends and associates were frightened, and the evidence presented was confusing and contradictory. Roland West said that on the Saturday night, as Thelma had left to go to a party at the Trocadero nightclub given by Stanley Lupino and his daughter Ida, he had jokingly said he would lock her out if she didn't return home by 2 a.m. She left the party and got a lift home at 3.30. A driver dropped her outside the café. Mr West admitted that he had locked all the doors, but said that Thelma had a key. The maid confirmed this. But it transpired that the doors had been locked on the *inside* and she couldn't get in. So it looked as if Thelma had spent the night in the garage with the car engine running, trying to keep warm, and that the fumes had killed her on Sunday morning and not Monday. But why hadn't West sounded the alarm when he didn't see her on Sunday?

However, according to a different account, Thelma had telephoned someone on Sunday afternoon, said she was still in her party frock from the previous night, and was coming over to their house with a surprise guest – but she never arrived. Another witness reported seeing her driving in Hollywood on Sunday night, in her own car, with a 'dark-complexioned man'. At the Trocadero party she had been in good spirits, although her ex-husband had snubbed her. They had a row, and on the way home she told her driver she was 'frightened of gangsters'.

MYSTERY OVER FILM STAR'S DEATH DEEPENS
Murder, Suicide, Mishap? Police Cannot Decide

The head waiter at the Trocadero got a threatening postcard telling him he would be kidnapped if he gave evidence. So where had Thelma spent the rest of Sunday, and where had the dark man materialized from?

A further witness reported her coming into their drugstore on Sunday to make a telephone call 'in a distressed state' and accompanied by the mystery man. Her evening shoes had unmarked soles, so it was clear that she hadn't walked from the point where her driver had dropped her off after the Trocadero party and walked all the way up hundreds of steps to the garage. Also, if she had wanted to kill herself, would she really have done it in an open car, when next to it in the garage was a sedan with closed windows? And furthermore, would she have left the garage windows open?

'DARK MAN'

Rumours were rife that organized crime had wanted to get involved in her café, and were pressing her to let them open up a crooked casino upstairs there, where Thelma's rich and famous friends would be fleeced. It was well known that a few months earlier she had had an unpleasant experience involving a blackmail threat: two anonymous writers demanded money or she'd be dead, killed by 'The San Francisco Boys'. Thelma hired a bodyguard for a while until it seemed that they were not going to carry out the threat. So who was the 'dark man'? She had told friends about a new romance involving 'a businessman from San Francisco', but nobody knew who he was. Was this man a gangster putting pressure on Thelma to give in to the Mafia? Had he killed her on Sunday night and then arranged the body in the car to look like suicide? And why didn't Roland West, her partner, suspect anything?

The eventual verdict was 'death by carbon monoxide poisoning', but it did not record whether Thelma had really meant to die or not.

SINATRA: ME AND THE MAFIA

America's Top Mafia Hoods Are Frank's Pals

Frankie and Friends

WHEN MARIO PUZO wrote the best seller *The Godfather*, everyone thought that one sequence in it was a sly dig at Frank Sinatra. And when the film was released, the stories started all over again. They revolved around one of the minor characters, an Italian-American singer who is desperate for a part in a film. He comes to the Godfather at his daughter's wedding and asks a favour: will the Mafia help him? When the emissary sent by the Godfather is told where to get off by the Hollywood tycoon, the film producer finds his prize racehorse in pieces in his bed the next day. So guess who got the part.

All this was taken by many people to be a re-working of the legends about how Sinatra got his first film role (for which he later won an Oscar) in *From Here to Eternity*. It was 1953, and Sinatra was in trouble. His

voice wasn't good, and he had been released from both his television and his recording contracts. He heard that Columbia were casting, and started his campaign to get the part of Maggio. Now different versions of the process take over. One says that the Vice-president of Columbia was in New York when Frank arrived at his apartment and offered to do the part for nothing. After much consideration, it was decided that it would place the studio in a favourable position with Ava Gardner (then Sinatra's wife) and so, very reluctantly, they gave him a test. He got the part for the basic rate. Another version of the saga is that, after Ava's efforts on his behalf had failed, Sinatra reputedly asked someone to ask his acquaintance Frank Costello to ask around the Syndicate to put some pressure on the studio. Sinatra still denies this. Either way, this tactic didn't work. According to a third version, Sinatra saw Harry Cohn personally and begged for the part for just $1,000 a week. It seemed as if Eli Wallach was lined up for it when Frank flew off to join Ava on location in Nairobi. A telegram arrived telling him he could have a test, so he flew back to Los Angeles, took the test, and returned immediately to Ava. Meanwhile Eli Wallach signed to do a play, making himself unavailable, and the rest of the picture had been cast. Finally Sinatra got another telegram to say he could have the part for a mere $8,000. He agreed.

Either way, it is doubtful whether he would have played the role had he not been so outstanding in his first screen test.

PRESIDENTIAL LINK

Judeth Exner had been a girlfriend of Sinatra, and in 1960 flew with a party of his friends to Las Vegas for the weekend. That weekend she met John Kennedy, brother-in-law of Sinatra's buddy Peter Lawford. She remained on good terms with Sinatra, and through him met Mafia boss Sam Giancana. Sinatra had feverishly supported the Democrats, and after Kennedy was elected had put together a concert which helped to pay off their campaign debts. Judith's affair with Kennedy was no longer much of a secret, and Sinatra was a regular guest at the White House. Exner's

EXPOSED: SINATRA'S GANGSTER FRIENDS

relationship with Kennedy ended in the spring of 1962, and Hoover tipped off Kennedy that Sinatra had Mafia connections. By the end of 1962, the FBI and other government departments were asking for an investigation into Sinatra's affairs, but this was firmly vetoed by John's brother Robert, then Attorney-General. Was he protecting the President? Anyway, Sinatra was no longer welcome at the White House.

In 1963 it was discovered that Sam Giancana had been a regular guest at a resort hotel partly owned by Sinatra. Sinatra was threatened with an inquiry – or else he would lose his gaming licence in Nevada. Sinatra later claimed he sold his share in the hotel on the advice of Jack Warner, head of the film studio, who said it was bad for his image. Whatever the truth, Sinatra did lose his gaming licence. In 1969 and 1970

the New Jersey Commission of Inquiry into Organized Crime eventually dropped all charges against him after he put in an appearance and gave evidence. In 1972 a Select Committee in Washington, investigating how far organized crime had penetrated sport, questioned a Mafia witness who claimed that Sinatra had shares in two hotels as a front for a Mafia boss. Sinatra refused to be subpoenaed to appear, left America, and turned up in Monte Carlo, where he accepted an 'invitation' to give evidence. He did so brilliantly, and handled the committee like the members of an orchestra he had to whip into shape. He was asked if he thought the Mafia existed and gave them a famous answer, 'I suppose it does exist. But I am not aware of a tremendous amount of crime.'

The appearance was a total success, and the *Daily Mail* reported that his friend Nixon had phoned to congratulate him. Sinatra's political ambitions had now switched to the Republicans after being spurned by the Kennedys. After winning the election, Nixon invited him to sing at the White House.

NEW SENSATION

Sinatra had by now sold his interests in a racetrack after discovering that, besides Dean Martin, his partners were two Mafia bosses, but he nevertheless found himself caught up in yet another sensation. During the trial of eight Mafia members, reference was made to a theatre in which he had performed. In court was exhibit 181, a photograph, and a few days later *Life* magazine published it: it showed Sinatra surrounded by members of the Mafia, including Carlo Gambino. Sinatra himself said that Gambino's

daughter had asked for a snap and then 'eight or nine men had suddenly appeared in a group'.

Early in 1981 Sinatra applied to have his gaming licence in Nevada restored. Appearing before the Gaming Board in Las Vegas, he had a lot of explaining to do. He acknowledged his friendship with known gangsters, but played it down. He called character witnesses like Kirk Douglas, and there was an affidavit from Bob Hope saying, 'I consider him to be a dedicated public citizen.' The Chairman granted Sinatra a licence, saying, 'I'm not saying he's a saint by any means, but we have not found any substantive reasons why he should not be granted a licence.' Reagan, for whom Sinatra had raised half a million dollars at a pre-inaugural gala, said: 'We've heard these things about Frank for years and we just hope none of them are true.'

SINATRA'S MAFIA FAN CLUB

Showbiz

Sad Suicides

The reasons why stars commit suicide can usually be pretty easily categorized. Often it is the fear of being phased out of the public eye, of no longer being beautiful enough to be photographed or fashionable enough to be cast in interesting parts. Or, in many cases, the private reality of their world is so far removed from what the public believes that they can no longer go on trying to keep the two separate. And the reaction in the press is always the same, be it the death of Lady Barnett, respectable doctor and caring mother of a handicapped son, or of Carole Landis, popular film star. All their friends supply quotes like: 'I just can't believe that she would do such a thing ... why didn't she tell us?' Suicides can't face telling anyone anything any more.

Carole's 'I'm Sorry' Note
POLICE SAY SUICIDE

So Sorry

CAROLE LANDIS was a five-times-married actress whose career wasn't exactly moving in leaps and bounds. Carole had met Rex Harrison in London when she was filming *The Noose*, a time when she hinted at her depression in interviews, implying how, in spite of leading a glamorous life, she was really unhappy. Her suicide at 29 was a tidy affair. She wrote a note to mum, then took an overdose. The body was found by Rex Harrison, who did his very best to avoid the ensuing scandal. Gossip columnists Hedda Hopper and Louella Parsons were furious when Harrison and Lilli Palmer later attacked Hollywood: *they* felt that Harrison had got off lightly over Carole's death. At the time of Carole's death a variety of stories circulated, including one that she was suffering from incurable cancer, and another that she had recently had a disastrous romance with a young G.I. The note which Harrison read on 5 July 1948 when he arrived at the house in the afternoon made no mention of him. It merely said:

❝ Dearest Mommie. I am sorry, really sorry, to put you through all this. But there is no way to avoid it. ❞

THE REAL TRAGEDY OF LADY ISOBEL

LAST WORDS OF LADY B..

'Please help me—I can't stop stealing'

Lady Barnett

ISOBEL BARNETT first came to the public's attention as a panelist on television on 'What's My Line?'. Her first few contributions were rather stilted and formal, but she soon developed a breezy style that became very popular. She was great friends with Gilbert Harding, and they made an odd couple, the lady doctor and magistrate and the grumpy, taciturn bachelor. They appeared on hundreds of quiz shows and panel games together, and she gained a reputation for her charm, tact and middle-class respectability. She seemed to stand for all that was terribly comfortable about English society, and spent a busy life giving lectures, after-lunch and dinner speeches, and performing much work for charity.

In August 1980 the newspapers carried a small report that she had elected to go for trial by jury on a charge of shoplifting, and in October of that year she made front-page news as the evidence unfolded in court. She was accused of stealing a tin of tuna fish and a carton of cream, together worth 87p, from her village store. The court found her guilty and imposed a £75 fine. After the case she faced the journalists bravely enough, but she confessed to one, Mary Griffiths of the *Sun*, that she just couldn't stop stealing, and asked for help. She was convicted on a Friday, and on the Monday morning was discovered dead in her bath. Nobody who knew this highly intelligent, well-organized woman could believe that she had spent the last few years of her life feeling lonely and fighting the compulsive urge of petty pilfering without being able to ask anyone for help. After her death, newspapers carried editorials suggesting that perhaps fines were not the right way to deal with what was, after all, a psychiatric illness.

Spitfire Splutters Out

LUPE VELEZ, the Mexican film star, was billed by her studio as the Spitfire and she lived up to her title with her legendary temper and outrageous behaviour. Throughout her career she was never out of the headlines for more than a few weeks at a time, starting with her affair with Gary Cooper, her leading man in *Wolf Song* in 1929, and throughout her relationship and later marriage to Johnny Weissmuller. Lupe dressed crazy, acted crazy, kept pet chihuahuas with which she carried on a running conversation whilst cycling round town, and cooed to seventy-five canaries at home. She loved boxing, to the extent of clambering in the ring to give the fighters encouragement. She punched people in restaurants who annoyed her, and gave Weissmuller boxing gloves after their marriage so that he could punch *her*

if she ever walked out on him again. After their divorce (she described her husband in court as a 'furniture-breaking caveman'), she had a number of affairs and her career entered something of a decline.

DEEPLY RELIGIOUS

In 1944, aged thirty-four, she had another stormy liaison with a 27-year-old actor. He turned out to be something of a cad and Lupe ended up pregnant. When he said that he would marry her only in order to legitimize the baby, Lupe broke off the engagement, telling reporters, 'I like my dogs much better than him. I am taking them to New York.' In reality Lupe set about planning her suicide meticulously; in spite of her extravagant public image she was deeply religious and would not contemplate an abortion, preferring instead to kill herself and her unborn child. She took an overdose of sleeping pills and left a note addressed to her lover: 'God forgive you and forgive me too. But I prefer to take my life and my baby's before I bring shame on him or kill him. How could you, Harold, fake such great love for me and our baby when all the time you didn't want us?'

SLEEPING PILLS

There are two versions of how Lupe's body was discovered. The world press wrote a scenario along the lines of Lupe putting on her blue silk pyjamas and retiring to bed in her pink boudoir and falling asleep, never to waken again, with a suicide note on the silk pillowcase beside her head. In Kenneth Anger's *Hollywood Babylon* he gives a different story. The sleeping pills had made Lupe feel sick and she had rushed to the bathroom. When the police were called in the morning, they found the Mexican Spitfire dead with her head down the toilet. Either way it was a sad end for the girl whose favourite party trick was to lift up her dress and show off the full extent of her charms – and Lupe never wore underwear.

DEATH AFTER TIFF
Lupe Velez Broke Engagement And Took Poison

Jean Harlow's wedding night
THE SHOCKING TRUTH

Bern Bows Out

THE MARRIAGE of Jean Harlow, the Blonde Bombshell, and Paul Bern, quiet, sensitive top producer (almost twice her age at 40), pleased almost everyone in Hollywood in July 1932. The studios regarded it as a good match because Bern was a top executive at MGM and it seemed a good business arrangement.

ODD COUPLE

The smart social set were pleased because they were trying to create the impression of a film crowd that led respectable conservative lives, playing down the reputation that the town had got during the twenties as a place where wild behaviour, drugs, and excessive drinking were commonplace. Harlow and Bern made an odd couple; but he was a popular man, highly sympathetic to actors, who had worked his way up from a clerical job. Jean respected his advice and he certainly helped push her career.

Two months after they had tied the knot, Bern was found dead on September 5 1932, having shot himself. On finding the body, the butler called MGM, and the head of the studio, Louis B. Mayer, arrived. When Mayer read Paul's suicide note, he knew that trouble lay ahead. It said:

❛ Dearest Dear ... unfortunately this is the only way to make good the frightful wrong I have done you and to wipe out my abject humiliation. I love you ... Paul. You understand that last night was only a comedy. ❜

To the outside world Paul and Jean had seemed perfectly happy, and the note made no sense at all. Under intense police questioning Jean refused to reveal what it could possibly mean. The next day, a lady named Dorothy Millette, who claimed to be Bern's first wife, drowned herself. Jean inherited Bern's wealth and house, but received sacks of hate-mail at the studio from people who thought she was responsible for Bern's death. She never revealed publicly what had gone on, even under pressure from her studio. Years later the full saga unfolded when, after her death in 1937 at the age of 26, her agent, Arthur Landau, decided to tell all.

In the early hours of the morning after her wedding, Jean had called Arthur and asked him to drive over to her house and take her to his. Landau and his wife discovered that Paul Bern had beaten Jean with a cane and bitten and bruised her legs and thighs. After she was treated by a doctor they returned her to Bern's house, and when they found him sprawled asleep naked on the floor, saw immediately where the problem lay – Bern was decidedly underdeveloped.

The morning after her beating, Bern and Harlow posed for photographers at their wedding reception, attended by everyone who was important in Hollywood. Privately, she asked her agent to set about arranging a divorce as soon as a respectable length of time had elapsed. Jean and Paul lived the next few weeks out as the perfectly happy newly-weds in public, although in fact he was seeing a doctor about his sexual inadequacies and they were having fights. He couldn't understand why, if he'd married the sexiest lady of the day, she couldn't arouse him enough to make love. The night before his suicide, he had appeared in the bedroom wearing a contraption which he thought might compensate for what nature hadn't provided him with. This just distressed Jean even more – hence his suicide and the sad little note she always refused to explain.

Showbiz Slayings

Director Peter Bogdanovich observed after his friend Sal Mineo had been murdered, 'They [the police] always try to blame murders on drugs or sexual behaviour to lead to the conclusion that the victim was just asking for it anyway. The rationale just makes it simpler to live in Hollywood.' As the following stories show, there is nothing like a murder to spark off rumour and innuendo.

Sweater Girl in Tight Spot

FILM BUFFS disagree about the exact location of the discovery of Lana Turner: some say the soda fountain at Schwabs in Hollywood, others the drugstore over the road from the High School, where Lana had sneaked across for a malted milk in the middle of classes. They also disagree about her age – but that's because she started playing extremely sexy parts while still a naive teenager. Although her intellectual education may have been incomplete when she left school and plunged into the world of the starlet, her physical development was such that from the moment she appeared on the screen at fifteen she caused a sensation. Never had a twinset clung to the female form in such an extraordinary manner, and she was christened the first of the Sweater Girls.

PERSONAL COST

For all her visual appeal, Lana wasn't well equipped emotionally to deal with life as a film star, and her first marriage at nineteen to bandleader Artie Shaw resulted in a nervous breakdown two months later. The next year she made *Ziegfeld Girls*, which established her reputation, and throughout the forties and early fifties she was consistently one of the top female box-office draws. But this success was at some personal cost: her second husband, Stephen Crane, married her when she was pregnant, and they divorced when their daughter, Cheryl, was less than a year old. By the time Cheryl was ten, mommy had married twice more, and the little girl spent a lot of time being shunted around to various private schools.

Lana had a little black book or two of lovers, including Frank Sinatra, Tyrone Power, Howard Hughes, and Victor Mature. She told gossip columnists that she just didn't seem to know how to pick men. However confused her domestic life, it seems that studio technicians always found her pleasant to work with.

TOUGH GUY

During the fifties her career took a nosedive and she appeared in seventeen straight flops. In the spring of 1957, while feeling depressed, she took a phone call from a man she had never met, who suggested that they go out on a blind date, mentioning friends that they had in common. He was Johnny Stompanato, an associate of known gangsters, an ex-marine with a big line in hot and heavy chat and a wonderful ability to persuade rich, lonely ladies to lend him money to finance his gambling. He was the kind of guy who exposed a lot of chest, acted tough, and certainly knocked his girlfriends about. He and Lana started having an affair, and when she came to England in late 1957 to make *Another Time, Another Place* with Sean Connery, Stompanato followed. He picked fights with everyone, accused Connery of getting too close to Lana, and got knocked out. Eventually the Special Branch of Scotland Yard encouraged him to leave the country, much to everyone's (including Lana's) relief. Cheryl then arrived and spent Christmas with her mother.

PASSIONATE

In spite of the fighting, Lana was smitten with Johnny: after all he had a wonderful record as a Hollywood stud. She wrote him passionate letters which were

BEDROOM KNIFING DRAMA

Lana Turner's Daughter Knifes Man

HOLLYWOOD PUTS ON A REAL-LIFE DRAMA

later to become such a major embarrassment that it is a wonder she ever sent anyone so much as a postcard again. After a holiday in Mexico together, they returned home to carry on fighting. Lana had been nominated for an Academy Award for her portrayal of a guilt-ridden mother in *Peyton Place* – the kind of performance she spent many years perfecting. However, she refused to take him to the Awards dinner, and he resented this deeply. Stompanato was O.K. as a lover, but not at all the kind of partner you paraded in front of your peers at the top film event of the year. She didn't get the Award; nevertheless, *Peyton Place* was doing well and her career seemed to be on the up. But at home things had reached rock bottom. On the night of Friday 4 April 1958, she and Johnny had a furious row, during which he threatened to disfigure her. As the pair of them rushed out of the room, Johnny ran straight into a carving knife wielded by Cheryl, who had been listening on the other side of the door. Lana was thirty-eight, and believed Johnny to be forty-two. He turned out to be thirty-two. Cheryl was just fourteen. What happened next was like a scene from a B movie. Cheryl called her father, the police arrived, journalists arrived who had heard the murder call on their car radios, and, most important of all for Lana, Jerry Geisler, top lawyer to the stars, arrived and took charge of Lana's and Cheryl's stories. Lana pleaded with the police to charge her instead of her daughter, but to no avail. Cheryl was kept at the police station and Lana returned home to speak to the press.

Next day newspapers round the world carried headlines like JOHNNY RAN INTO KNIFE, and the *News of the World* commented, 'From some angles it was a tragedy strangely reminiscent of *Peyton Place.*' Cheryl was reported as saying to the police, 'I wish I was like my mother, who at least is able to cry.' The teenager remained unmoved publicly by the whole episode. Her father told the press, 'I'm proud of my Cheryl; she only did what anyone else would have done.'

LANA TURNER'S CHILD KILLS STAR'S LOVER

Johnny's body was claimed by his gangster friend Mickey Cohen, and buried a few days later with full military honours. According to the *Daily Mirror*, servicemen of the American Legion fired guns, hoisted flags, and paid a silent tribute to the murdered man, 'for Stompanato was an ex-marine as well as an ex-gangster'. Mickey Cohen released to the press a stack of letters written by Lana to Johnny, the sad romantic ravings of an immature woman. He also showed the press letters from Johnny to Lana professing his love, but strangely enough these had never been posted. It was alleged that Cohen had stolen the letters from Stompanato's flat in order to terrify Lana.

MILITARY HONOURS FOR STOMPANATO

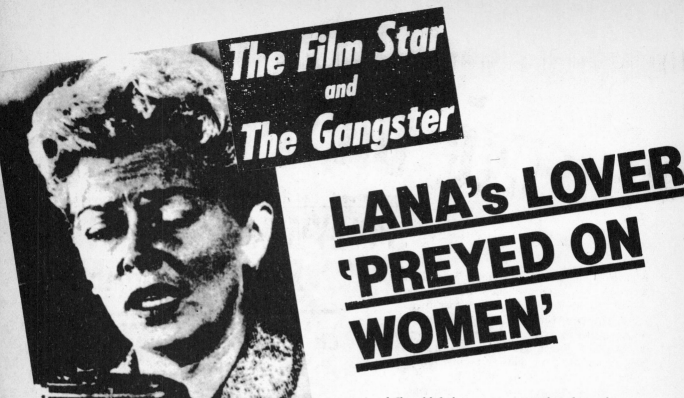

The Film Star and The Gangster

LANA's LOVER 'PREYED ON WOMEN'

and Cheryl left the court to await their fate at home, and girls screamed at the press to take pictures of them because 'they were prettier than Lana'. After less than an hour the verdict of 'justifiable homicide' was delivered; in other words, Cheryl had killed Johnny to prevent her mother from being murdered.

JURY say CHERYL WAS JUSTIFIED

The inquest, a week after the killing, was sensational. First of all it was broadcast live on American television, and second, Lana Turner gave the performance of her life in the witness box. Although the press had been filling pages with her pathetic notes to Johnny for the previous few days, she didn't crack up in court. The *Daily Mirror* carried a report by Lionel Crane, 'the only British newspaper staff man in Hollywood', who breathlessly gushed: 'Film star Lana Turner sat for sixty-two minutes in a packed, sweating court here today, telling every detail of a night of horror.' He also informed fashion-conscious readers that Lana wore 'a trim grey costume'. Her evidence led up to the quarrel with Johnny, and she told the court, 'He said when I say you will hop, you will hop. You will do everything I tell you or I will cut your face or cripple you.' Every sob, sip of water, and gasp, was watched by millions of viewers glued to their television sets. Cheryl didn't take the stand but submitted a signed statement. Mickey Cohen caused uproar in court when he refused to identify the body, claiming that it might result in him being accused of murder. This device meant that he was relieved of having to give evidence. A man stood up and accused Cheryl of killing Johnny because she was in love with him. Lana

Such a scandal would have crushed other women, but Lana carried on working. The sick result of the publicity was that *Peyton Place* did better business and the studios rushed out the picture she had made in England to cash in on the whole affair. From then on, Lana's screen roles tended to mirror what had happened to her in real life. She starred in *Imitation of Life* as a mother who neglected her daughter, making a fortune out of it, and again in *Madame X*, the story of a woman accused of murdering her lover.

DELINQUENT

Perhaps the biggest loser in the whole sordid story was Cheryl. After the inquest the trial itself was just a formality, but in 1960 she was made a ward of court and was later placed in a home for juvenile delinquents.

Seaside Slaying

ON THE MORNING of Sunday 2 November 1975, a poor Italian family took a trip to the seaside suburb of Ostia outside Rome, where they were building a simple house. On a football field by the side of the track, they discovered the body of one of the European cinema's best-known directors, Pier Paolo Pasolini, whose films, including the beautiful *Gospel according to St Matthew*, *Theorem*, *Salo or the 120 Days of Sodom*, and *Decameron*, had been as controversial as his death was to be. The skull was completely smashed in, and the body was identified by the name written inside the jacket.

Pasolini knew the slum area where he was found well; he often picked young people who lived there to appear in his films, and used it for sexual assignations. Pasolini had boldly written of the problems of homosexuals, making no secret of his own sexual preferences. Furthermore, he was a well-known communist, and only a few weeks before his death he had written a series of newspaper articles attacking his compatriots, saying that they had become obsessed with crime and had abandoned genuine values for those of the bourgeois consumer society. On the fateful evening, Pasolini had dined at a friend's house and, ironically, discussed how much he hated violence.

DEVASTATING INJURIES

A few hours after his death, the police announced that a 17-year-old boy, Giuseppe Pelosi, had confessed to the crime and had made a statement saying that Pasolini had picked him up late on Saturday night in a bar. In the early hours of the next morning, Pelosi clubbed him to death and then ran over the body in Pasolini's sports car. Pelosi claimed he hit Pasolini after the director had made sexual advances to him.

When communists in Rome put up commemorative posters in the city on the day of Pasolini's funeral, they were defaced to read PIG and a Jesuit priest was arrested and charged. Many of the left-wing sympathizers at the funeral believed that Pasolini was not murdered by the young boy alone and that it was the work of the fascists, against whom the director had consistently spoken out. Journalists speculated whether such devastating injuries could really have been inflicted by one person, but the mystery was never solved. Was Pasolini too outspoken for his own good?

Youth confesses after Decameron director is killed

X-FILM KING MURDERED

What the Butler Saw

THE MURDER of director William Desmond Taylor on 1 February 1922 caused a scandal in Hollywood that lasted for fifteen years or more. The case was never solved and, as the months passed, so many famous names (mostly female) were involved that it seemed certain the police would never be able to unravel the dead man's affairs. Taylor was the President of the Screen Directors' Guild, a well-read, charming man who said he was forty-four (but was probably older) and who enjoyed considerable success with women. When his butler Peavey found him dead on the living-room floor, the newspapers at first concluded that revenge or jealousy had been the motive, as he had not been burgled. A neighbour who heard the butler's screaming telephoned two leading actresses of the day: seventeen-year-old 'sweet young thing' Mary Miles Minter, and the comedienne Mabel Normand. Mabel rushed round to Taylor's house, telling reporters that this was at the request of detectives because she had been the last person to see the dead man alive, but in fact she was desperately trying to remove incriminating letters she had written him.

LOVE LETTERS

Mary Miles Minter, when told of the tragedy, also rushed round to the house but was unable to get in because of the crush of reporters and police. Recognized by the crowd, she went to see the body in the mortuary. Mary too had wanted to remove letters from Taylor's flat, and the detectives had found a particularly juicy one promising the lucky Desmond undying love, signed 'Mary'.

Mary and Mabel both eventually owned up to their love for Taylor, although it was never clear if in Mary's case it was actually reciprocated. He had had an enormous clash with her mother, Mrs Shelby, after mum had discovered her virginal teenage bread-winner was besotted with a middle-aged man. Mary Miles Minter was under contract to Paramount, as was Taylor, and the company were concerned when Mrs Shelby announced that she did not want Taylor to direct her nubile young daughter again. Nevertheless Mary continued to pen purple prose to the man of her dreams, expressing the hope that they could be married when she was twenty-one. Another rumour going round town was that Mrs Shelby and Taylor had had an affair and she had been distraught to discover he had been dating her own daughter at the same time.

The police found plenty of evidence that Taylor had numerous affairs: there were signed portraits, a

ANOTHER FILM TRAGEDY.
MYSTERIOUS MURDER OF BRITISH EX-OFFICER.
STARTLING REVELATIONS.
"News of the World" Special

collection of pornographic photos, plus a drawer-full of ladies' undies – treasured trophies; one piece of frilly silk was initialled MMM.

UNDERWEAR CACHE

The neighbours described hearing a 'loud noise' after Miss Normand's departure the previous evening. A woman reported seeing a man with an odd walk leave Taylor's apartment, and she thought that possibly it was a woman in drag. The police, however, were playing down the underwear cache they had found, saying it could have been used by the butler, who was due in court on a charge of indecent exposure and was a known homosexual. The *News of the World* hinted at the drug angle of the case:

❝ Detectives are investigating a report that Taylor recently attended a number of so-called "hop parties" where people addicted to the drug habit gathered, and morphine, opium, and marijuana were used freely by those present ... Male and female reputations may be scorched or smirched before the investigation is over, and all the sins of the cinema colony may be revealed. Dope fiends will figure in the tale, as well as strange effeminate men and peculiarly masculine women ... all Hollywood is being raked over, and all queer meeting places of movie actors, ... and directors, such as restaurants, beauty parlours, studios, dens where strange drugs are common, and others where men and women sit in circles drinking curious drinks, are being investigated. ❞

Mabel Normand was trying to play down her role in all this, saying, 'His friendship was that of an older man for a girl who liked outdoor sports that he liked.' This produced a laugh or two, for it was well known

that Mabel had a drug problem, and one theory about the death was that Taylor had told the police of the dealers supplying her, and one of them had bumped him off. Another theory was that he had started to get drugs for Mabel, and had been killed by the dealer he had thereby done out of business. Then there was the mysterious male secretary, Sands, who had disappeared a few months earlier after forging Taylor's signature on some cheques.

As police inquiries proceeded, an amazing story unfolded. Taylor's real name was William Cunningham Deane-Tanner. He claimed he was born in Ireland in 1887, but the truth of this claim was questioned when it was pointed out that he had married an actress in New York in 1902. In 1908 he walked out on his wife and daughter and the antique shop he had been running, and they never saw him again, and his wife divorced him for desertion. Four years later his brother Dennis did the same, walking out on his wife and family too. Over the next few years their movements are mysterious, but they spent some time prospecting for gold in the Yukon and in Colorado. Some newspapers said at Taylor's death that he had fought in the British army in the First World War, serving as a captain in France. Others said he was in the Canadian Flying Corps at one time, but that he never left Canada. Anyway, around 1919 he had turned up in Hollywood and made a name for himself quickly, first directing episodes of *The Diamond from the Sky* series, and then important features like *A Tale of Two Cities* for Fox, and *Huckleberry Finn* for Paramount. Many people thought that the missing secretary, Mr Sands, was his brother in disguise. Several years later, in 1937, Dennis's long-lost wife reappeared on the scene with a photo of Dennis she had suddenly 'found' which proved that Dennis and Sands were not the same. Or did it? Who knew where Dennis was?

CAREERS OVER

Either way, the events of February 1922 ruined the careers of the two women involved – Mabel and Mary. Whether Mrs Shelby had had an affair with Taylor or not, she too was dragged through the muck by the papers. Mum and Mary rushed off to Hawaii to get away from it all, and the studios rushed out two pictures of Mary's, capitalizing on the rumpus. They did reasonably well, but Mary made only four more pictures before she retired, fat and miserable, from films. She and her mother then got involved in a court battle with each other over money. Mabel didn't work any more and died of TB in 1930. When, a few years later, the police went through the evidence removed from Taylor's flat, the frilly undies marked MMM had disappeared.

CLAUDINE TO SPIDER: BANG! BANG!

The Ski-racer and the Town Which Took Sides

VLADIMIR SABICH, known as 'Spider' within the skiing fraternity, was a popular resident of Aspen, Colorado. Twice world ski-racing champion, 31-year-old Spider had earned enough from endorsements to have a large investment portfolio and a $250,000 house built by his brother Steve, a local contractor. But by March 1976 his four-year relationship with French-born singer and actress Claudine Longet was going sour. For the past two years they had lived together, with her three children by her marriage to singer Andy Williams. Now friends reported them rowing in private as well as in public. Claudine, who had been a lead dancer with the Folies Bergère in Las Vegas when she met Williams, had separated from him in 1970 and divorced him (after fourteen years' marriage) in 1976.

Claudine was considered a bit of an intruder in Aspen, where Spider was the hero who lived in a chic community with Tina Sinatra and John Denver as neighbours. Although residents protested that Aspen (nicknamed the 'cocaine capital' of the USA) didn't

deserve its reputation as a pleasure place for the rich and powerful, nevertheless expensive chalets filled the valley and there was a bar on every block in town. Early residents who flocked there for the simple outdoor life and excellent skiing now complained that it was so expensive they were having to leave. But the community of 60,000 was a close-knit one; they liked to think that everyone was entitled to their privacy and they were pretty 'laid-back' folk. But for a town that claimed to be prim, they had some exotic ways of letting off steam. One was an end-of-season 'bare breast' competition where, after consuming large quantities of drink and drugs, girls whipped off their T-shirts in front of a panel of male judges. Another festive occasion was the Winterskol, a winter party when guests plunged nude from a ski-jump into a swimming pool.

On 21 March 1976 Spider was in the bathroom of his house when Claudine appeared carrying a gun that belonged to him. After some conversation it went off and he fell to the floor, dying from a gunshot wound in the abdomen. Claudine tried to resuscitate him while her three children waited outside for the ambulance, but to no avail. The whizz on skis – who was reputed to be the model for Robert Redford in the film *Downhill Racer* – was buried after a packed funeral service. His distraught parents did not attend, although Claudine had called them and told them how sorry she was for the 'accident'. A few days later they turned up at the house and asked her to leave.

At her first court appearance and every subsequent one, Claudine was accompanied by her ex-husband Andy, who totally supported her in public. On 8 April she was charged with the manslaughter of Sabich, a charge which carried a possible ten-year jail sentence and/or a $30,000 fine. She was released on $5,000 bail. Frank Tucker, the District Attorney, claimed that a diary of Claudine's which police had taken from the house would show the rocky state of their relationship. He said he also planned to subpoena Claudine's 12-year-old daughter, Noelle, to give evidence. Claudine's story was that she was putting a sweater away in Spider's closet when she found the gun. Out of concern for her safety when she was alone in the house, she asked him to show her how to use it. It had gone off by mistake and the incident was 'a tragic accident'.

Rocky Mountain Murder?

Immediately Aspen became the focus for media attention. Its image had already suffered a bit of a jolt when a pulp novel had described the town as a place where sex, money and power culminated in violence and murder. Reporters descended in swarms, and at the preliminary hearing in June the judge banned the public and press on the grounds that it might not be possible to hold a fair trial with rumour and speculation flying around. Claudine pleaded not guilty and the trial was set for August. The next day the judge decided to allow transcripts of the proceedings to be released. Tucker declared that a ballistics expert would testify that the bullet which killed Spider had been fired from four to six feet away; Claudine's lawyers claimed that they would demonstrate that the safety catch on the gun was broken.

The trial was postponed, and Claudine continued to live in Aspen even though local opinion was running strongly against her and many residents and friends of Spider wanted her to leave. She bought a Victorian house and decorated it with pictures of her children and Andy Williams – no pictures of her dead lover.

The trial was eventually set for January, and Claudine refused to discuss the case with reporters. In December the Colorado Supreme Court had ruled unanimously that the District Attorney could not use her diary or the results of blood and urine tests (which were performed on her on the day of the shooting) as evidence in the forthcoming trial. The diary had been taken and the tests performed without the necessary court orders. Tucker, undeterred, announced that he still planned to proceed with the prosecution.

At the start of the trial, finding a jury proved to be an enormous problem. It took a week to find unbiased local citizens. Claudine was said to be 'heartbroken' as day after day the witness box was filled with prospective jurors (including the Mayor) who said they thought she was guilty. Only two people stuck up for her, and they were disqualified on the grounds of prejudice in her favour. A sign of how strong local feeling was running were the bumper stickers up and down the valley proclaiming, 'It's all Claudine's fault.'

After all the fuss of finding a jury, the trial itself proved to be something of an anti-climax, with only three and a half hours of testimony. In spite of the District Attorney claiming to have a witness who would testify that Spider had made a $100 bet with him that Claudine would be out of his house by April, the judge ruled out this line of questioning. Dressed conservatively, Claudine and Andy Williams both sobbed while she gave evidence. She claimed that, contrary to Spider's friends' claims that the relationship was at an end, they were the best of friends and loved each other very much. She didn't know if she had loaded the gun correctly, but Spider assured her that the safety catch was on. After it had gone off, she was distraught and tried to help him while waiting for an ambulance. A detective claimed that when she recounted the incident to him at the time, she had described how she said 'Bang bang' when the gun went off; Claudine denied this. Andy Williams also denied saying right after he'd heard about the incident: 'She's a crazy chick who likes to drive fast, ski fast and take chances.'

51st Way to Leave Your Lover?

After almost four hours the jury decided she was guilty on a lesser charge, that of criminal negligence, which carried a maximum sentence of two years' jail and a $5,000 fine. On 31 January Claudine was sentenced to thirty days, to be served at a time of her choice, and two years' probation. Andy Williams cried and said he had hoped that she would not have had to go to jail. Although local opinion was pleased that at least she'd been convicted of something, the sentence was only as long as that normally given to drunken drivers in the county. Claudine decided not to appeal and went to serve her sentence in April 1977. Meanwhile Spider's family were furious at what they called 'a bungled investigation'. His brother Steve took to calling up magazines to let journalists know that they felt Claudine had been let off lightly. Father Vladimir told a reporter, 'Justice has not prevailed.'

While Claudine herself claimed she was the victim of a district attorney who was 'more concerned with his own ambitions than truth and justice', it emerged that the lieutenant who had illegally seized her diary had resigned under pressure. The banned blood tests were now rumoured to have shown traces of cocaine, and the diary was said to detail her affairs with other men as well as Spider. On leaving jail in May Claudine was slapped with a $1·3 million damages suit by Spider's family. She was rumoured to be considering writing a book about her experiences, which the Sabich family said 'would be a pack of lies'.

COLD-SHOULDERED

A year later Claudine continued to live in Aspen, rarely going out in public. Feelings still ran high about the shooting – a friend of Spider's had dumped manure on the back seat of her Mercedes and poured brown stain all over the roof. The house Spider lived in remained unsold, and his brother Steve was planning to move to Florida. The 'ambitious' district attorney, Frank Tucker, was indicted for misuse of public funds: apparently, he'd paid for an abortion for a 17-year-old girl who he claimed was hired as an undercover agent. The loving ex, Andy Williams, came to stay with Claudine during a rugby festival in town. But many people wondered just how long she could face putting up with so many cold shoulders.

WHO KILLED SAL MINEO?

Switchblade Kid Knifed

THE IRONY of Sal Mineo's murder wasn't lost on the press. At the time he was rehearsing a stage play in which he hoped to relaunch his career – it was entitled *P.S. Your Cat is Dead*. He'd won his first Academy Award nomination for playing James Dean's friend in *Rebel without a Cause*: in the film the police shoot him, not realizing that his gun isn't loaded. Irony number three: Sal was the son of a Sicilian coffin-maker.

Sal Mineo grew up in New York. After being expelled from school at nine, he made his debut on Broadway as a child actor in *The Rose Tattoo* and *The King and I*. From the age of fifteen he mostly played juvenile delinquent parts in Hollywood, earning himself the nickname 'the switchblade kid'. He received his second Academy Award nomination in 1960 for the part of a young Israeli in *Exodus*. He even had a gold record in 1957 with 'Start Moving', which was in the British charts for eleven weeks.

The movie parts stopped coming in, but Sal had to pay huge back-taxes, about half a million dollars. He moved to smaller apartments and started appearing on the stage, occasionally popping up on television. According to his friend, director Peter Bogdanovich, 'Sal was a reminder of the fifties people preferred to forget.' He gave Bogdanovich a book which he thought would make a good film, adding that he realized he was too old to play the lead – it turned out to be *The Last Picture Show*, which really launched the director's career. On the night of his death on 12 November 1976, he was stabbed as he got out of his car at his apartment off Sunset Strip; the killer had been waiting. The murder set off panic in Hollywood: people feared the start of another Sharon Tate/Manson Family-type vendetta against the famous. Police offered various theories; that he had been stabbed by an ex-convict whom he had befriended, or by a cheated dope-dealer; they even issued a statement saying that he might have been killed by an ex-lover, since 'he was pretty active in the gay community' – but it seems that these were all cover-ups for lack of a real answer.

Showbiz
Legendary Deaths

Show me the death of a famous star, and I'll show you a conspiracy theory. For every simple overdose, fatal illness, or death by exhaustion, the press have cooked up intrigue, missing evidence, and cover-up allegations. Judy Garland believed she was a victim of the studio system which made her an addict at sixteen; she couldn't bear to think that she might at forty-seven be responsible for her own actions. We want Monroe to be the victim of the same system as Judy, and when another Monroe death theory appears, we all rush out and buy it. More people have seen films by Valentino, Garland, and Monroe after their deaths than they ever did while they were alive. By dying, they completed the image we wanted them to have.

Uppers, Downers, and Dorothy

THE SCANDAL about Judy Garland lay not so much in her death as in her tragic life-style, which dated from her days as a child star. Judy's problems were different to those of the average American teenager. Of course she had some of the regular worries of a thirteen-year-old – puppy fat, falling in and out of love – but no one of her age had to work like Judy did at MGM.

Signed up by Louis B. Mayer when she was thirteen, the studio immediately started to create myths about their young protégée which were to confuse her for the rest of her life: they changed the date of her birth, making her a year younger; they changed and 'improved' her family background in their carefully manufactured press releases; and they sent her to do special exercises so she would stand straighter and look taller.

SPECIAL DIET

Judy claimed that as a chubby teenager she had been put on a special diet by the studio to lose weight, and that Mayer himself had ordered amphetamines to be

HOW JUDY DIED —AN OVERDOSE

JUDY GARLAND DIES IN LONDON

Coroner decides it was an accident

ground into her food to reduce her appetite. In Christopher Finch's book *Rainbow: The Stormy Life of Judy Garland*, her sister Virginia confirmed that this went on, saying, 'Nobody realized it was *speed*!' Garland also said that after giving them pills to work late the studio supplied pills to make their stars go to sleep, that this régime led to her nervous collapse, and that Mayer had her treated in a psychiatric hospital. She believed that Mayer and her mother were ganging up against her, although this is something the rest of the family don't agree with. Certainly she was addicted to drugs by the age of sixteen, when she was chosen to play Dorothy in *The Wizard of Oz*; but despite all the slimming pills she had taken, she had naturally sprouted breasts and the studio firmly bound them down to keep their little girl looking little just a bit longer. Even then the pills were beginning to cause some of the problems which were to be so highly publicized in her thirties and forties – her tantrums, her chronic insomnia, her arrival at the set in no condition to work, and her failure on occasions to turn up for work at all. Her personal life was scarred by overdoses, suicide attempts, and failed marriages.

MATTER OF CONCERN

In March 1969 she married Mickie Deans, her third husband, at Chelsea Registry Office in London. The wedding made the headlines because the reception was at Quaglino's and few of their friends turned up. For those who were close to her, her condition was a matter of concern: she was a 47-year-old pill freak who just couldn't be persuaded to eat. One Saturday night she and her husband didn't go to the theatre as they had planned. Instead, she went to bed early, and when he joined her she seemed asleep. On the morning of Sunday 22 June, he found the bathroom door locked, and, when it was broken down, Judy dead on the toilet. The coroner recorded a verdict of accidental death. Her funeral attracted more curious onlookers than her sad last wedding reception a few months earlier.

JUDY GARLAND'S LAST WORDS HER FINAL EXCLUSIVE INTERVIEW

–8 Hours Before Death She Talks About:

- Her New Husband
- Her Stage Career
- Her Drug Habit
- Her Happy Future

Star's husband tells of locked bathroom

In "The Sainted Devil" with Nita Naldi.   As "The Sheik" with Agnes Ayres.   In "Blood and Sand" with Nita Naldi.

VALENTINO DEAD

SHEIK REPORTED POISON VICTIM IN MYSTERIOUS VENGEANCE PLOT

Riots over Rudy

Nobody wanted to believe that Rudolph Valentino died from a simple perforated ulcer, one of the countless other people who died straightforward, unremarkable deaths on Monday 23 August 1926. The moment The Sheikh drew his last breath, the riots and rumours started. His death was every bit as spectacular as any part he portrayed on the screen. To understand why over 10,000 women were hysterical on the streets of New York over a man who had never uttered a single word in a film, you have to remember that in the age of the great silent film stars, looks and expression were everything. As David Robinson wrote in *The Rise and Fall of the Matinée Idol*: 'In their Valhalla of beauty it seemed normal that all thought and feeling found expression in expansive mime and mobile features. Eyes were for flashing and rolling and hooding with languorous lids; lips were for curling ...'

He had started off as a dancer, and had hung around Hollywood for a couple of years before he had his first success in *The Four Horsemen of the Apocalypse*. Another Rudy smasheroo was the wonderfully silly *The Sheikh*, where, in flowing robes, he rushes an English lady off her feet in the middle of the sand dunes, and turns out to be an earl in disguise. No matter how much the popular press attacked Rudy and implied he wasn't *that* masculine, it made no difference to his career. No matter that he had disastrous marriages and a non-existent sex life, on screen Rudy photographed as simply the most erotic man in the world. No matter that he was a bit cross-eyed, going bald, and pudgy, he died at exactly the right moment to ensure immortality as the first legendary film star death, after a career that had lasted only five years. His fans didn't want to separate the real Rudy from the screen Rudy; an ulcer just wasn't the way The Sheikh would have wanted to die. So the fact and fantasy surrounding his death became entwined; and everyone felt much better about it: it kept the fans happier, and it certainly sold a lot more newspapers.

He died at either ten past twelve or three o'clock according to the different reports. The *Daily News* started with the rumours immediately: VALENTINO POISONED? BROADWAY HEARS! There were stories that 'the great lover' had died from arsenic poisoning, the work of a jealous lover, or, according to the *Daily Mirror*, after 'fisticuffs' or 'a shooting'. Immediately every woman he had spoken to telephoned a

FOLLIES GIRL SAYS RUDY ASKED HER TO MARRY HIM

newspaper and claimed they were to marry. Two ladies committed suicide in sympathy, and so did a young boy. Actress Pola Negri apparently 'fainted at the news', recovering sufficiently to inform the press that they had been 'engaged'; she then had a relapse, and fainted again, this time in front of all the photographers. Her floral offering spelt out her name and was eleven feet across, just to make sure that those cameramen got the message. A dancer called Marion Kay Brenda announced that Rudy had asked her to marry him, saying, 'He told me that Pola Negri was a very charming person, but that he had no intention of marrying her'. Poison rumours persisted

Doctor Denies Arsenic Story; Pecora Ready to Act

There flew along Broadway yesterday sinister reports that Rudolph Valentino, idol of the screen, who died in Polyclinic hospital after a week's illness, came to his death by arsenic poisoning.

in spite of doctors' reports, and the *Daily News* asked provocatively, 'Did Valentino die like a victim of the Borgias, from whose land he came?'

When Valentino's body was taken to lie in state, 10,000 people rioted to see the body, injuring over a hundred and wrecking the funeral parlour. According to reporters, 'They were beaten back by the clubs of policemen . . . they were like the gallery gods at a championship prize fight.' Meanwhile his ex-wife Jean Acker had admitted to journalists that, although she and Rudy hadn't spoken for six years, she saw him fifteen minutes before he died. Actress Norma Talmadge rushed into print with her version of their friendship: VALENTINO AS I KNEW HIM . . . HIS CHEERY FAREWELL FOLLOWED BY HORROR OF CALL TO DEATHBED, offering such tantalizing little titbits about the star as MADE WRITING OUTLET FOR TINGLING NERVES. It seemed The Sheikh could only write 'when his nerves were tingling and his brain power suppressed'. Norma thought he would have made a good journalist or author; but his death filled more columns of text than he could ever have tingled from his pen in life.

10,000 RIOT TO SEE RUDY

MARILYN MONROE FOUND DEAD

Sleeping Pill Overdose Blamed

Blonde's Death Makes Others Rich

Marilyn Monroe was found dead early in the morning on Sunday 5 August 1962. She died too late for the last editions of the newspapers, but as Sunday is always a slack news day, editors all round the world knew that for once in their working lives they would have no trouble deciding what to make the big splash on Monday morning; and they had a whole day to put together lavish photo-reports and distressed quotes from the star's 'friends' throughout the world. MARILYN MONROE FOUND DEAD – SLEEPING PILL OVERDOSE FOUND was a favourite banner headline, although the *Daily Sketch* in London came up with a nice alternative in 'GOODNIGHT HONEY', allegedly her last words to her housekeeper on shutting the bedroom door. Vatican Radio paid a tribute, adding 'a person can be poisoned by the environment from which he or she draws the sap of physical and spiritual life'. *Il Tempo* newspaper in Rome was more forthright: 'Who killed her? Let's be honest – we killed her, the everyday people, the cinema spectators, the readers of illustrated magazines.' *Pravda* declared she was 'the victim of a decadent society' – predictable enough. Then the fan magazines started churning out Marilyn specials: HER TRAGIC LIFE, THE SEX SYMBOL, HER MANY LOVES. All the implications were that sad Marilyn was unable to cope with life and had therefore committed suicide. The coroner returned a verdict of death from an overdose of Nembutal (a powerful sleeping pill). Pat Newcomb, who had spent Friday night and all day Saturday with Marilyn, took 250 calls from journalists from all over the world seeking quotes – and that was only in the first eighteen hours after the death was announced.

At the time of her death, Monroe had been fired from *Something's Got to Give*, but after talks there were plans to reinstate her. She had been offered the lead in a musical on Broadway, had turned down the lucrative chance to appear in Las Vegas, and, although her dependence on pills was widely known in the film business, was being actively pursued to star in more pictures. So was she really depressed enough to take her own life? At the time she was seeing a doctor and a psychiatrist who were both prescribing more pills, and most people preferred to believe that, even though the coroner's and the toxologist's reports differed in some details, she simply forgot how many pills she had taken.

DEATH INDUSTRY

This theory didn't reckon on the Marilyn Monroe death industry. Nothing as simple as an overdose would sell millions of books, so there had to be a more complex answer. Journalists noted that her housekeeper took a long holiday in Europe after the death and was no longer around to talk, and that another best friend had also conveniently left the country. Two weeks later *Time* magazine wrote that her finances were in a bad way, and that she had managed on only $20 a week pocket money for two years. The *Los Angeles Herald Examiner*, however, said her estate was worth at least a million dollars. Nobody seemed to agree. Scandal sheets asked how the housekeeper could have looked into the locked bedroom from the garden and seen the body, when it was well known that Marilyn kept the curtains closed day and night to prevent Peeping Toms. And why had she been found naked, when informed sources claimed 'she always slept in a bra'?

The Marilyn rumour industry really got going in 1963 when *Newsweek* hinted at a manuscript written by Ezra Goodman that was too controversial to find a publisher. From then on there was a spate of in-depth investigations, conspiracy theories, mystery lovers, wire-tappers, extra husbands, and so on. Warhol and Salvador Dali portrayed her on canvas, while people who had never met the blonde started tapping out their intimate revelations. One was Norman Mailer, who advanced the theory that Marilyn was killed by secret agents acting to prevent her affairs with President Kennedy and his brother Robert, then US Attorney-General, from becoming public. Another was Robert Slatzer, who came out of the woodwork to

WAS MARILYN KILLED BY SECRET AGENTS?

announce he had been married to Marilyn for four days and they had always remained 'very close'. He came up with his version of her death. Slatzer reckoned she had hoped to marry Robert Kennedy, and said that a secret police report existed which contained a statement from Robert in which he didn't mention that he was having an affair with Marilyn, but said that his brother had sent him to Los Angeles to try to prevent the distraught actress from telephoning his brother at the White House any more. According to Slatzer, there had 'been talk in the coroner's office of murder', and the author claimed he later met a workman who told him Monroe's house had been bugged. *Midnight* magazine later speculated that wire-tap expert Bernard Spindel had compromising tapes involving Monroe and Robert Kennedy, and that rumour suggested the house had been bugged at the request of Jimmy Hoffa, leader of the Teamsters' Union. Frederick Lawrence Guiles in *Norma Jean* didn't name Robert Kennedy but referred to him as 'the lawyer', and claimed that his affair with Monroe had been going on for some time, during which she discovered she was pregnant and had an abortion.

NUDE PHOTOS

Nor did the cashing-in stop there. In 1980 *Penthouse* magazine published nude photographs of a well-developed girl in her early twenties frolicking in a bedroom with an equally well-equipped fellow. Other shots, deemed to be too advanced for its readers, involved a vibrator. The magazine claimed that these were frames from a pornographic film Marilyn had made early in her career.

A further means of money-making was discovered by the lady who bought the vacant vault next to Monroe's in the cemetery, placed an ad in the paper, and sold it for around £10,000 (the rest of the vaults were going for £1,300). That just about sums up Monroe's death: a good profit was had by all.

GOODNIGHT HONEY...

NATALIE FORESHADOWED OWN DEATH?

Knock, Knock, Who's There?

AT 7.45A.M. ON SUNDAY, 29 NOVEMBER 1981, the harbour patrol off Catalina Island in California made a gruesome discovery. It was the body of film star Natalie Wood, floating one and a half miles away from her 60-foot family yacht, *Splendour*. Natalie was wearing a red nightgown, a ski jacket and socks, and had apparently drowned while trying to scramble to safety – her hands were covered in scratches, as if she'd been trying to grab hold of something. The dinghy belonging to the *Splendour* was found nearby. Her husband, actor Robert Wagner, who had called the harbour patrol when he found she was missing in the early hours of the morning, was distraught. So

was the co-star of the film which she had been shooting, Christopher Walken. Wagner and Walken had apparently been involved in a heated argument on the boat when Natalie slipped away in the dinghy to her death. Like so many Hollywood deaths, this was immediately the subject of great rumour and speculation, especially since many journalists implied that Miss Wood and Walken had been romantically involved during the filming of *Brainstorm*, on which they'd been working since the previous September.

Natalie's whole life had revolved around the movies, and so her death seemed a disturbing echo of the drowning scene she had played in *Splendour in the Grass*, one of her biggest successes, in 1960. Natalie had started in films at the age of four, and between the ages of six and seventeen she had worked continuously. She starred in classics like *West Side Story* and *Rebel without a Cause*. It was noted that the latter film seemed to have a curse which had plagued everyone who had worked on it. Co-star James Dean had died in a car crash; with Natalie's death, all the leading actors and actresses (except one) plus the producer and director had been struck down. Wood had appeared in lots of pretty dreadful films, as she was the first to admit, but throughout her career she had turned in some fine performances and had been nominated for an Oscar three times.

ACTIVE LOVE LIFE

Born Natasha Gurdin, Natalie Wood's romantic life had been as active as her professional one, and she was rarely out of the gossip columns. She met Robert Wagner in 1957 and they married at the end of that year, spending a week of their honeymoon on his yacht. In 1960 her career reached its peak, with *Splendour in the Grass* (it was during the shooting of this film that she revealed her fear of water: when it became known that her double couldn't swim, Natalie became terrified of doing a drowning scene). She became romantically involved with her co-star, Warren Beatty, and she and Wagner announced a 'trial separation' in 1961. In 1963 she was briefly engaged to Ladislaw Blatnik, a millionaire, but it came to nothing. Then in 1969 she met actor Richard Gregson, who was already married. After his divorce, he and Natalie were married and spent two years together before she ran into Robert Wagner again on a trip to Europe on the *QE2*. At the end of the trip they announced that they were in love again, and they remarried in July 1972. At the time of her death it looked to outsiders as if 43-year-old Natalie had finally settled down, with one child by her marriage to Wagner and one each by their previous marriages.

But were they really the happy couple they seemed to be in all the Hollywood fan magazines? Why would anyone with such a chronic fear of water get into a small dinghy in the ocean in the middle of the night? Why were Wagner and Walken having such a row that no one noticed her slip away from what was not a very large boat? Rumours were fuelled by the report that people on a nearby boat said that they had heard screams of 'Help me' for twenty-five minutes in the middle of the night. Then, they said, they heard people from a third boat say, 'We're coming to get you,' and so they assumed that everything was now in order and went back to sleep. However, the owners of the third boat denied ever saying such a thing. The question remained – had it been Natalie calling for help?

Gradually a picture was pieced together of the events of the Saturday night which had led to her death. The coroner, Dr Thomas Noguchi, announced that after performing an autopsy he had found that the actress had a high alcohol level in her blood (higher than the amount allowed for driving in California) and that in his opinion she had slipped and fallen into the water while fleeing from an alcoholic row. He said she was drunk and incapable of saving herself when she fell into the sea. Noguchi was thought by some of the Hollywood establishment to have overstepped the mark with his version of what had happened on the fateful night, and to have caused the relatives of the dead woman needless distress. On the day she was buried, the manager of the restaurant in which the three had spent the Saturday night, said that they had left his premises so drunk that Natalie had slipped on the dock outside the restaurant.

It emerged that Walken, Wood and Wagner had sat down to dinner at about 7p.m. amicably enough, but had ended up having a furious row, possibly over the attention that Natalie had been receiving from fellow-diners who sent over bottles of champagne. Anyway, on their way out they had been seen smashing their champagne glasses against the wall of the restaurant. Now another story surfaced: Natalie had checked into a Catalina hotel on the Friday night, with Walken and without Wagner. Both the Los Angeles police and Robert Wagner denied that this was true, and said Walken had spent the evening on board the *Splendour*. At the same time, fears grew for the completion of *Brainstorm*. If the producers decided to scrap the film – with only less than two weeks' work needed to finish it – then they could be submitting one of the biggest insurance claims ever. The film had cost over $10 million and there were doubts as to whether a double could satisfactorily stand in for the dead star.

TORRID ROMANCE

The *National Enquirer*, undeterred by denials about Walken's whereabouts on the Friday night, painted a very different story to the one put out by Wagner. They alleged that Natalie had been having a torrid romance with Walken, which had started during the filming of *Brainstorm*. According to the *Enquirer*, Natalie, Walken and the captain of the *Splendour* had all got drunk on Catalina on the Friday and then checked into a motel. Natalie and Walken were seen together in one room by a member of the motel staff who came to help her light a heater that she was

ACCIDENT OR SUICIDE

having trouble with. He said the two stars were deep in conversation. That night the weather was dreadful and they were unable to rejoin the yacht, which Wagner moved to Isthmus Cove. On the Saturday the three rejoined the boat, and then in the evening they decided to go out to dinner. It was thought that the row in the restaurant had been over the fact that Natalie had been flirting with Walken in front of Wagner, and that when they returned to the *Splendour* it continued. Natalie went to her stateroom and after a while Wagner went to the small guest-cabin; but on waking at 1.30a.m. and finding her and the dinghy gone, he telephoned the restaurant manager to see if

that the controversial coroner had been suspended for thirty days over the way in which he had handled both the death of Natalie Wood and that of William Holden. While the District Attorney considered whether to investigate Noguchi's behaviour, his bosses refused to reveal all the allegations against him. The suspension had been triggered by the Screen Actors' Guild, who had complained that Noguchi had sensationalized the deaths of the two stars. Frank Sinatra had written a letter to Noguchi's superiors, calling for his dismissal and saying that the coroner was constantly seeking headlines for himself. Noguchi certainly was a well-known figure in Los Angeles – he

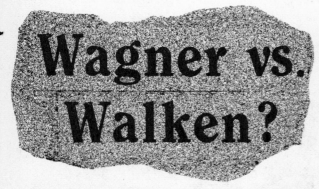

Wagner vs. Walken?

he knew where she was. After a two-hour search on land proved unsuccessful, Whiting, the restaurant manager, phoned Wagner and the harbour patrol. The question still remained: why did it take so long for anyone to phone for help, especially when the patrol could have reached *Splendour* in five minutes? As it was, they didn't find her body for another four hours – and one and a half miles away.

JEALOUSY

No one will ever know what really went on aboard the *Splendour* that night. The *Enquirer* said that Wood and Walken's affair was well known to the crew, who apparently had a pet joke: 'They're going to have to clean up their act, RJ's coming in again.' Both Wagner and Natalie were jealous – he of male attention paid to his beautiful wife, and she of scenes in his smash-hit TV series, *Hart to Hart*. She frequently insisted that steamy scenes be cut. Other reports said she had been miserable for some time before the tragedy and, in spite of trips by Wagner to the film-set in North Carolina, had continued the affair with Walken.

Either way, Walken and Wagner weren't saying anything. But Dr Thomas Noguchi, it turned out, had said far too much. In April 1982 it was announced

had performed autopsies on such stars as Marilyn Monroe and Sharon Tate – and had attracted trouble since he was appointed in 1967, when he was alleged to have prayed for airliners to crash to make him more famous.

Finally the police disagreed with Noguchi's theory that Natalie had died while fleeing from a row. They said there had never been an argument on board the *Splendour*. Truth or whitewash? No one will ever know.

Showbiz

Drugs

Martyrs to their work, victims of police harassment, or mindless morons? From Sid Vicious to the Rolling Stones, drugs and rock music are a volatile combination as far as newspapers are concerned. It is O.K. for lyrics to be suggestive, as long as you don't hear the records on the radio. It's O.K. to stage concerts where people get beaten up by bouncers and are crushed until they're sick, but at the same time we expect singers and musicians to 'set an example' as far as drugs are concerned. We always talk about fame-and-drugs as if it is a phenomenom that started the moment rock-and-roll arrived in the fifties. The truth is that from the day a silent film star became the image of the moment, he embarked on a life-style where drugs were one of the options.

Wild Child of a Junkie
Poppa

IN FEBRUARY 1980 things came to the crunch for TV star Mackenzie Philips. The twenty-year-old daughter of sixties rock star John Philips (founder of the Mamas and the Papas) had been going through a rough patch on the CBS top-rated show 'One Day at a Time', when the producers – alarmed by rumours of her drug-taking and ill-health – had told her to take six weeks' rest. On returning to the show at the end of 1979, she didn't seem to have reformed her ways, so she was told to resign 'for personal reasons' or be thrown off the set. In February she eventually left 'by mutual agreement'. An executive at CBS was quoted as saying: 'I consider this firing to be a step towards saving a child's life. The kid's in real trouble.'

The trouble was that Mackenzie was a legendary junkie – just like her dad. By the late seventies he was said to have sold most of his possessions, including works of art, a couple of houses and half-a-dozen cars (including four Rolls-Royces), all to buy heroin. Mackenzie herself was reputed to have spent $300,000 in one year on her drug habit. John's addiction to heroin went back to the mid seventies when he was in London to write the musical score for the David Bowie movie *The Man Who Fell to Earth*, but he'd been using drugs since the end of the sixties. By 1977 he was taking cocaine to get off heroin, and he subsequently became addicted to a whole variety of pills. He had to sell his future royalties in order to finance drugs that were costing a million dollars a year by 1980.

Mackenzie kicked off set

EXOTIC CHILDHOOD

It didn't take an analyst to see that Mackenzie's problems stemmed from her exotic childhood. Her mother, Susan Adams, was a socialite, and her parents divorced when Mackenzie was just three. John remarried twice – first to Michelle Philips and then to actress Genevieve Waite. At first Mackenzie attended a trendy 'free school' in Los Angeles at which she later claimed she'd smoked pot by the age of eleven. Then she was sent to a far stricter private school, but she rebelled against her mother and ran away to live with her father at the age of twelve. Her mother then sent her to a Swiss finishing school when she was fourteen, but by this time she'd formed a band and appeared in the movie *American Graffiti*. Father John was said to have written 'Too High on Arrival' for his highly sophisticated drug-taking fourteen-year-old. By the age of fifteen Mackenzie had appeared in another film and soon after was offered a part in 'One Day at a Time'. In 1978 she owned her own house in Laurel Canyon and had surprised all her friends by suddenly marrying a record-business gofer after dating producer Peter Asher for two years. Her father tried unsuccessfully to stop what turned out to be a doomed marriage. On Mackenzie's eighteenth birthday CBS weren't too pleased to find out that she'd been found semi-conscious on the street in Hollywood and been arrested for disorderly conduct under the influence of drugs or alcohol. It was rumoured that the programme had been asked to send doctors to her house in the middle of the night.

ALL IN THE FAMILY

DRUG COUNSELLOR

John and Mackenzie toured high-schools in New York in 1981, counselling against drug use. She claimed she wanted to help others not to make the same mistakes she had. John gave evidence at a hearing conducted into the abuse of heroin and alcohol in New York State, supporting Governor Carey's contention that a heroin crisis existed.

Mackenzie, who by now was divorced, said she wasn't bitter towards her father for her childhood. She'd had two overdoses before seeking hospital treatment, but had now formed a new band and was trying to re-launch her career. John, meanwhile, was starting a movement called 'Musicians against Drugs' and re-launching the Mamas and the Papas – only this time around, life was going to be very different.

Like Papa, like daughter

Her fellow actors reported her as a pleasant person to work with, but one who was constantly ill, hoarse and obviously suffering from the effects of too much cocaine. After she left the show, her manager said she was seeing a psychiatrist and claimed that Mackenzie was now 'straightened out' and merely suffering from the strain of trying to launch a singing career at the same time as working on a TV show. In March 1980 Mackenzie and her husband split up.

Her father's situation continued to deteriorate, in spite of friends like Mick Jagger trying to help. On the weekend of 4 July that year he had a crash near his holiday house on Long Island, where Jagger was a house guest. It resulted in thirty-five stitches in his head and a charge of conspiracy to traffic in narcotics. In September he checked into a psychiatric hospital in New Jersey to try and fight his addiction. He was so sick that there were no good veins below his elbows, and there was a danger he might lose the use of his hands. He was a 45-year-old wreck. His wife Genevieve joined him on the treatment programme – luckily their baby, Bijou, was not an addict, because Genevieve had undergone a detoxification programme shortly before his birth. John's brother Jeffrey also checked in for treatment, as did Mackenzie in December – her cousin had recently died of heroin. As the whole family were weaned off drugs, they were also put on a special diet and a programme of physical exercise.

Human Wreckage

WALLY REID, matinée idol, died insane in a padded cell in a mental hospital in 1923, aged thirty. He started out in films as a prop man, occasionally operating the camera, and became the clean-cut star of a string of car-racing comedies. The studio wanted to keep junkie Wally working – allowing him to inject himself on the set, but 'only in the presence of a guard'. But Mrs Reid had had enough and in 1922, when Wally's condition deteriorated further, she had him admitted to a sanatorium and announced to the world what was killing her husband. He was addicted to morphine.

BLIND EYE

A year later Reid was dead. His wife started a nation-wide campaign against drugs, giving the police the names of Hollywood pushers and even starring in an anti-dope film produced by Thomas Ince called *Human Wreckage*. Of course the Hollywood bosses financed the film: a bad image of what went on in their town wasn't good for profits, and so they publicly backed Mrs Reid's attack, while privately turning a blind eye to drugs as long as stars churned out their required quota of pictures per year.

WALLACE REID.
FAMOUS CINEMA STAR SERIES

The fan magazines, however, couldn't cope with the bald truth that their Wally was a piece of human wreckage. They started printing carefully woven little scenarios explaining away his dependence on the needle. One claimed that 'infected teeth and pain-relieving narcotics led to his demise'. Another version was that he had received a blow on the head while filming in 1919 and had started drinking to excess.

WALLACE REID captured the feminine hearts of America in the early "twenties." Infected teeth and pain-relieving narcotics led to his demise.

When his life became a round of non-stop parties at home, he could no longer combine work and booze, so he turned to dope. According to one magazine he tried a self-cure, which seemed to take the form of long walks up mountains and working out with a special trainer.

But the truth is probably nearer the story told in Kevin Brownlow's book on the early days of Hollywood, *The Parade's Gone By*. There was an actor on the Sennett lot whom everyone remembered as a 'really nice' fellow. When actors used to arrive for work with a hangover, he'd say, 'I'll give you something for that.' And he did, killing Mabel Normand, Wally Reid, and Alma Rubens with his special form of kindness.

WALLACE REID

Wally Reid was the idol of millions of fans. In 1919, he was happily married and was building up a huge fortune doing the work he loved. And then he received a blow on the head. The caboose in which he was riding to a picture location jumped the track in the Big Tree country and the star was injured.

Wally began drinking to excess. His fair weather friends turned his home into a road house. To hold up under the strain of party life and picture work, Wally began to take dope. He studied pharmacy so that he could administer his own drugs.

When he found that the habit was getting the better of him, he tried to cure himself by taking trips into the mountains, training under a special trainer, and entering a sanitarium. But it was too late! One day he collapsed on the set where he was allowed to "use the hypodermic only in the presence of guards". He died in 1923, a victim of the drug traffic.

PARIS POLICE PROBE OLIVE THOMAS' DEATH

Olive and the Dead Rat

ONE OF THE first victims of drug-taking in Hollywood didn't necessarily use the stuff herself. Silent film star Olive Thomas's death in Paris on 10 September 1920 was mysterious for a number of reasons. Why should a 20-year-old girl, whose career was going well, kill herself with an overdose of mercury?

One half of what was described in all the fan mags as 'the ideal couple' (her husband was Jack, actor brother of Mary Pickford), Olive left Broadway to star in a number of comedies in Hollywood in which she always looked exquisitely beautiful. So what was the ex-*Vogue* model doing in such unlikely haunts as the

BROADWAY DIMS LIGHTS FOR NOTED SCREEN STAR

appropriately named Dead Rat Club in Montmartre? PARIS POLICE PROBE OLIVE THOMAS'S DEATH vied with BROADWAY DIMS LIGHTS FOR NOTED FILM STAR in the tabloids. Then came the rumours, the first of which concerned the questioning of an American army captain, Mr Spaulding, who had started to serve a six-month sentence at the Santé prison in Paris for selling cocaine. The word went out that Olive's name was among his contacts. Journalists noted that it was just 'one more sorrow in the misfortunes of the Pickfords' as husband Jack collapsed with grief. What *had* the star of The Flapper been doing in the Dead Rat? And why did she insist on going to several more low dives in Montmartre when it closed at 1 a.m.? On returning to her hotel at 4 a.m. she had seemed 'very excitable'. Later that morning the maid found her dead. A doctor in Los Angeles said she had been suffering from 'a nervous complaint' and had taken an overdose of drugs which he had prescribed.

STIGMA

The Pickfords themselves, who were busy trying to establish themselves as the smart set in the film colony, had some explaining to do. Mary, Olive's sister-in-law, issued a denial of drug rumours, but reporters were starting to dig up little bits of muck about Jack, the remaining half of the 'perfect pair'. While Mary was being criticized for rushing out of a divorce and straight into a marriage with Douglas Fairbanks (when it was still being questioned whether the divorce was final) and Lottie, the other Pickford sister, was also in the middle of a divorce, Jack's troubles went back to his days in the navy during the First World War. Apparently he had been recommended for 'disenrollment from the navy as undesirable', and it was alleged that he was involved in a racket where rich young men got berths away from the action. In the end he got an ordinary discharge, but the stigma remained. It was rumoured that the pretty young Olive had been scouring Paris for drugs for Jack who was the addict in the family, and because she couldn't score, she had killed herself. Nobody has ever found out what really went on in the Dead Rat.

Mitchum Mops Up

ONE OF MY favourite picture captions accompanies a truly 'posed' shot of Robert Mitchum hunched over a mop, and reads: 'Up with the sun, film actor Robert Mitchum finds himself with an unaccustomed weapon

– a mop – tidying up the cell block in Los Angeles County Jail where he is serving a sixty-day sentence on marijuana charges.'

PARTY RAID

This was February 1949; and if there's one star you really can't imagine would ever choose to be linked with a mop, it's Robert Mitchum. Considering that drug-taking was common in Hollywood, and that contemporary stars like Errol Flynn used morphine when they needed that extra energy to get their act together and walk out onto the set, Mitchum felt that he had been picked on when, the previous August, police had raided a party he was at and charged him with possession. At that time he had made the transition from cowboy films to starring in *The Story of G.I. Joe*, and the last place he wanted to learn his lines was the L.A. County Jail.

PUBLICITY

Mitchum felt he had been framed. But he had been signed for a big picture by RKO, and the boss was Howard Hughes, who decided that to plead guilty and to do time would cut down on adverse publicity. Hughes was adamant about this, which is odd when you think of what the bad publicity at her daughter's trial did for Lana Turner – it made her recently released film, *Peyton Place*, do very well. He engaged Jerry Geisler to handle the case, who was more used to getting people off than getting them locked up. Bob expected the worst, and was reported as taking to court 'a small case containing a shaving kit and toothbrush'. A further embarrassing aspect of the case was that at the time of his arrest he had been due to give a talk for National Youth Week.

SERVING TIME

During his time in jail, the press reported that he had to 'wear prison garb' and was only allowed two visitors weekly. However, serving time didn't harm his career at all, much to everyone's surprise.

ROBERT MITCHUM GOES TO GAOL: 'NO PRIVILEGES'

POP GROUP THAT
THE WORLD

Punk Passes On

SID VICIOUS was the member of the Sex Pistols
with whom even the rest of the group found it pretty
hard to cope. Much has been written about the band
by the popular press, embellished by their manager
Malcolm McLaren, and plenty more was stoked up by
the various record companies they signed with, but
Sid did actually seem to live out his life like a tediously
hysterical press release.

NOTORIOUS

Looking back at the heady, exciting early days of punk
rock in 1976, it seems difficult to really believe that
the Sex Pistols and their fans posed such an
overwhelming threat to civilization as we know it –
but they certainly attracted that kind of response in
the press. It wasn't until every town in the country
boasted a few safety-pin-wearing young people, and
punk bands could be heard the length and breadth of
the land, that the Sex Pistols began to seem like the
pretty average band they really were. But in 1976 and
1977, when their records were getting banned on the
radio and concert halls refused to let them perform,
they became wonderfully notorious, just because they
couldn't do *anything* without someone, somewhere,
getting upset about it. The band had been formed in
late 1975 and Sid Vicious (real name John Ritchie)
joined it in February 1977, after the release of their
first record, 'Anarchy in the U.K.', which reached
number twelve in the charts. Sid replaced Glen
Matlock and pretty soon made it clear that he didn't
think that playing a guitar demanded very much
talent or effort. After EMI dumped the band (they had
created a rumpus by swearing on a live television
programme the previous November) they signed with
the A&M label, who shortly dumped them again, with
a £75,000 pay-off. In May 1977 they signed with
Virgin records and released 'God Save the Queen',

which was promptly banned by the BBC. Nevertheless
it got to number two in the charts, and they followed
it up with 'Pretty Vacant', which also reached the top
ten. So, regardless of the sneers of the popular press,
the band had a definite appeal and were selling a
considerable number of records. Their first album,
'Never Mind the Bollocks', released in November
1977, was banned by Smiths, Boots and Woolworths,
and a record store owner was prosecuted when he
decorated the window of his shop with album sleeves
bearing the offensive word.

VIOLENT

The first signs that all was not well with Sid occurred
on the band's tour in the summer of that year. He had
attacked rock writer Nick Kent with a bicycle chain,
cutting Kent's head badly. Malcolm McLaren had sent
a telegram to the rock music paper *Melody Maker*
generally praising Sid for his behaviour. The violence
of their songs started to become a reality at their gigs,
and several concert halls refused to let him play.
Members of the band were themselves attacked, and
when they toured America in January 1978 Sid was
mutilating himself and cutting his arms with a knife
on stage. He had been carried off the plane on arrival,
unconscious from a mixture of drink and drugs. Nor
was his girlfriend Nancy Spungen, a dancer, much
help: Sid told journalists, 'Nancy was great because
she and I were the same – we both hated everyone.'

Early in 1978, at the end of their abortive American
tour, the band split up. Two of them flew to Brazil to
see the Great Train Robber Ronnie Biggs; meanwhile
Johnny Rotten was thought to be starting a new band.
In October Vicious hit the headlines, without playing a
note. Nancy was found dead in the bathroom of their
flat at the Chelsea Hotel in New York, with a large

SHOCKED

SID VICIOUS KILLED HIMSELF ON PURPOSE SAYS HIS MUM

SID VICIOUS IN MURDER DRAMA

Girl friend is found stabbed in a hotel room

I GAVE SID THE DRUGS

knife wound in her stomach. Sid was arrested and charged with murder. His mum's comment was, 'I called her nauseating Nancy. She was a bad influence on my Sid.' Sid was placed on a detoxification programme to try to get him off heroin, and he celebrated his release on £25,000 bail by telling reporters, 'I'm longing for a slice of pizza.' Sid and his mum went to a party at his new girlfriend's flat, and during the evening Sid injected himself with heroin and went into a spasm. Because he seemed to recover, nobody called an ambulance. On the morning of 2 February 1979 he was dead. His next-door neighbours in Maida Vale, London, told the *Sun* he had been 'peaceful and polite' and 'no trouble'.

A year later on the anniversary of his death, Sid's mum, Mrs Anne Beverly, collapsed from an overdose. When a film featuring the band entitled *The Great Rock and Roll Swindle* opened in London in June, she gave an interview to the *News of the World* in which she claimed she had bought the drugs that killed her son. Described as 'wearing punk clothes' and 'owning a 750 c.c. motorbike', punk 48-year-old momma explained she had bought heroin for Sid on the street in New York, and it had turned out to be unusually pure. After his detoxification programme his body just couldn't handle such a massive dose, and he died. His mum said, 'I suppose it was fate really. He died because I tried to help him.'

Finance

Finance

Noisy Crashes

There are two types of noisy crash: those of companies whose downfall made front-page news, and a different kind – the recalling or cancelling of cars and planes that suddenly become an embarrassment to their makers. Penn Central is a story of gruesomely chaotic mismanagement, while the Lancia, Concorde, Brabazon and Pinto stories seem to reflect dubious investments.

Lancia

TUV 183P

Rusty Cars Crushed

IN JUNE 1979 an irate motorist left his Lancia in a car park in Guildford, having daubed all over it the slogan LANCIAS RUST LIKE HELL. A week later Prince Philip mentioned this in a speech, saying he thought such action struck a blow for good design. This wasn't exactly music to the ears of Lancia executives, who had sold around 43,000 cars in Britain since 1973. Then, in an exclusive story on 9 April 1980, the *Daily Mirror* revealed another rust story that left the company with even more egg on its collective face.

DANGER

The report declared that the Lancia Beta range, which sold for around £7,000 a car, had developed a serious rust problem which meant that, in extreme cases, there was a danger of the body coming away from the chassis. According to the *Mirror*, Lancia were spending about £1 million to recover faulty Beta models and crush them as scrap. The plan was to do this without the customers finding out. Lancia agents had been instructed to look for rust-damaged cars and offer to buy them back at prices above their true

EXCLUSIVE
LUXURY CARS IN RUST RIDDLE

paid £950 for this car. Then crushed it..

market value. 500 cars had been sent from all over the country to a scrapyard in Somerset and the *Mirror* said that 400 more were on the way. They recounted stories of Lancia owners who had sold their second-hand cars for between £800 and £950, assuming that the dealer would resell them. They were shocked to discover that their family saloon had now been reduced to cubes of tin. Lancia refuted the *Mirror*'s allegations that a total of 3,000 cars were to be scrapped and that some of the cars were relatively new. They replied that in most cases the cars were six to seven years old, and that the fault had been eliminated. They offered a six-year corrosion guarantee on all their models, and said that the car-crushing operation had merely been a 'goodwill exercise'.

Death by the Gallon

THE SUNDAY TIMES of 12 February 1978 carried a horrific story entitled 'Death in the Company Balance Sheet'. It related how a Californian jury, after seeing the balance sheets for the Ford company's Pinto car, decided that Ford had sold over two million of a particular model knowing that it had a severe design fault in the petrol tank. This fault made the car a potential fire-bomb if it was involved in a crash. But Ford had calculated that the cost of altering the Pinto was about $137 million. This was set against $49.5 million which they reckoned they would have to pay out after accidents in which an estimated 180 people would burn to death, a further 180 would receive serious burns, and 2,100 cars would go up in smoke. In other words, they decided to take the risk and see if their profits were used up in compensation.

52 OPERATIONS

Richard Grimshaw was just thirteen when he was given a lift in a brand-new Pinto. It stalled and was hit from behind, and the petrol tank (situated only seven inches from the rear bumper) split and burst into flames. The driver was so badly burned that she died in hospital, and Richard had undergone 52 operations by the time of the court case five years later, leaving his face a mess of scar tissue. He said after the hearing that he would rather be able to live a normal life than have the awarded £66 million. It was the highest personal award ever made. Although Ford had paid

out for people burned in Pinto cars before this case, Richard's lawyers produced the balance sheet in court to show that Ford had consciously and wilfully disregarded the safety of their customers. Ford threatened to fight the settlement, calling it 'unreasonable and unwarranted'. It was later reduced to about £3 million by a Superior Court judge. By 1978 Ford had recalled 1,500,000 Pintos to have their fuel tanks modified.

£66m damages: the car that carried death in the boot

BATTLE OF THE MILLIONAIRES
Armoured cars in ballot to decide who runs a railway

From DON IDDON : New York, Tuesday

MR. ROBERT R. YOUNG, self-made multi-million-aire and close friend of the Duke of Windsor, meets Mr. William White, president of the New York Central Railroad, to-row in a showdown for of the famous line, 600,000,000 (about

"the Battle er the Cen-ress." The

Albany, he line.

"nise ro-

Mr. R. R. Young.

All Change
for the Line to Disaster

THE CRASH of the Pennsylvania Railroad Company on 21 1970 was the largest bankruptcy ever (in terms of assets involved) in American history. The story of how two giant railroad companies merged and set themselves on a course of unmitigated disaster is enough to cheer up even the most hardened critic of British Rail.

CUT-THROAT

The problems which affected the railway system in America can be traced back to the end of the Second World War. Too many companies were competing for too little territory, and services and stock often overlapped. Business was cut-throat, and in 1954 the *Daily Mail* informed its readers that 'a battle of the millionaires' was taking place to gain control of the New York Central Railroad. Armoured cars were used to ship the ballot forms to the shareholders, as one of the contenders did not like to trust their precious load to the unreliable rail system. Mr Robert Young gained control but, finding the problems of the job insurmountable, committed suicide. The idea of merging the New York Central and the Pennsylvania railroads had first been discussed around 1957, but it did not actually taken place until 1968, when it became the largest railway conglomerate in the world.

RIVALRY

Later that year they were joined by the New Haven Railway. At that point, the massive company had a staff of 100,000 workers, over 4,000 engines, and 180,000 passenger coaches and trucks. At the time of the merger the company's shares were quoted at 84 on the New York Stock Exchange, and Stuart Saunders, the head of the new conglomerate, was voted Businessman of the Year. But the problems that would culminate in a disastrous crash after only two years were just beginning. First of all, the two companies had been bitter rivals; one New York Central driver had called his Penn counterparts 'the dirtiest men in the business'. In the reorganization the structure was ruled by a Penn man with a New York Central man below and a Penn man below him, and so on. This was not likely to promote working harmony. Secondly, the chief of New York Central, Alfred Perlman, who was made joint head of the new company with Saunders, did not hit it off with his partner. But apart from personality differences, the real problem was that the new company was simply too big and cumbersome. The computer used for freight could not cope, so firms took their business elsewhere, often choosing road haulage instead.

DERAILMENTS

After the merger there were 5,000 combinations of new routing; and when this proved too much for the clerks, thousands of trucks ended up in the wrong yards. In 1968 a coal train of over 100 trucks was 'lost' in the system for ten whole days before it could be tracked down. Business was not helped by a terrible winter at the end of 1969 which froze the engines up and destroyed miles of track. There were, on average, 2,300 US derailments a year. As business declined, the company started to borrow money to keep afloat, and executives who had been hired for their knowledge of freight and railways found themselves learning more about international banking. The $87 million profit of 1968 was reduced to $4.4 million by 1969 and a loss of $30 million in the middle of 1970 when the company stopped trading.

RECORD LOSS

Then came the crash, involving assets of over $4.6 billion. The *Daily Mail* reported that a Manhattan management consultant had designed a set of rubber railway officials which were to be placed in the ticket offices of Penn Central so that frustrated customers could beat them up. A record loss of £179 million was announced for 1970 when financial experts came to try and unravel the books.

CONCORDE DOOMED

The Big Bird
That Never Took Off

IN 1962 Britain and France, in a rare act of cooperation and general goodwill, announced that together they would develop and build a supersonic aircraft called Concorde. The project was budgeted at a joint cost of £170 million, but in 1964 costs had already risen to £250 million and they had doubled by 1968. By 1973 the development costs of the most sophisticated passenger plane in the world stood at £1,065 million.

PRESTIGE

Nevertheless, the building programme commenced after test flights had proved successful, and Britain was firmly divided into pro- and anti-Concorde camps. Even Concorde wallpaper went on sale. Pro-Concorde people argued that its technological achievements placed us ahead of the Americans and, apart from the employment the project offered, it was vital for our international prestige. If Britain was to continue to have a viable aviation industry, we had to proceed with the project. Anti-Concorde people complained on cost and environmental grounds. They even took whole page advertisements in newspapers to state their case, in which they were supported by members of the French 'anti-bang' lobby. *Private Eye* argued that in the Middle East many of Concorde's proposed routes were just as quickly covered (at less cost) by using conventional subsonic planes. Noise was always a problem with Concorde, and no matter how many people thought she looked beautiful in the air, thousands more did not want the unspeakable racket of the great bird taking off within earshot. After fighting strong opposition in New York, Concorde was eventually allowed to land at Kennedy airport.

In 1977 the Public Accounts Committee, which supervised Government spending, said that it thought production of Concorde should stop after the first sixteen had been completed; the programme had already cost the British taxpayer £560 million in development costs and £200 million in construction costs. One MP called the plane 'a flying overdraft'. In April 1979 the last Concorde took off from the factory runway near Bristol; sixteen had been built altogether in ten years, and only nine were in use. Even though no more planes were to be built, it was estimated that the British Government would be spending up to £80 million over the next four years on spares that had to be supplied under guarantees. It was said that the Government would write off the costs of British Airways' Concordes in return for eighty per cent of the profit when they were in operation. Then in 1980 it was announced that so far BA hadn't made profits on Concorde; in fact they lost £30.5 million between January 1976 and March 1979. Losses continued to rise, with the company facing a Concorde deficit of £4 million on the financial year 1979–80, double that of the previous twelve months.

INQUIRY DEMANDED

In 1981 the argument was still raging. A House of Commons committee said that it suspected the Department of Industry of trying to make the costs of British Airways operating Concorde look less than they really were, and claimed that the expense of running the plane had been played down while the expense of scrapping the project had been played up. MPs wanted an independent inquiry to look into Concorde's future prospects, and they implied that any benefits industry had gained from the development of the project had already been realized.

Finance Gamblers

All these men are larger than life: Bunker Hunt, who dreamt of controlling the world supply of silver; the irrepressible Clarence Saunders, the supermarket genius who took on the Stock Exchange single-handed and lost; and Colombo, the bank clerk who couldn't resist playing with his employer's money. Under the guise of business-as-usual, they all attempted to get a lot for a little and ended up losing it all.

Bunker Engineers Bullion Coup – Then Collapse Follows

NELSON BUNKER HUNT is the kind of fellow reporters love to write about. He may look like a chubby, friendly cowboy, but he is a financial killer, according to the *Sunday Times* the reputed model for JR in the television series 'Dallas'. He is a big chap and he thinks big. Why put small plans into operation when, albeit at some risk, there was a chance for him and his brother Herbert to control the world supply of one commodity – silver?

Nelson already owned a million acres of Texas, Oklahoma, and Montana, one of the largest independent oil companies in America, and oil reserves worth £1 billion, when he and his brother decided to start buying up silver; by January 1980 they had got their hands on half the world's bullion. When the *Daily Express* visited him, it was claimed that his profits had increased by £50 million while the photographer took four snaps of the portly Nelson buying a racehorse (he already had 650). The horse cost a mere £70,000 and he called it 'Double Your Fun'. At that point he was still doubling *his* fun, owning silver worth more than £2,000 million and going up in value by the minute. The price of silver rose to an incredible $52 an ounce, and it was said that Nelson and his brother had been known to take charter planes loaded with silver to London if there was a chance of making a few cents per ounce more profit.

Luring Hunt from his bunker

Then came the crash in March 1980, and headlines screamed SILVER BARON NELSON LOSES BILLIONS. The great silver caper came tumbling down about his ears. Nelson saw £2 billion wiped off his paper profits when the price of silver crashed from $50 an ounce to $10.5. His losses triggered off near-panic on the American stock market, with people just dumping shares at any price. The *Daily Telegraph* commented that Bunker Hunt's collapse tarnished the reputations of some big names on Wall Street, and he faced total losses of around $235 million.

MIXED FORTUNES

On April Fool's Day Dr Armand Hammer, an American billionaire and art collector, as thin and elegant as the Bunker Hunts were fat and tasteless, announced that the fall in silver prices had made him the fastest £50 million he had ever pocketed. Bunker Hunt had gambled £1,000 million that the price of silver would continue to rise, but Armand Hammer disagreed. He had committed his company's assets to the theory that the price would come crashing down, and had now made as much profit from the fall of silver as Hunt had made from its rise. But while some gained, others lost: newspapers announced that a gang of thieves who had stolen ten tons of silver worth about £3¼ million now had rapidly decreasing assets on their hands.

In May the Bunker Hunt brothers appeared before a Government committee in Washington to explain their version of events. They denied that they had tried to corner the world's silver market, but were met with scepticism. The House subcommittee had already heard evidence from the Chairman of the Federal Reserve Board, who had said that it did seem as if there had been an attempt to control the supply of silver. If successful, the brothers would have been able to dictate the price of the precious metal.

In October 1980 Nelson Bunker Hunt emerged from his bunker, the huge ranch he owned in Texas. Journalists had been trying to interview him for months and had now found him – only to hear that the house was mortgaged up to the hilt.

BUNKER HUNT'S 'HOUSE OF SILVER' FALLS IN RUINS

'Bunch of Welchers'
Cause Supermarket Crash

BORN IN AMERICA in 1881, Clarence Saunders rose from being a simple grocer's assistant to owning his own chain of food stores. In 1919 he began to build a chain of self-service grocery stores called Piggly Wiggly, which rocketed Clarence into immortality as the inventor of that great twentieth-century institution, the supermarket. Clarence the Supermarket King let some of his success go straight to his head and built himself a pink folly outside Memphis. As his success grew, so his shares began to arouse interest amongst speculators. Piggly Wiggly seemed like a good investment. However, several small businesses operating under the Piggly Wiggly franchise (but not owned by Saunders) went broke, and this gave unscrupulous investors the chance to initiate the rumour that the parent company was in trouble to try to force the share price down. This would mean that they would be able to buy shares cheap and, when the rumour turned out to be untrue, sell them at considerable profit. Saunders, who was relatively inexperienced in the devious ways of the American Stock Exchange, instinctively understood what was happening and acted in order to protect his own stock and that of his shareholders. He borrowed $10 million and started to buy up Piggly Wiggly shares.

'SHORT SELLERS'

Many of the shares he bought were from 'short sellers'; that is, stock which the seller had borrowed from the real owner, in this case often Clarence himself. At any time the owner of the stock can recall it from the borrower, so the borrower's intention is to gamble and hopefully make money on the price of the stock before it is handed back to the real owner.

CREATING A 'CORNER'

The lender participates in this transaction because he hopes to create a 'corner' (owning almost 100 per cent of the shares in a company) by discreetly buying up floating stock and simultaneously selling it short (lending it out). When the time is right, he will call for the return of all his shares, and then the short sellers must rush round trying to lay their hands on the number of shares they owe him. If there are none available (which is likely because the owner will have secretly mopped up all the spare shares), they then have to buy shares from the owner to pay him back,

and he can set the price as high as he likes. Regulations drawn up since the Piggly Wiggly affair now make this almost impossible to achieve, but Piggly Wiggly is a good example of how the impossible was nearly brought off.

HIGH SHARE PRICES

So Clarence and his army of twenty brokers set about buying up Piggly Wiggly stock and succeeded in driving the price of his shares higher than it had ever been. There was a rumour that he was trying to create a corner, but he was cleverer than anyone suspected. He advertised his shares at $55 each, although they stood at $70. No one could understand this manic move, but Clarence realized that he would not succeed if he owned too many shares; once the price fell he would not be able to offload any.

DOWNFALL

He sold them on an instalment plan, handing over the certificates after six months. As the buyers could not re-sell until they owned the certificates, no spare shares floated on to the market, and the short sellers were placed in a really tough position with nothing for them to buy. In the middle of March 1923, Saunders felt he had created a 'corner' and he sprang the trap, calling for the delivery of all his stock. His shares immediately rose to $124, but fell to $82 before the day was out because of rumours that he was to be investigated by the Exchange Governors. He asked for a settlement of $150 a share, and then $250. The Stock Exchange announced that they were removing Piggly Wiggly from their lists, and that they were giving the short sellers time to find more floating shares, rather than cash, in which to pay back Saunders – the very thing he did not want. He called the Stock Exchange a 'bunch of welchers' and got enormous support from the press and public. He was in a bad way financially, unable to raise the cash to repay the money he had borrowed because the Stock Exchange refused to deal in his shares. More rumours were started about the state of his company's accounts, which didn't help matters, and all those who had volunteered to buy stock to try and help him out of the crisis withdrew. Early in 1924 he was declared bankrupt.

Colombo

Mombelli

How Lloyds Bank Just 'Lost' 33 Million Pounds

MARCO COLOMBO was earning £9,000 a year as a currency dealer working at the smallest overseas branch of Lloyds, in Lugano, when he managed to run up the largest losses ever incurred by an English bank. There were red faces all round in September 1974 when the head office of Lloyds International in London discovered what their Swiss employee had been up to. They ended up around £33 million worse off than when the year had started with Colombo behind his desk with a brand new diary.

In the spring of 1974 he had started to speculate in foreign currency in the bank's name in what are described in banking terms as 'forward' deals (i.e. buying and selling currency based on an estimated future price). Colombo began by contracting to buy 34 million American dollars which he would pay for in Swiss francs in three months' time. He assumed that the dollar would drop and he would make a tidy profit by buying back his francs with cheap dollars. But instead of dropping its value went up, and that one transaction alone cost Lloyds about a million pounds. Colombo never gave written confirmation of telephone deals but merely kept a note of them in his diary, so his manager, Mr Mombelli, had no idea of what was going on. After the disaster of his first foray into the field of high finance, you would have thought that Colombo would have been scared off. But he was the masochistic sort, and relentlessly continued with more

and more telephone deals in currency in order to try to end up in profit. In July 1974 the Swiss Government declared that all banks had to announce their foreign exchange deals at the end of each month. A telephone call from a foreign banker to Lloyds in London in August hinted that something 'odd' was going on in Switzerland at the same time as Colombo was desperately trying to straighten out the books. He and Mombelli were recalled to London, where officials discovered to their horror that another 235 million pounds' worth of deals were still unpaid. Their chief exchange-dealer gave up his Bank Holiday weekend and, with Colombo at his side, spent several days secretly trying to unravel the mess, manipulating the currency market brilliantly and making quick profits to minimize the losses. He managed to eliminate about 200 million pounds' worth of debts, but when Lloyds made the incident public, it wiped £20 million off their London shares. The City guessed that to lose £33 million Colombo must have been speculating with up to £500 million, described as 'absolutely fantastic figures' for a branch that only had about fifteen employees. In 1975 Colombo and Mombelli appeared in a Swiss court on charges of violating the Swiss banking code. Mombelli, who claimed never to have understood what his worker was up to, was characterized by the judge as 'a disaster'. Both men got a suspended sentence and a £300 fine. After all, they had never pocketed any money, and Colombo claimed that if his deals had been allowed to go through as he had planned, Lloyds would have ended up with a large profit. Somehow I'm not convinced.

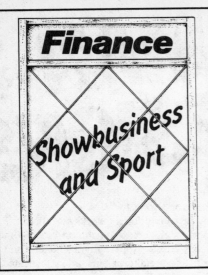

What's in a name? Quite a lot if you are Muhammad Ali and allow your name to be rented out to endorse products and occasionally organizations. For David Begelman, his name meant the kind of box-office successes which would allow his employers to overlook the 'small' matter of some forged cheques and welcome him back with open arms. Crook or not, he was good for business. And given the fast and persistent popularity of rock and roll, it was only inevitable that allegations of financial impropriety would arise – again and again.

Close Encounters
of the Embarrassing Kind

THE STORY STARTS in the mid sixties when Judy Garland and her husband Sid Luft brought a law suit against her (then) agent, David Begelman of CMA, alleging that money owing to her had not been paid – a total sum of £50,000. The action was later dropped; Sid and Judy split; she remarried, and died in London in June 1967.

Cut to September 1976, and David Begelman is now President of Columbia Pictures' film and television divisions. Since 1973 he has rescued the company from a serious financial state with successes like *Shampoo* and *The Deep*. He earns a salary of around $250,000 a year and has perks worth another $150,000. Although half his salary may be going in tax, he has small consolations, like Columbia paying the rent on his house. Only one blot on David's horizon – he needs cash. Why? Who knows, but one clue could be the fact that in the early sixties he was known to have gambled heavily. Indeed, he owned up to the fact that he had been a 'compulsive loser' to the

HOLLYWOOD WITH THE LID OFF

tune of $60,000 and rumour said it was more: that on one occasion a rich pal had flown out $300,000 in cash to Las Vegas to bale out Mr B. Nobody knew if Begelman was still gambling – if he was, it was very private – but he certainly mixed with a crowd who had a *lot* of money.

In September 1976, a cheque was issued by Columbia pictures for the sum of $10,000, payable to the actor Cliff Robertson, specifically on Begelman's orders. He then took the cheque down to his local bank, having forged Robertson's endorsement, and cashed it. Nothing more would have happened if the next February Cliff had not been sorting through some business papers and spotted a letter from the accounts department of Columbia informing him that for tax purposes they were notifying him of the $10,000 he had received from them in the previous tax year.

The Fall, Rise and Fall Of David Begelman

BEGELMAN RESIGNS

Robertson investigated and discovered that he hadn't worked for Columbia, and therefore wasn't owed any money. He hadn't even received the cheque to which he was not entitled. His accountants rang Columbia and asked for a copy of it, whereupon his agents received a call from Begelman saying a young man in the company had stupidly forged it, and they had sacked him after deciding not to press charges. Would Robertson agree not to call in the police? Robertson was prepared not to go any further until he rang the bank and asked who had cashed the cheque. On discovering it was Begelman, he called in the police, who did nothing. He then called in the FBI, who did nothing too.

SUSPENDED

Suspicion grew and Begelman was called before the board to explain. He owned up, saying that only one cheque had ever been forged. They suspended him on full pay and began a thorough investigation into their financial affairs. They also put out a woolly statement which did nothing to dispel the growing rumours; it did not say Begelman was involved in forgery. Suspended on 3 October, Begelman mysteriously told *Newsweek* magazine, 'Any judgement I made I stand by.' Meanwhile the cost of having their books carefully audited had set Columbia back a cool $250,000, and it was discovered that Begelman had lifted about another $74,000 from the company by forging cheques and fiddling his expenses.

'COMPLETELY CURED'

While all this brow-beating was going on, several interesting things were happening. One was that the board were deluged with telegrams urging them to keep Begelman on, since Begelman had taken Columbia through a period when it had made about $100 million in profits, and many thought him the best man to continue to provide the shareholders with good dividends. Secondly, Begelman started visiting Judd Marmor, the top shrink to the stars. This psychiatrist saw Begelman for six weeks and then produced a report for the board which announced that he was 'completely cured'. Apparently his actions had been the result of emotional problems, and constituted a 'temporary period of self-destructive behaviour' which was unlikely ever to be repeated. This was music to the company's ears, particularly as their film *Close Encounters of the Third Kind* had just opened and was fast becoming the highest-grossing film at that time in the United States. It was Begelman who had got the film together. The board offered him his job back, and at first he refused, preferring the earlier offer they had made of making him an independent producer on the payroll without all the hassles of running a company. In late December 1978 he changed his mind and accepted the job of President back again.

OUTCRY

There was an immediate outcry. The whole affair was picked over in *New West* and *New York* magazines, and all the allegations concerning Judy Garland's finances resurfaced. By the second week of February Begelman had resigned, accepting the company's offer of work and the same salary as an independent producer. The police were thwarted as Columbia refused to press charges against him. The Begelman scandal also brought out into the open many disputes concerning the film companies' accounting methods that had been simmering for some years. Many actors, directors and producers spoke out for the first time and claimed that the books were often 'cooked'. Begelman may perhaps have forced some of the worst offenders to clean up their act a little. Begelman is now President of MGM, and is liked and widely respected for his many box-office successes.

COLUMBIA CHIEF IN PROBE

Stars of the drama: Muhammad Ali, "I'm innocent"; Harold Smith, hunted by FBI; Don King, under investigation

Boxing and Banking
Just Don't Mix

IN 1974 MUHAMMAD ALI met one Harold Smith, who hung around the champion long enough to persuade him to start a club for young boxers from poor families in Los Angeles. Smith converted a garage in Santa Monica and, using Ali's name, ran a successful, if charitable, venture, getting government grants in the process. Smith had been a rock concert promoter, and his ambitions extended beyond merely helping underprivileged boxers get a step up the ladder. In 1978 he started MAPS (Muhammad Ali Professional Sports), a promotions company that organized fights. MAPS, on the face of it, seemed a sensible project for Ali: it gave the young boxers from the club something to aim for, and linked them to a highly professional match-making organization. But it wasn't only the magic of Ali's name that attracted boxers to the Smith stable, but the insanely huge purses that Smith paid out at fights, very often in cash.

ALLEGED EMBEZZLEMENT

Smith had all the trappings of an extremely rich man. In a business not noted for its personal restraint, he was outrageously lavish. He owned a large house, a racehorse, two private planes, and a boat. All went well until the end of January 1981, when the Wells Fargo bank alleged that someone had embezzled over $21 million from two of their branches in Los Angeles.

Smith had disappeared. Another missing face was that of Benjamin Lewis, a former employee of Wells Fargo and a director of MAPS. The FBI started a hunt for the two men. On the run, Smith said he would answer all the charges and declared that he was being hunted by the 'Japanese Mafia'. He also asserted that one of the bank's own employees had taken the money, and that the bank had a team of gunmen tracking him down. Needless to say, Wells Fargo retorted that this little scenario was bordering on the ridiculous.

HEAVY LOSSES

According to the American magazine *Sports Illustrated*, Smith made heavy losses on his fights. So where did the endless supply of ready cash come from? Wells Fargo said that someone with intimate knowledge of their computer system broke the codes and carried out a complicated swindle, extracting money from twelve accounts which ended up in the hands of MAPS. They suspected Lewis of carrying out the transactions.

NOT INVOLVED

Meanwhile Ali's name, which he had rented out for a good cause, was being dragged through the mud, although by the time the scandal broke he was no longer involved in it: having fallen out with Smith over the fact that he could not see the books, he had removed his name from the list of directors – but not from the title MAPS. Ali said, 'After all this is over, it will make a hell of a movie.' I doubt he will want to star in it.

105

Finance

Super Salesmen

What makes a super salesman? These characters all had a single-minded drive to take advantage of what was not theirs to sell. They could be deemed clever and resourceful – selling trust funds, trademarks, and patents is not, on the face of it, illegal. It's not what they sold but how they sold it that makes these men less than desirable business partners. They also seem to be free of moral restraint, from any regret for having transgressed the spirit of laws and values.

KING CORNFELD ACCUSED OF FRAUD ON INCREDIBLE SCALE

Bernie Cornfeld, Ageing Hippie

IN THE LATE 1950s Bernie Cornfeld was a trust fund salesman *shlepping* round the American bases in Europe when he hit on a brilliantly simple idea. He decided to convert the unit trust scheme into a massive operation funded by thousands of small investors. By pooling all their contributions he would be able to use the capital to make a wide variety of investments in which the small dabblers in finance would not otherwise have been able to participate. He founded the Investors Overseas company, IOS, in 1960, registering it in Panama. By operating outside America and England, he bypassed many dreary laws and regulations; similarly, the first unit trust fund he set up, ITT, was registered in Luxemburg, a country not known for its stringent attitude to currency and

their money moved around in such a way that it was 'laundered' for them as well as making a profit in the process. Locked in a Swiss bank was a list of investors known only to Bernie and a few close colleagues. All this gave the conventional banking world a lot of misgivings, and in 1966 the Swiss police tried to investigate IOS activities in Geneva, but without much success.

ASSUMED NAMES

By the end of the sixties IOS had formed its own banks, thus gaining even more control over the movement of funds. In 1970 there was a convention of the top ninety-seven salesmen in London, and according to Jim Hougan, author of *Spooks*, over half these men, including the top 'associate' of the year, used assumed names. IOS was beginning to get bad publicity – the police had raided some of their South American offices, and in 1969 there had only been a £10.3 million profit instead of the projected £25

NAKED TYCOON AND GIRL WHO SAID 'NO'

tax controls. Bernie's theory was that many small investors would receive the same financial advice as millionaires, and he set up teams of salesmen, whom he called 'associates', to go and win him those vital clients. Operating outside America enabled him to pay his salesmen on a higher commission basis than was allowed by American law, and he also offered them the chance to buy stock in the company; but as its value rose, this became an offer that would cost them dear. Cornfeld then created the Fund of Funds, with two classes of stock. As he held most of the common stock, which carried the voting rights, he effectively ran this fund as he wished.

'LAUNDERED' MONEY

He bought the Villa Elma, which Napoleon had built for Josephine, to house IOS in Geneva. At its height, IOS held funds approaching £1,000 million and claimed to be able to triple your money in three years. Often the same 'small investors' whom Bernie used to boast that he was helping (he said he was a socialist) were in fact wealthy expatriates avoiding tax and members of organized crime syndicates who wanted

million. It meant that a lot of people cashed in their holdings, leaving IOS with a potential cash flow problem. In spite of Bernie's ravings about 'little people', about twenty-five per cent of all the holdings in IOS were in the hands of one per cent of the investors. It was at this point that IOS was approached by Robert Vesco, a man who specialized in building up huge financial conglomerates. Vesco offered to bail them out with a loan on condition that Bernie left and sold his shares to Vesco. Cornfeld had no option but to comply.

In 1971 the *Sunday Times* published the result of their year-long inquiry into Cornfeld's affairs as a book entitled *Do you Sincerely Want to be Rich?* It alleged that Cornfeld had misled investors, used brochures that added to this confusion about what really happened to the investors' money, and sold shares in the company to benefit the directors rather than the shareholders. Vesco retreated to Costa Rica, where he remained surrounded by bodyguards and avoiding extradition. Meanwhile IOS more or less collapsed.

Bernie Cornfeld returned to Geneva in 1973 and was arrested on charges of fraud and issuing bogus brochures. Earlier that year, he had been in the news when he was convicted in London of indecently assaulting a young lady at his home. 'Twenty years of sex and this is the first time it's happened,' he said. 'I expected to have sexual intercourse with her.' Then in May he appeared before a Swiss judge who said that over eighty former employees had complained of illegal business practices at IOS. He was held in custody. After eleven months about 100 of his friends, including actors Tony Curtis and George Hamilton and Bunny person Hugh Hefner, raised £680,000 to get him out on bail. He then financed the film *Jackpot* which sank without trace, but this did not stop Bernie from buying Pickfair, Mary Pickford's house in Beverly Hills, where he proceeded to run his investments while awaiting trial and further charges from the Swiss authorities. He was reported as claiming to be worth about £12 million despite the collapse of IOS.

In June 1976 he married Lorraine Armbruster, an ex-model, two months before she was to have their child. He was back in court to hear further charges arising out of the collapse of IOS in 1977, but the following year he was delighted to hear that most of the outstanding fraud charges against him had been dropped. Finally, in October 1979, all remaining charges were withdrawn and Cornfeld left the country on a round-the-world second honeymoon.

SEX DRIVE

Bernie was nothing if not an elderly hippy, a chubby, bearded fellow with an over-publicized sex drive that made up for what he lacked in hair. By the end of 1975 he had an amazing total of sixteen women living with him. He said he liked to make love two or three times a day, preferably with two girls at once. 'My tastes are simple,' he declared. He was distressed by Women's Lib and commented, 'A woman's role is to take the tedium and monotony out of an otherwise dreary day.'

A Small Man Making a Big Mark

IN JUNE 1980 the *Sunday Times* revealed the strange story of a man who claimed he was a modern-day Robin Hood. Doctor Robert Aries owned up to getting enormous pleasure from what he described as 'tweaking the noses' of multinational companies like ICI, Marks and Spencers, and de Beers. No target was too large or formidable for the ingenious Doctor Aries. His secret was to register the trademarks of large companies before they got round to doing it themselves. They then had to buy the rights back off him at whatever price he dreamt up. His most famous coup was in 1972 and involved Exxon, the giant oil company. He knew that Standard Oil of New Jersey (as it was then called) were thinking of changing their name. After some in-depth research he discovered that Exxon was the new title they had chosen. He immediately registered it in France, which automatically gave him the rights to trade as Exxon in twenty-two other countries. To buy back the rights to use their name Exxon had to cough up, and it was rumoured they paid over £1 million.

BUSINESS METHODS

Another Aries trick was to 'persuade' laboratory workers to come and work for him and reveal the development work they had been involved in. Then he marketed the new product before the drug firm who had been doing all the research work on it. He also took out patents on drug compounds that he knew (from research workers) would be needed to develop and market new products. He then sold these compounds to the drug companies at *his* price. A further Aries speciality was to research the trading methods of large companies and then threaten to expose them if he found any evidence of tax-avoidance or price-fixing schemes. They had to pay for his silence.

£50 MILLION

Aries has owned over 3,000 trademarks, including de Beers, Revlon, and Celanese, in various obscure parts of the world, and has filed more than 400 patents. His enemies called it 'technological crime' and 'blackmail', and in 1980 the *Sunday Times* estimated that over £50 million had passed through his hands. He has been exiled from America for twenty years, banned from

Switzerland, and jailed in France. Sometimes the trademarks that Aries had registered for under £1 each were owned by companies who refused to buy them back. Then, it was said, he was often just satisfied to be given an expensive lunch by the Chairman. After all, enough suckers had already provided him with a string of racehorses and an art collection. One of his private jokes was to photograph himself outside the offices of any company he was doing battle with and then send a copy to the top fellow in the organization. When interviewed by the *Sunday Times*, he said, 'I am not a crook'.

Finance Fakes

The point of these fakers is that they aimed for the big time. Not for Alves Reis the usual petty attempt to float some forged five spots on the market. Nothing less than the issuing of a whole fake currency would suffice – and he actually got it produced by the people who were printing the real money. Ivar Kreuger, too, was nothing if not sweeping in scope and vision – he managed to dupe the political and business leaders of Europe. Graham Barton aimed high and got his 'fake' on the front page of a national daily. Clifford Irving knew that the world was desperate to know more about Howard Hughes, true or false. We accept what we want to accept.

The Million Pound Banknote Bluff

AFTER THE First World War, Governments were deseperate for money to pay off their debts and paper currency was pouring out at a fantastic rate. What better time for an unknown swindler to involve the highly reputable British company of Waterlows in one of the biggest banknote frauds of all time? It cost Waterlows over half a million pounds and dragged them through the courts in a most embarrassing fashion.

MASSIVE FRAUD

Alves Reis was a businessman who had already equipped himself with a forged degree from Oxford. In 1924 he was imprisoned in Lisbon for embezzlement, and it was there that he dreamt up his revenge: a massive fraud against the Portuguese Government. Portugal was relying on Angola to help solve its financial problems, and Reis found that the Banco de Portugal was issuing notes far beyond any capital they held, and that this new money was being used without a proper record of the serial numbers being kept. He then forged a contract which said that an international group of financiers was to lend Angola a million pounds. In return for this they would get the right to print currency for Angola worth that amount. Then Reis chose two partners, Marang and Bandeira, but he omitted to tell them how the money would be used. In December 1924 Marang went to see Sir William Waterlow with forged credentials, and asked

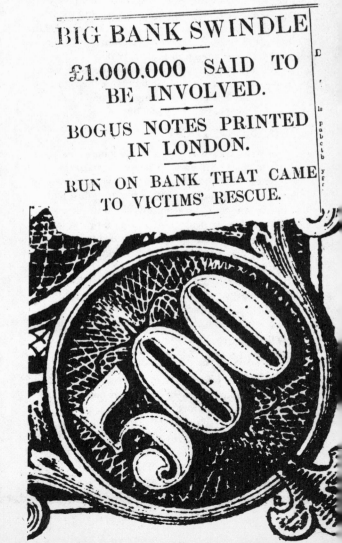

BIG BANK SWINDLE

£1,000,000 SAID TO BE INVOLVED.

BOGUS NOTES PRINTED IN LONDON.

RUN ON BANK THAT CAME TO VICTIMS' RESCUE.

ECHO OF BANK-NOTE FRAUDS.

LAWSUIT AGAINST PRINTERS.

SIR W. WATERLOW A WITNESS.

him to print some 100 million escudos' worth of notes. (Waterlows had already printed Portuguese banknotes; in fact they worked for banks throughout the world.) Sir William said that this would be difficult, but that at a pinch they could be printed from the Vasco da Gama plates which the company had already used to print notes for the Banco de Portugal. Meanwhile the printers had checked with their agent in Lisbon, who sent them a coded message telling them to be very careful. But Marang was able to persuade Waterlows that their agent was not important enough to know of the high-level decisions made in Portugal. He suggested that Waterlows should write to the Governor of the Banco de Portugal and that he would deliver the letter by hand. It is hard to believe, but the trusting Sir William actually fell for it. Marang returned with a forged reply, and Waterlows noticed that it was on different paper from the usual letters from the Banco de Portugal, and that it was written in English instead of Portuguese. It said that the money should be printed and that any further correspondence should go through none other than Mr Marang. Sir William believed the letter's instructions to be genuine, but nevertheless sent a letter through the post to the bank. Incredibly enough, it never arrived.

Marang told Waterlows to use the same serial numbers as they had used on their previous batch of Vasco da Gama notes, saying that when the notes arrived in Lisbon they would be over-printed with the message 'For circulation in Angola only'. All went according to plan and the notes were printed.

FOREIGN EXCHANGE

At this point Reis owned up to Marang and his other accomplice and told them what they were going to do with the money: they had to get it into circulation. This they did by setting up their own bank and dealing in foreign exchange. They also got black market traders to exchange the forged notes for real ones on the streets. The money started to go to their heads – Reis, for instance, bought himself a lavish home and large amounts of jewellery for his wife. Then the rumours started, and at the beginning of December 1925 one bank found it owned four pairs of Vasco da Gama notes, all with the same serial numbers. The bank belonging to Reis was raided and the police found him and his accomplices in the cellar.

PANIC

Over a million pounds' worth of forged notes had already gone into circulation. What could the Government do? People started to panic and changed the real Vasco da Gama notes as well as the fake ones. After all, they had both been printed by the same printer, Waterlows, with the same plates, so how could anyone tell the difference? Finally the notes were all recalled. The English papers picked up on the story, featuring the British involvement in another country's currency crisis. Luckily Sir William Waterlow told the Portuguese Government that the second batch of notes had been printed with a secret printer's mark, so the forgeries could be detected on close inspection.

DAMAGES

Reis and Bandeira were tried in Lisbon in May 1926 and received long jail sentences followed by exile. The lucky Marang had escaped before the trial with £500,000. Four years later, Waterlows were back in the headlines, this time over a lawsuit. The Banco de Portugal sued them in the British courts, asking for damages caused by negligence. Waterlows were ordered to pay over £500,000. On appeal the damages were reassessed – upwards. They then had to pay £610,392. Newspapers carried the story and referred to the hapless Sir William as 'the man who fell for a huge banknote bluff and it cost him £900,000'. Reis wasn't in the headlines again until his death. He died completely broke in 1955.

Howard Hughes Speaks!

Mute Millionaire Speaks

'I ONLY WISH I were still in the movie business, because I don't remember any script I ever saw in Hollywood as wild or as imagination-stretching as this autobiography yarn has turned out to be.' So said Howard Hughes at one of the most bizarre media events ever televised, his first interview in fifteen years. Naturally Hughes was never in vision – he was just a disembodied voice at the end of a telephone line being questioned on TV by seven reporters. His answers solved the publishing scandal of the century, but they never revealed the other big secret he kept to his death: what he looked like. After deciding fifteen years before that he wanted to be alone, what had produced this dramatic change in Hughes, the world's most famous recluse? Why was he speaking to millions of viewers on 9 January 1972?

The story started two years before in Ibiza, where Clifford Irving, an American novelist, lived with his wife Edith. Irving had spent the previous few years travelling round the world wherever he fancied, but he had never made much from his writing. He had been to art school before university, a training that would come in very useful in the following months.

ELUSIVE

He told a friend, Richard Susskind, that he had decided to write the autobiography of Howard Hughes. The only trouble with his plan was that he executed it without the help of the elusive Mr Hughes, who had rarely been seen publicly since 1960 and spent most of his time shacked up in hotel suites guarded by trusty Mormons. Irving wrote to his publishers and sold them the idea of an 'official' autobiography of Howard Hughes written with the millionaire's approval. Irving's gamble was that when the book appeared it was most unlikely that Hughes would come out of hiding to refute it. McGraw-Hill were persuaded to send Irving a large advance to pass on to Hughes as a payment for allowing taped

Irvings

interviews, and another huge sum to Irving to cover an advance on the manuscript plus his expenses. Irving then forged a passport for Edith, his wife, in the name of Helga Hughes and she departed for Zurich, where she opened an account in the name of H. Hughes and deposited the money. From then on, the Irvings spent both his advance and Hughes's payment in an orgy of good living. Clifford had a terrific time in top hotels all around the Caribbean, Europe, and Central America, sending back to the publishers forged letters purporting to be from Hughes to Irving in order to show that the two men were having meetings and carrying out interviews. He began to construct his book from newspaper cuttings and the transcript of a book which one of Hughes's former executives, Noah Dietrich, was writing secretly in Los Angeles. Because Noah's stuff had never been published, it gave Irving lots of detail about Hughes's private life which greatly added to his book's authenticity. Much encouraged by the material they received, McGraw-Hill announced on 7 December 1971 that they had sold the serialization rights to Time-Life, who would print three long extracts in *Time* magazine.

'FAIRY TALES'

This was when Irving's beautiful gamble started to go badly wrong. He was under pressure to complete the book because another publisher in New York had announced that he too had a Howard Hughes autobiography and that his was 'official'. Then Hughes telephoned Frank McCulloch, an old friend who worked for Time-Life, and told him Irving's book was a fake, but to his horror top executives at Time-Life decided to go ahead and publish, arguing that Hughes's phone call was typical of his paranoid behaviour in the past and that it was perfectly normal for him to deny any involvement in a project once it displeased him. This forced Hughes into the televised press conference, where he denounced both books as 'fairy tales'. The reporters had to resort to trick questions to make sure that the man they were questioning really was Hughes, and they asked him about a wide range of subjects, including his health and his appearance. But Hughes's main preoccupation was to prevent any book about him from appearing in print. The net closed in around the Irvings, even though McGraw-Hill still stuck by their story after

Hughes's press conference, saying they were going ahead and publishing, and had received signed letters from Hughes about the whole project. They had submitted these letters to a handwriting expert, who informed them that the signatures were genuine.

Swiss find $442,000, order Irvings arrested

On 31 January Swiss police issued warrants for the arrest of Edith and Clifford over irregularities in the H. Hughes account, alleging fraud. In court Irving finally agreed to submit samples of his handwriting and experts, reversing the previous opinion, said the Hughes letters were faked. Danish singer Nina van Pallandt (ex-Nina of the Nina and Frederick singing duo) stated that on one occasion when Irving had been with her he told everyone he was seeing Hughes.

Irving admits hoax

By 11 February Clifford had admitted the hoax, and a writer called Jim Phelan told McGraw-Hill that Irving's book contained material from the book he had been ghosting with Noah Dietrich. A copy of the transcripts had been given to Noah's middleman in the deal, a Hollywood character called Stanley Meyer, and he had passed them to Irving. Meyer had also told Hughes's lawyers about Noah's book (Dietrich had signed a no-book contract when he left Hughes), ensuring that Jim Phelan's book would get blocked by the lawyers and never see the light of day.

give in to court

DRAMA BEHIND MATCH KINGS DEATH

FINANCIER BROKEN BY THE ECONOMIC CRISIS

Swedish Moratorium on Private Firms' Debts in Operation Today

WORLD—WIDE REPERCUSSIONS

Matchmaker Cons Leaders of Europe

IVAR KREUGER, who was known around the world as the Match King, shot himself in his luxurious Paris apartment in March 1932. Europe's newspapers were full of expressions of regret at the demise of a man generally regarded as one of the great financial geniuses of the time. Although it was hinted that his empire had been having some problems, it was not until several weeks later than the public gradually became aware that Kreuger, friend of many of Europe's top politicians and a multimillionaire, was probably the greatest swindler of all time: some experts estimated that during his life he had misappropriated £142 million.

Ivar Kreuger was born in 1879, and after training as an engineer he built up a substantial construction business before taking over the family's match firm in Sweden in 1917. From that date onwards, he developed a theory which was to rule his business activities: in order to exploit the match market to the full, he had to have a monopoly in each country where his products were sold. First of all he started buying up and amalgamating other match-making companies in Sweden. This gave him better credit than the Government of France, for these were financially bleak days for countries devastated by the First World War, and many Governments were having a great deal of difficulty in finding the money to rebuild their economies. So the climate was right for

114

Kreuger to offer giant loans to interested countries in return for match monopolies. Between 1925 and 1930 he lent France about £18¼ million, Poland between £6 and £10 million, Rumania £7½ million, Yugoslavia about £22 million, Hungary £36 million and Turkey £2½ million. In 1930 he lent Germany £31¼ million.

FORGED BONDS

These are incredible sums of money, and the transactions seemed even more bizarre when accountants, many years after Kreuger's death, started to unravel his business operations. He simply operated a pyramid of paper companies, over 400 in all. He borrowed money in order to lend it, and forged millions of pounds' worth of bonds to raise more cash. Kreuger tried to cover up one fraud with another, even spelling names incorrectly on fake documents. But these were not noticed, so great was his reputation and so influential his friendship among leading financiers and politicians of the day. Nevertheless, things were starting to go badly wrong with his operations. His companies were earning less than two per cent profit on their turnover, and yet he was paying out share dividends of five, seven, and even ten per cent. His affairs reached a critical point in 1930 with the onset of the Depression, and he found it increasingly hard to get credit. He took control of the Ericsson company; but a fall in the price of Ericsson shares made ITT suspicious, and when they inspected the books they found that the true value of Kreuger's assets was negligible, consisting mainly of claims on other companies. By then they had taken him on their board and put up £2 million to buy Ericsson. They demanded that Kreuger should return this money, which of course he could not do. His advisers told him to cash some Italian bonds which they knew he kept in his private safe. But before a meeting was held to discuss the matter, he was found shot dead. When they opened the safe, they discovered that the bonds were cheap forgeries.

'FINANCIAL WIZARD'

Several rumours surrounded his death. Some people thought that he had sold some of his securities, faked his death, and had another body substituted for his own. After his death 165,000 shares in his companies were sold in a morning, and the *Daily Mirror* commented, 'His death will have repercussions in stock markets all over the world . . . he was a financial wizard beaten by the world economic crisis.' Accountants were still trying to sort out the mess in 1954, but one thing had become crystal clear: the 'financial wizard' had been nothing but a plain crook.

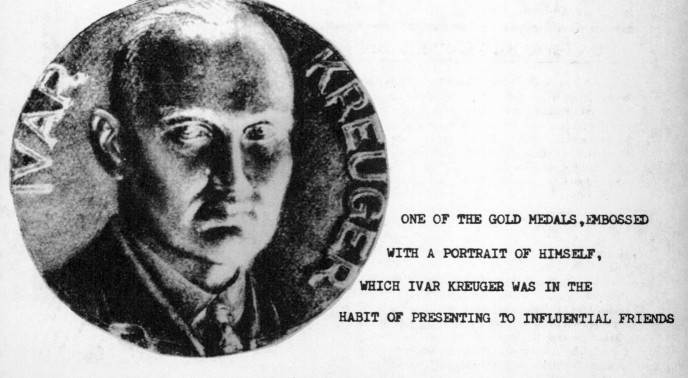

ONE OF THE GOLD MEDALS, EMBOSSED WITH A PORTRAIT OF HIMSELF, WHICH IVAR KREUGER WAS IN THE HABIT OF PRESENTING TO INFLUENTIAL FRIENDS

Finance

Less Than Proper

We all know just what behaviour is expected of us. It's the same for public figures, but more so. If you are in the public eye, if you're the President's son, the press and the officials will be scrutinizing every move. If you're a religious leader, your flock looks to you for moral example. Yet they're surprised every time they're caught red-handed. But after all, what's a scandal without the denial?

CARDINAL CODY'S MISTRESS ?

The Cleric and Cousin 'Sis'

A SCANDAL ERUPTED in August 1981 when it became known that one of America's leading Catholics, Cardinal John Cody of Chicago – the largest archdiocese in the country – was under investigation by a Federal Grand Jury. This was the first time in the history of the Catholic Church in America that such a high-ranking official had been suspected of criminal wrong-doing. In September the *Chicago Sun-Times* revealed the result of an eighteen-month investigation they had conducted into the financial affairs of Cardinal Cody and accused him of diverting over $1 million of Church funds to a step-cousin, 74-year-old Helen Dolan Wilson, as well as paying her a secret salary from Church funds from 1969 to 1974. The crux of their allegations implied that the Cardinal had used money which should have been spent as donations to visiting clergy and for his household expenses to buy his relative an expensive apartment in Florida and keep her in Designer clothes. Using Church funds (which are tax-free) to benefit an individual in this way is an indictable offence.

The initial five-day exposé in the *Sun-Times* saddened many Catholics. But Cody was not without some enemies within his flock, and when it became known that he had failed to answer Grand Jury subpoenas which had been pending for some months, even his supporters felt that if he at least responded to his accusers by making his financial records available, it would have stemmed the growing tide of criticism at the high-handed way he seemed to conduct his business affairs.

At the time of the *Sun-Times* articles Cody was seventy-three and nearing the age when many Cardinals customarily retired. He and Wilson – he called her 'Sis' – seemed a bizarre couple to have been the centre of such charges of lavish expenditure. They had known each other for over sixty years, and were cousins by a family marriage in 1913. They grew up in St Louis and had been childhood friends. In 1927

Chicago, and Helen Dolan Wilson followed him in 1969. In 1967 she had been photographed with him and Pope Paul VI in Rome during the ceremony of induction into the College of Cardinals.

AUTOCRAT

Cody's image underwent a change in Chicago, where Cody controlled an annual Church budget of $220 million, and where (in spite of the prevailing spirit of directives from the Vatican) he failed to allow his clergy or the parishioners any great amount of participation in deciding how Church funds were spent. He was an autocratic man who kept the handling of Church finances very much to himself. His liberal image was somewhat diminished when he closed four inner-city schools and spent a lavish $4 million on a closed-circuit TV system. He was also resistant to letting his priests have a say in parish affairs. Things came to a head in 1971 when a

Woman kept on diocese funds?

Helen had married and had two children, but she divorced in 1939. Since then she was said to have lived on her alimony of $1 a month plus $50 a month child support. She admitted that in 1961 Cody had lent her $21,000 to buy a vacation house in Florida. She paid back less than half this amount before selling it in 1972 for $110,000 and buying a luxury condominium in Boca Raton, Florida, for $61,000. It was said that although she drew a salary from Cody's office for some years, she had never been seen there. Her apartment in Florida was currently valued at around $250,000 and she wore smart clothes and furs, and belonged to an expensive country club. None of this seemed to add up to a life-style financed by her meagre income. The *Sun-Times* also alleged that her son, an insurance broker, had benefited by commissions totalling over $150,000 from insurance policies taken out by the churches in St Louis, New Orleans and Chicago under Cody. They also claimed that Helen was the beneficiary of $100,000 life-insurance policy taken out by Cody.

Cody had a reputation of being a tough cookie under his rather frail exterior. He suffered from heart trouble and was under constant medical supervision. After serving in St Louis he moved to New Orleans, where he established a liberal reputation by pursuing a policy of integration in church schools. In 1965 he moved to

dissident group, the Association of Chicago Priests, voted to censure him because they felt that he had not fully represented their views on the subject of Church reform at a meeting of bishops.

It was revealed that although Helen Wilson had moved back to St Louis from Chicago in 1975, Cody visited her frequently. He was also said to have visited her apartment in Boca Raton. Wilson had helped Cody to redecorate his three-storey offical residence in Chicago to a lavish degree, and even used it as a summer forwarding address when she was travelling. As millions of minds boggled over the exact nature of a relationship between two senior citizens whose friendship spanned over half a century, charitable minds assumed that it had always been platonic, and that since her divorce Mrs Wilson had pursued the one group of men who could not threaten her in any way, the clergy. Nevertheless, given the sums of money involved, it did seen to be a very *special* kind of relationship. She retorted that the *Sun-Times* allegations made her seem 'like a tramp or a kept woman'. Cody's lawyer responded by saying that his client was answerable only to God and Rome and certainly not to journalists.

But questions were growing about the way that Cody had administered two funds in particular. A system operated within the Church in Chicago called the Corporation Sole, which meant that he alone had legal control of the Church's assets within the diocese, and could decide whether or not to pass details of financial transactions down to his priests. Many claimed he was withholding information, which, although he was perfectly entitled to do so, had led to a growing amount of criticism. Most importantly, it was rumoured that if Cody was formally indicted, it could not bode well for the tax-free status of the Roman Catholic Church and that other investigations might follow. Cody himself was not thought to draw a high official salary; it had been about $12,000 a year in the 1970s, certainly not a sum which would keep Mrs

Wilson in the style to which she now seemed accustomed. Apart from quoting Jesus and saying he forgave his attackers 'seven hundred times seven times', Cody would not comment on the allegations at all. Neither would the Government. Cody claimed that he had lent Wilson money from his own savings. The Chicago Catholic newspaper accused the *Sun-Times* of harassing their Cardinal, and *The New York Times*, while applauding the journalistic scoop of the *Sun-Times*, pondered on the timing of their exposé. Had they deliberately tried to make it coincide with subpoenas to strengthen their story? The *Sun-Times* was said to have documents to back up all their allegations, but so far had not published them. A controversial priest and sociologist, the Rev. Andrew M. Greeley, had just published a novel, which (by enormous coincidence) revolved around a financial scandal concerning a Chicago archbishop and his step-cousin with whom he was having an affair.

CODY RESIGNS

Greeley denied he had helped the *Sun-Times* with their inquiries and refused to comment on the Cody affair. As the Grand Jury subpoenas relating to Cody's finances remained unanswered for eight months, fresh ones were issued. Five banks were asked to supply information as the inquiry broadened. The *Sun-Times* alleged that this was to try and obtain information which the Grand Jury had been unable to get directly from Cody. Mrs Wilson had already been subpoenaed and handed over financial statements to the Jury. Now the Government was said to be looking at other aspects of diocesan funds, including the insurance policies for which her son had acted as broker.

HEART ATTACK

The Chicago diocesan office said they had received about 10,000 letters since the scandal broke, the majority supporting Cody. It was rumoured that the Vatican was possibly going to retire the Cardinal on his seventy-fourth birthday in December 1981 and was looking into a face-saving way of doing so. It was said that Cody had secretly offered his resignation to Pope John-Paul II, but it was rejected. His last public appearance was at Midnight Mass on Christmas Eve, but his health was steadily declining and he died on 25 April 1982 of a heart attack, after which it was thought that the Federal investigation would be dropped. Cody left a letter saying he forgave his critics but that God would not be so lenient.

President's Son Faces Probe

MICHAEL REAGAN, the President's eldest son (by his first marriage to Jane Wyman), started being a major embarrassment to his image-conscious dad in February 1981. The press revealed that he was under investigation for allegedly diverting funds invested in a gasohol development project to his own personal use. Michael was said to have offered and sold stock in a company that was planned but never incorporated, and as a result was the subject of inquiries on the part of both the Los Angeles County District Attorney's office and the California Department of Corporations. They wanted to get to the bottom of how Michael Reagan had used the $17,500 given to him by four investors in his 'company', Agricultural Energy Resources, of which he was sole owner and which he operated from his home. While Michael's attorney told the press that it was a complex situation and that his client was sure to be exonerated, search warrants were issued.

It turned out that, at the same time as giving 250 campaign speeches for his dad, Michael had been setting up the business which was selling gasohol equipment to grain farmers. A former world-class boat salesman, who was said to have a 'persuasive' personality, Michael claimed that no one would be interested in his business affairs if his name had not been Reagan. Facing charges of using the $17,500 for his own expenses, he complained: 'I've lost my money, my business and seventeen pounds. I'm a victim.' He claimed to be over $10,000 in debt as a result of his legal fees.

While the District Attorney's office were close to making a decision whether to prosecute or not, another facet of Michael's business activities emerged. He said he would now abandon his career as a wheeler-dealer after it had emerged that he had been using his father's name to seek defence contracts. In December 1980 he had been employed as marketing vice-president at Dana Inalls Profile Inc. of Burbank California. In March 1981 he telephoned several military installations, including the airbase in Oklahoma which supervises the maintenance of the President's plane, asking how to get on the 'approved' list of contractors. He then followed up his call with a letter which said; 'I know that with my father's leadership at the White House this country's armed services are going to be rebuilt and strengthened. We at Dana Inalls Profiles want to be involved in that process.' The letter was described as 'dubious sort of behaviour', and it duly appeared in the *Oklahoma Times*. At first the White House brushed the whole issue aside, but later in the day they announced that Presidential Counsel Fred Fielding would be advising all four of the Reagan children on possible conflicts of

Prez's son in trouble

interest. Michael was most upset when a reporter compared his rather silly behaviour with that of Jimmy Carter's bizarre and embarrassing brother Billy. Finally Michael got let off the hook when the DA's office said that they'd cleared him of complicity in a stock fraud scheme, and they'd decided that, rather than being a participant, Michael Reagan was a victim. The investigation found him guilty of 'technical' violations of state security laws because it was asserted he encouraged friends to buy stock when he was not a licensed security salesman. As Michael had not made any profit out of the deals, it was decided not to press criminal charges. It also turned out that in fact Michael as well as his friends had lost money in the venture.

Along with his good news, Michael had to face some not-so-good news when newspapers revealed that a year previously the DA's office had said it was investigating him as part of a broader inquiry into the business activities of a certain Richard Carey. Carey was charged with selling worthless stock while fraudulently claiming to be the son of the Governor of New York. Former Hollywood actress Terry Moore also claimed after Carey had married her in Mexico that he had run off with $200,000 of her money and her Rolls-Royce. Michael Reagan was said to have steered customers to Carey, and had accepted a cheque for $4,000 from one investor, as well as explaining in at least one meeting with potential investors that he assisted Carey in a promotional capacity. Finally Carey was arrested at Los Angeles airport and faced with twenty-six charges of grand theft, twenty-four counts of sale of securities by false representation, two counts of forgery, and one charge of bouncing a cheque. With the White House now 'advising' Michael Reagan on how to conduct his business affairs, it remains to be seen what kind of 'new friends' he makes.

AS A FAVOR TO MY FATHER

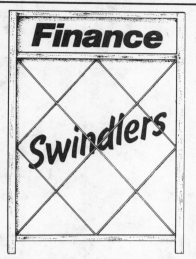

Finance Swindlers

These swindlers are a pretty unattractive lot. Look at their photographs and you get no hint of the incredible powers of persuasion they could exert over their fellow men. Time and time again, con men like Ponzi or Stavisky talked their way out of trouble, and smooth managers like Parker talked themselves into their next million. What they all have in common is an amazing combination of guts and gall – for most of us, a fortune is a sum of money we could retire on; for these men, a fortune was *never* enough. Setting up and carrying out a spectacular business manoeuvre gave them more pleasure than anything.

DID COL. TOM CHEAT ELVIS?

THE KING

A Good or a Greedy Manager – Courts to Decide

THROUGHOUT ELVIS PRESLEY'S life he never at any stage hinted that his relationship with his manager and mentor, Colonel Tom Parker, was anything other than a happy and lucrative arrangement. On his death, however, a different story began to emerge, and many questions were raised in court that didn't seem to be receiving satisfactory answers from those in charge of the fortune earned by the talents of Elvis Presley. In spite of the fact that Elvis was reputed to have earned over $1 billion during his career, his estate was rumoured to be a paltry (by his standard) 10 million.

Elvis left all his money to his daughter, Lisa Marie, who will inherit his fortune when she's twenty-five. She was just twelve in 1980 when a court battle commenced between the executors of the will, including her mother Priscilla, and the man who helped Presley earn it, Colonel Tom Parker. Attorney Blanchard E. Tual was appointed by the Memphis court to protect Lisa Marie's interests, and as he started his investigations into Presley's business affairs, Tual started to ask a lot of embarrassing questions about the Colonel.

According to Tual, Parker had not always acted in the singer's best interests, and had sometimes displayed an amazing lack of business acumen. For example, he had never got Elvis to register with the performing rights society, Broadcast Music Inc., and so Presley had lost out on a fortune in royalties from the

LOST MILLIONS TO MANAGER

broadcasting of songs which he himself had composed, such as 'Love Me Tender' and 'Don't be Cruel'.

Tual had been appointed to protect Lisa Marie after the executors of the will had asked the Memphis probate judge in May 1980 to agree to let them hand over *half* the estate's annual income to Parker. They claimed that this was the cut which he had taken while Presley was alive. Tual filed a report in December 1980 which said that Parker's commissions on Presley's earnings had been 'excessive' even by the standards of the traditionally steep cuts taken in the music industry by managers and promoters (25 per cent was allegedly more the norm). As an example of a deal that Parker had struck which did not favour his client, Tual cited the one made with RCA in 1973, in which Parker negotiated a flat royalty rate of 50 cents per record regardless of price – half of that given to other star performers like the Rolling Stones and Elton John. He also arranged for RCA to buy Presley's master tapes at the absurdly low price (given that they were priceless and represented over 700 songs which had been in the charts) of $5 million. A merchandizing deal split the income 40 per cent in Parker's favour and only 15 per cent in Presley's, while the deals on the royalties and the sale of the masters were split 50–50. It was later revealed that, incredibly, the deal did not include an audit clause, and Parker, trusting RCA's book-keepers, did not request one. Tual claimed that Elvis was simply a hopeless businessman and left everything to Parker, and that Parker in turn didn't know how to maximize the money which was pouring in, and that far too large a sum went in taxes which could have been minimized in the hands of a better financial brain. It was also said that Parker had received gifts from record companies when making deals.

CASE PRESENTED

In August 1981 Tual presented his case to the Memphis court. He sought to prove that Lisa Marie's interests would be neglected if Parker were allowed to take a 50 per cent cut from the estate's earnings, and also that Parker should be forced to repay to the estate the earnings which he had built up from it since Presley's death.

By now, news of Albert Goldman's shattering book on the King was leaking out, and a very different picture of the relationship between the singer and his manager was being revealed. Elvis was 'naive, shy and unassertive', whereas Parker was 'aggressive and tough'. Parker claimed that his family were carnival people from West Virginia, but it was disclosed that he was born Andreas Cornelius van Kuijik in Holland and had emigrated to the United States when he was twenty. He was given the courtesy title 'Colonel' by a Tennessee Governor, and had started out by managing country-and-western singers before latching on to Elvis in 1955 when the boy was just twenty and Parker forty-six. For the first eleven years his commission had been the regular 25 per cent, but then he and Presley did a deal in 1967 which doubled it. It was surmised that Parker's entry into the United States might have been one reason why he never let Presley perform overseas – the Colonel might have had great trouble with his documentation. It was said that in the twenty-one years they had worked together the two men had never eaten dinner together. At Elvis's funeral Parker had showed up in a gaudy Hawaiian shirt and baseball hat.

The Colonel was greedy

Another deal that Tual cited as not being in Presley's best interests was when Parker signed for the singer to appear in Las Vegas in 1972. The hotel manager claimed that Parker had gambled an incredible $1 million in one year in the resort. It seemed that the low performance fee was compensation for free food and drink, travel round Las Vegas (which can't exactly be a fortune), as well as a suite of rooms all the year round which must have suited Parker's hobby – gambling.

The probate judge ruled that Parker's compensation was excessive, and ordered the executors to stop dealing with him and to start litigation within forty-five days to recover money owing to them. RCA refused to allow the estate to audit their books for the period 1973–8 because they said that Parker, acting on Presley's behalf, had agreed with their accounting. It turned out that of the $5 million which he'd received for his master tapes, Presley's tax advice had been so poor that he was left with only 1·25 million. It also emerged that Parker had other agreements

and by RCA, and the executors of the will found themselves in the contorted position of filing against Parker in one court while contesting the IRS in another.

In January 1982 Priscilla filed a court petition in San Francisco, asking for a full accounting of all Presley's earnings and claiming that Parker owed the estate more than $5 million from illegally negotiated contracts. Attorneys alleged that Parker had broken a little-known Californian state law which said that anyone managing an artist must register with the California State Labour Commission before negotiating contracts on their behalf, or else pay a fine equalling everything earned in commissions while representing the artist; if the manager decided to opt for a trial, he must post a bond equal to the sum in dispute. The attorneys who had been appointed to sue RCA and Parker on Lisa Marie's behalf were asking that this law be applied to Parker's earnings from the early seventies. The statute was little known in Tinseltown circles, and caused both merriment and slight anxiety if indeed it turned out to be a way of trapping unscrupulous managers.

'EQUAL PARTNERS'

In March 1982 Parker started to fight back. He asked a Nevada court to liquidate the estate, now said to be worth $25 million, and to award him half, claiming that he had never been 'employed' by Presley but had been his equal business 'partner'. He said that he 'had no choice ... but to protect the assets which Elvis and I worked so hard to build'. Parker also asked for the return of $1·6 million which Elvis had withdrawn from the partnership in 1976 in order 'to meet financial demands'. According to Parker, Priscilla and the other executors had been only too happy for him to continue to run Presley's business after the singer's death, until they had heard the highly critical reports from Blanchard Tual, Lisa Marie's legal guardian.

In 1982 Graceland was turned into a museum, and the public had to pay to tour it. This was said to be a necessity 'for financial reasons'. As the courts continued their investigation into the tangled affairs of Presley and Parker (who admitted that neither he nor Presley 'were much good at paperwork'), the Colonel told a reporter that all the mud that had been slung in his direction had upset him deeply. He claimed that his whole relationship with Presley had been based on the homespun philosophy of 'a buck for you and a buck for me' – the only trouble was that it soon became 'a million for you and a million for me'.

with RCA – quite separate from Presley – which had paid him $400,000. Tual was now asked by the probate judge to prepare a full investigation into the Parker-Presley business dealings within ninety days.

CLAIM FOR MILLIONS

Now the IRS got in on the act by issuing the estate with a tax demand for $14·6 million. They claimed that the estate was owed millions in royalties: about half a million by a Parker-owned company, Boxcar Enterprises; about 6·7 million from RCA records; nearly 3 million from Chappell Music; 1·25 million from film rights; and 1·35 million from residual rights to TV specials. The IRS claimed that Parker hadn't given Presley a fair amount of revenue from his many and varied sources of income and hadn't paid him any income from royalties at all for the last four years of his life. These claims were contested both by Parker

GET-RICH-QUICK MAN.

MILLIONAIRE IN A FEW MONTHS.

Ponzi's Postal Prizes

CHARLES PONZI was transformed within weeks from a humble office clerk in America to a chap whom ladies swooned over and cheering crowds besieged. He had made a very simple observation when poring over his mail at work in 1919: a Spaniard had sent his employers some American postal coupons to pay for some goods he was ordering by post; the coupons had been bought in Madrid for one cent each, and were redeemable in America for ten cents – an amazing profit.

TEENAGE THIEF

Ponzi had always had delusions of grandeur. He started his career as a thief while still a teenager in Italy, and when he was eighteen he got together £100 and emigrated to America. Working as a waiter, he was caught fiddling the bills and dismissed. He became a bank clerk and started forging customers' cheques. Luck ran out again for Ponzi and he spent the next three years learning how to forge better in jail. On leaving jail, he got a job as a clerk and invented the great postal coupon swindle. He rented a room and went into partnership with a man in Madrid. He borrowed $250 from friends, bought coupons abroad, cashed them in America, and paid his friends back $375. There was a rush of investors eager to join in Ponzi's little scheme, and within a month the queue outside his office was so long that he had to pay three young ladies to serve potential customers with coffee and frankfurters. Newspapers produced headlines like GET-RICH-QUICK MAN A MILLIONAIRE IN A FEW MONTHS and THE MYSTERY MAN – PONZI'S AMAZING SYSTEM, for Ponzi did not let on how he was giving investors this incredible return on their money. Reporters guessed, however, and wrote STAMP WEALTH – HOW MR PONZI IS SAID TO QUADRUPLE MONEY, and described the ex-waiter as 'a dandy' who owned a 20-acre estate which was guarded by Doberman dogs. Money was pouring in at the rate of $250,000 a day, and they had so much waiting to be banked that it was stashed in cupboards and litter bins; sixteen clerks tried to cope.

ARREST

Meanwhile the postal authorities launched an inquiry and discovered that although the entire issue of postal coupons over the past six months accounted for less than a million dollars, Ponzi had accumulated ten times that amount. The *Boston Post* leaked the story and other papers followed with headlines like WHIRLWIND FINANCIER IN TROUBLE, featuring pictures of the smart Mr Ponzi chewing on a cigar. His supporters urged him to sue the papers, the police started an investigation and, after learning of his previous forgery conviction, arrested him on 13 August 1920. His clients were so sure of his innocence that they attacked the detectives. At the trial it turned out that he had tricked about 40,000 investors into parting with over $15 million.

DEPORTATION

He pleaded guilty and was sentenced to five years' imprisonment. In jail he received a sack of mail each month, some from people threatening to kill him when he was released, but many from well-wishers who sent him more money to invest. He sent his creditors Christmas cards and promised he would pay them back. Unfortunately for Ponzi, he had no sooner stepped outside the jail at the end of his term than he was re-arrested on a grand larceny charge and locked up again till February 1934. On his release he was deported to Italy, and arrived back there with less money than when he had left as a teenager. He became a Blackshirt and worked in Rio de Janeiro for Mussolini's airline. After the war he worked as a translator and died poor at the age of sixty-six, leaving about £25 which was enough to bury him. The press commented, 'They fought to let him rob them', and remarked how the 'amazing' Mr Ponzi had ended up in a pauper's grave.

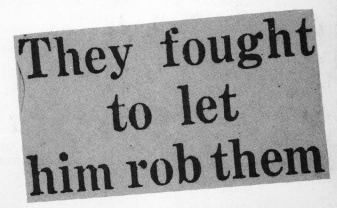

They fought to let him rob them

Influential Friends

ON 12 JANUARY 1934 English newspapers carried front-page photographs showing scenes of total chaos in Paris: five thousand people rioted, hundreds were injured, and the police arrested over 700 angry citizens. Trees were ripped up, pieces of railings and metal gates were torn out for use as weapons in the hand-to-hand fighting against the police. Meanwhile the French parliament sat behind locked doors debating the activities of one man, not even a Frenchman, who was responsible for the scene outside. Although they did not realize it, he was to bring about their downfall and cause a purge of top officials in the French Government.

The story of this man, Serge Stavisky, reads like a gangster film, and it is not surprising that director Alain Renais committed it to celluloid in the sixties, choosing Jean-Paul Belmondo to portray the greatest swindler and con man France has ever known. It is hard to reconcile a heart-throb's image with the contemporary newspaper descriptions of Stavisky as a rather short chap who wore high heels to boost his ego and too much powder on his face!

He was born in Russia in 1889 and arrived in Paris with his family when he was thirteen. His father was a dentist, but the son had more exotic plans for making money. He always liked to have gold in his hands rather than in other people's mouths. By the time he was twenty he had started in his chosen career – crime. Caught forging theatre tickets, he was lucky to have the charges dropped. At twenty-two he had raised enough money to take over a theatre in Paris, but then ran off with the cash. He liked money and women and managed to combine the two by living with several rich old women whom he robbed. Usually they were so infatuated with his charms that they were too embarrassed to press charges, even when he slashed one woman's face with a knife. Stavisky set himself up as a financier, operating a kind of public relations company promoting the activities of various businesses that he was involved with. By the time he was thirty the police had got sufficiently fed up with his activities for him to leave the country for a spell. When things quietened down, and the country was busy with the war, he returned to run nightclubs in Paris which catered for the wealthy, supplying them with sex, drugs, and gambling.

BRIBERY

A typical trick, for which he was arrested, was the altering of a cheque from 600 francs to 46,000 francs. While the case was being investigated, the cheque disappeared, and without the evidence the police were forced to release him. By now he had bribed friends in influential places. When he was caught cheating at gambling, he told the owners of the casino that he had bribed members of their staff, and that if they pressed charges, the casino would be ruined. The charges against him were consequently dropped. Arrested in 1926, he was again set free, this time 'for reasons of deteriorating health', but he made a 'miraculous' recovery within days so that he could spend New Year's Eve in a nightclub. He married Arlette, a model, in 1928, and together they moved in the smartest circles of Parisian society, giving lavish parties and dinners to which he invited his useful friends; Stavisky was now calling himself Serge Alexandre, in an attempt to live down his past.

PAWNSHOPS

In France pawnshops are run by the municipal authorities, and Stavisky soon developed a scheme involving the pawnshop in Orleans, whereby he bribed the manager to accept fake gems for which he was paid the price of the real thing. The trick was discovered, but up popped the manager a few months later running another pawnshop, this time in Bayonne, where Stavisky had 'persuaded' local authorities that a pawnshop was a good idea. He pawned his fake gems there, and also issued bonds on the strength of them which his rich friends talked up until they seemed to be worth a fortune; the Minister for the Colonies recommended Stavisky's bonds to insurance companies. It was estimated that he made about six million pounds from the Bayonne fiddle.

The whole of this time Stavisky was, astonishingly, still out on 'bail' from his 1926 arrest, but the police, led by Inspector Pierre Body, were close on his heels. The quaintly named Body used an informer called Jo the Terror to get hold of Stavisky's used cheque book with its stubs bearing the names of prominent people.

Stavisky knew he was trapped and fled in 1934 to Chamonix, selling some 'jewels' on the way. When the police trapped him in a rented villa, they heard shots ring out, and he was found seriously wounded. He died in hospital later. The *Daily Mirror* announced on 9 January 1934 that he was to have been arrested on a £6 million fraud charge, while journalists speculated that the figure involved was probably nearer £30 million. A Cabinet Minister resigned, and immediately the public accused the Government of protecting Stavisky. By 11 January the rioting in Paris had become extremely serious and the Public Prosecutor (brother-in-law of the French Prime Minister) was accused of being involved with the dead man. By February the Government had fallen, and 50,000 demonstrators took to the streets in marches organized by the French fascists, who were cashing in on the general unrest to stir up trouble. Eighteen people were killed, and 2,000 wounded.

NINE FOUND GUILTY

The inquiry proceeded after Stavisky's death, and in 1936 the courts found him guilty of fraud. Nine others, including a mayor, Government officials, a company director, and a general, were also found guilty and given sentences of up to seven years. A judge who sat in the Paris Appeal Court was found dead on a railway line the day before he was due to give evidence at the Stavisky inquiry. A month after Stavisky's death the chief of the French CID was sacked, and rumours flew about that he hadn't shot himself in the villa at Chamonix, but had been bumped off by the police, who were afraid that he might spill the beans about the head of the CID if they arrested him.

The English press described the affair as the 'greatest financial scandal in France since the 1918 War'. The influence of Stavisky lived on long after his death.

FIGHT TO SAVE STAVISKY'S LIFE

Hunted Banker Shoots Himself in Villa

DRAMA AS DETECTIVES BATTER DOWN DOOR

DOCTORS WERE EARLY TO-DAY FIGHTING DESPERATELY TO SAVE THE LIFE OF SERGE STAVISKY, THE HUNTED FRENCH BANKER, WHO SHOT HIMSELF AS DETECTIVES WERE BATTERING DOWN A DOOR TO ARREST HIM ON A £6,000,000 FRAUD CHARGE.

Politics

Politics

Questionable Conduct

It is a sad reflection on political life that, in compiling this section, one is almost swamped by choice. Unfortunately, the heady magic of power seems to have a strange, unsettling effect. Elected officials make new laws and freely break the old ones. They misappropriate funds for sexual pleasures, but they outlaw prostitution. They may or may not have homosexual relationships, but they won't lower the age of consent. They confuse the politics of power and the power of business. They just can't make the choice between 'for the people' and 'for myself'.

Sex on Congress Payroll!

The Secretary Who Couldn't Type and Wouldn't Answer the Phone

THE SCANDAL OF THE SECRETARY with *very* unusual duties broke in the *Washington Post* in May 1976 with the headline CLOSED SESSION ROMANCE ON THE HILL. Underneath was a cheesecake picture of 'secretary' Elizabeth Ray and another of her 'boss', Congressman Wayne L. Hays of Ohio, complete with his wonderful denial: 'Hellsfire! I'm a happily married man.' The reason that Elizabeth may have decided to talk to the *Post* about the bizarre requirements of her job could have been something to do with the fact that on 6 April Hays had informed her that he was going to marry Pat Peak, the hard-working chief of his Ohio office. On hearing the bad news, Ray was disgusted, lost her temper, and was shown out of Hays's office by the police. She then told everything to the *Post*, while Wayne, unaware of what was going on, invited her out to dinner to try and sort out his tangled love life. After their date he dropped her off and phoned later; unfortunately for Wayne, two reporters were listening in to the lovey-dovey chat about the couple's sex life. When the story broke with Liz's claim that she was kept by Hays in a $14,000-a-year job as a secretary whereas all she provided were sexual favours, the storm broke.

Although officially appointed a staff member of the House Administration Committee of which Hays was Chairman, she said she rarely visited the private office she had been given, and indeed supplied the immortal quote: 'I can't type, I can't file, I can't even answer the phone.' She called the committee she was supposed to be working on 'the out-of-sight committee', and said her real chore was to hold ad-hoc meetings with Hays *away* from all those filing cabinets that she didn't

Who's minding the office?

know how to use. She announced that she and Hays usually met for dinner about 7p.m. After a light meal, they'd return to her apartment, where Hays 'was a night-time snuggle'. According to Liz, he never stopped in the living room but walked straight in to the bedroom and carefully watched the digital clock, always returning home by 9.30p.m.

These revelations were the latest in a batch of similar, if less spectacular, stories of Congressional misconduct that had been appearing in the press. Others included charges of conflict of interest and of fiddling expenses. On reading the story, Thomas Henderson, chief of the Public Integrity Section of the Justice Department's Criminal Division, had to make a decision. If Liz Ray went to work every day, then there wasn't a problem. But if she turned out to be 'an amateur call-girl on the public pad', then Hays was in trouble: he could face charges of misappropriation of public funds and embezzlement.

WELL-KNOWN ABUSE

It was well known in Congress that Senators often abused the pay-roll system. Members and Senators received considerable allowances for their staff, and the fact that there was a central system for hiring and firing left this arrangement open for 'padding the pay-roll', to use a Washington term. Since nepotism had been made illegal in 1967, it was now common practice for members to persuade their friends to

employ their relatives, while not employing them directly themselves. Therefore many people were embarrassed by Liz Ray's frank admission of what was custom and practice around town, especially when she told journalists that she knew of ten to fifteen Capitol Hill offices with the same weird system of staffing. As the Justice Department launched their inquiry, the House Committee on Standards of Conduct (known as the Ethics Committee) also promised to make its own investigation.

STARLET

Things didn't look too good for Hays when the Staff Director of the Committee that Liz was supposed to be working for said he had never met her, and it turned out that the Committee, which had been set up by Hays, hadn't actually had a meeting since November 1975. Liz turned out to be a former stewardess and starlet, who'd arrived in Washington in 1972 and

worked for Illinois Representative Kenneth Gray. She had plenty of contacts, from rich restaurateurs to politicians. Barry Goldwater Jr was said to have given her a start in movies, and she claimed she had lunched with Hubert Humphrey. *Playboy* magazine was planning to feature a topless Liz in a forthcoming issue on 'The Girls of Washington'. On going to work in her unusual job for Hays, Liz did in fact sit down at a typewriter a few times. He paid for her to go on a typing course, but she only showed up for ten of the fifty classes – obviously otherwise engaged.

After his initial denial of the relationship, Hays decided to come clean in front of his 300 colleagues. While admitting their mutually voluntary relationship, he refused to agree with the story that she had been given the job in exchange for sex. He insisted that this was not the case and that she had been told to work a 'normal' day, and he declared passionately: 'Only time will tell whether Miss Ray has been successful in destroying my career. I pray to God she will not have destroyed my marriage.' (He had married Pat Peak just six weeks earlier.) Hays also claimed that Liz had threatened to blackmail him. In spite of his offer to retire after one more term, the damage had been done. He had seriously embarrassed his fellow Congressmen by getting caught out by a lady with a big bust and a big mouth.

BLONDE BOMBSHELL SECRETARY CAN'T TYPE

The Longs of Louisiana, Miz Blanche, and Blaze Star

THE LONG FAMILY dominated politics in the State of Louisiana for fifty years. Descended from a poor white family, they lived in a modest wooden house like most of the population and were thought of as 'middle class' simply because Huey, the sixth child, was a keen reader and eventually attended university. He supplemented his income by working as a travelling salesman in laxatives and kerosene lamps. He was desperate to enter politics, and managed to get on to the State Utility Regulatory Board by the time he was twenty-five. Louisiana was run by a powerful clique of men who represented all the leading companies and financial interests. They regarded Huey with horror; he seemed a country hick with no table manners, no social graces, and a hectoring style of campaigning. He ran for Governor in 1924 and narrowly missed getting elected, but succeeded in 1928. After a few days his wife moved out, taking the children. She too couldn't stand Huey's life-style. He certainly lacked finesse: when he was hungry, he would simply lean over and grab something off someone's plate, and he spent most of his life living in a series of hotels and dressing in rainbow colours.

Huey's politics were a bizarre combination of 'populist' theories and a fascist method of running the State. He represented the voice of small farmers against the interests of the giant oil and industrial companies. He called himself 'the Kingfish' and his slogan was 'Every man a king'. As Governor he implemented a number of reforms, including the introduction of free night-school for adults and free textbooks for school children, and he did away with the poll tax. He made significant improvements in the State's road and bridge systems. But all this was accomplished in a climate of total fear. Huey became a dictator who ran his State like his own business. Martial law was imposed on cities as the whim took him, and politicians took to wearing guns when they went to work. He censored newspapers and banned meetings of more than two people. In New Orleans, only the police were allowed to carry guns. He built a mansion which was a replica of the White House, so that 'he would know where every light switch was when he became President'. He also erected another monument to his reign: a hideous, grandiose, 24-storey Capitol building. By the end of his term, he was forced to travel with a posse of guards wherever he went.

In 1931 he installed a stooge called OK as Governor and got himself elected to the US Senate. At the same time as this public display of repression, Huey was formulating a radical solution to America's problems. He called it the 'Share the Wealth' plan, which proposed a system whereby the Federal Government would levy an annual tax to prevent any family from earning more than $1 million a year. This tax would be redistributed so that every family in America would have a 'homestead' worth $5,000 and a guaranteed annual income of $2,000. He wanted old-age pensions throughout the country, college grants, and a working week of thirty hours for eleven months a year. This was the era of the Depression, when the have-nots saw that American wealth was not reaching the worst victims, because of the lack of employment and opportunities. By 1935 Huey had four and a half million supporters of his scheme and 'Share the Wealth' societies were established in every single State. It was thought that in a Presidential election his party would severely damage the Democrats' chances. But Huey's combination of socialist politics and

totalitarian methods had made him many bitter enemies, and in 1935 he was shot dead in Louisiana before he had a chance to put his theories to the vote.

ELECTED GOVERNOR

The following year his brother Earl was elected Lieutenant Governor, and when the Governor resigned because of a political scandal, he assumed the job. In 1948 and again in 1956 he was re-elected Governor. Earl was a different kettle of fish to Huey, who had said of his brother, 'You have to watch Earl. If you live long enough, he'll double-cross you.' But Earl was not as dangerous as Huey. He was partly controlled by the fact that Huey's son Russell was elected State Senator in 1948. Earl ushered in free school lunches, paid teachers more, increased pensions, and built new hospitals. He looked like a fat, sweaty evangelist, and had inherited his brother's general lack of chic. He spent a lot of time mopping his brow with several handkerchiefs, and liked nothing better than to drive around the State purchasing crates of soft drinks, dozens of live hens, tons of fruit

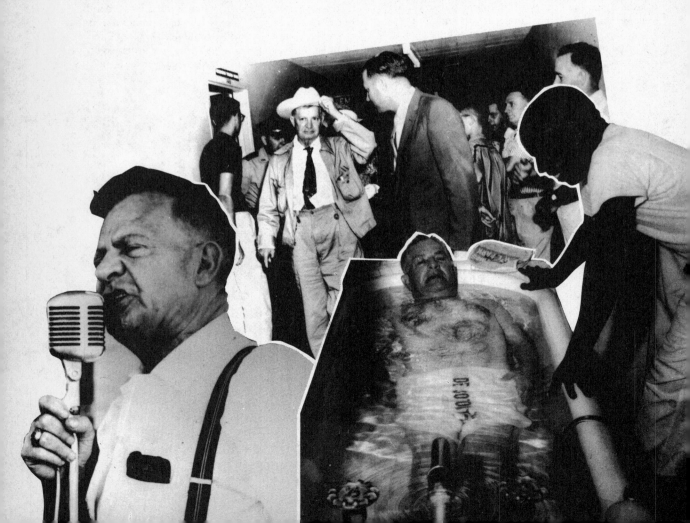

and other snacks. Towards the end of his second term, he worked out a way to get round the law that prevented anyone from running for Governor for a third term. He planned to resign a few days before the election and then stand again as an ordinary citizen.

TWO BIG MISTAKES

But Earl made two big mistakes in his bid for another dose of power. One was to try and force through the State legislature new voter-registration rules, which would have given the blacks (then mostly without the vote) a chance to take part in elections. This was promptly thrown out in a bitter and foul-mouthed debate. Earl's other problem lay at home. Miz Blanche, his matronly wife, had taken to having public fights with him. In 1958 Earl had sought solace in the Sho-Bar burlesque house in New Orleans, were he had met, and become extremely enamoured of, a stripper named Blaze Star, who the year before had been voted the 'Queen of Burlesque'. Earl told Blaze that he and Miz Blanche hadn't slept together for two years. She told him she was getting a divorce. He set her up in the Flamingo Hotel just outside town, and one day the pair of them were caught there together by the furious Miz Blanche. 65-year-old Earl asked Blaze to marry him, in front of an astonished audience at the Sho-Bar. Within a couple of weeks Russell Long and Miz Blanche had drawn up papers to have Earl committed to a mental hospital, and he was dragged out of his mansion and flown to a clinic in Texas. A judge let him return to Louisiana, providing he checked into another clinic. He arrived back, walked into a clinic in New Orleans and straight out again. On his drive back home to Baton Rouge Miz Blanche had his car intercepted, and he was returned, via a court, to another clinic. This time he got a judge to release him and immediately sacked the director of the Louisiana Department of Hospitals.

PARTY

Earl's behaviour was said to be rather bizarre. He ate a meal in public with Blaze with his false teeth in a jar on the table and a paper bag over his head. He decided to run again for the post of Lieutenant Governor. When he lost, he threw a wonderful party at the Governor's mansion for all the strippers from the Sho-Bar. Miz Blanche had already fled; and after Blaze had stripped, they returned to her flat, carrying of all the goodies they could stuff in the car. Earl then ran for Congress and got elected. A day later he died.

WHO KILLED THE PRINCE?

The Prince, Gun-Running, and an Unsolved Murder

A MURDER took place in Paris just before Christmas in 1976 which has never been satisfactorily solved. The suspects are still languishing in jail, and a political scandal was averted by postponing any trials until after the 1981 French Presidential elections. The reason for this delay was that the victim was a former Cabinet Minister, and a man whose business and political affairs overlapped in an unsavoury way.

DISTINGUISHED PAST

Prince Jean de Broglie, who was gunned down in a street full of Christmas shoppers, came from a family who had served under Napoleon. He had held four Cabinet posts under de Gaulle and had a distinguished naval career, helping to settle the war with Algeria. He had been a co-founder (together with Valéry, later to be President, Giscard d'Estaing) of the Independent Republican Party, whose aim was to rid France of the unsavoury association of politics, finance, and the underworld, which had characterized de Gaulle's years in power. But de Broglie didn't practise in private what he preached in public: at the time of his death he was on the boards of no less than forty-two companies, one of which was engaged in arms deals with Arab countries, and he owned plenty of real estate.

'SOLVED'

On 28 December the police had received a telephone call from an extreme right-wing group who claimed that they had killed the aristocrat because he was responsible for the occupation of France by 'African

scum'. The police now held eight people in custody and were convinced that the murderer was amongst them. Then the Minister of the Interior, Michel Poniatowski, a close friend of Giscard, took the unusual step of holding a press conference at which he said that the murder had been solved, even though the police had not yet charged anyone! The Minister said that the Prince had lent £500,000 to two of the men in custody, Patrick Allenet de Ribemont and Pierre de Varga, to enable them to buy a popular Parisian tourist restaurant. The loan had been covered by an insurance policy on the Prince's life: hence the

DEATH AT A DOOR

murder, which meant that the two men would not have to repay their debt. The Minister claimed that these two men had hired a policeman, Simoné (also being held in custody), to find a killer. Simoné, in spite of an unsavoury past including an attempt to shoot his mistress, had had a successful career in the police force. He came up with Frech, a thug from the Paris underworld. According to the Minister, Frech had confessed, and the two restaurant owners had admitted that they had phoned the police and put the blame for the murder on to the right-wing group.

SPECULATION

The next day doubts were expressed as to whether the case was as straightforward as the Minister's statements suggested. Journalists turned their attention to de Broglie's two partners in business, de Varga and de Ribemont. De Varga had served a prison sentence for fraud, and was said to be a possible double-agent and informer for the political civil service, the head of which was Poniatowski, the Minister who had leapt in and declared the matter closed. There was speculation that the Prince had been murdered to prevent him from exposing a massive fraud in French nationalized coal. De Varga had connections with those responsible for perpetrating the fraud. Another interesting point to emerge was that although de Broglie had negotiated peace with Algeria, he did business with de Ribemont who was a member of the OAS, an organization violently opposed to Algerian independence. He had also lent Simoné money which the policeman could not repay. All in all, these four men were unusual business partners.

FRAUDULENT

Further investigations found that de Broglie had a company registered in Luxemburg called Sodotex SA. It was a subsidiary of a fraudulent company which had cheated Spain out of £80 million in fictitious exports, its operations depending on tax havens. It was revealed that shortly before his death the Prince had been visited by the French secret police, who had warned him that his dealing in arms was upsetting a foreign power. Furthermore, de Broglie had borrowed £900,000 in the year before his death; it had disappeared without trace.

New twist to Paris death

A couple of months after the murder, the plot had more twists and turns than a French farce. The newspapers declared that the police knew in advance that de Broglie was to be murdered. It was alleged that they had known of seven previous attempts on his life, but had failed to alert him to the possible danger, and that they actually had agents on the spot when he was finally bumped off. Then events made it clear that someone was trying to cover up the truth: a car belonging to the restaurant was stolen and found dismantled, and the manager was attacked; de Varga's daughter received death threats; the Prince's castle was burgled; and a journalist writing about the case fell 'asleep' when driving down a street in the middle of Paris, and awoke to find he had crashed into a tree in a suburb!

In March 1977 de Ribemont was released on the evidence of documents which proved conclusively that the money he had borrowed from the Prince would not be covered by the insurance policy on de Broglie's life. That cash was to go to de Broglie's heirs.

In April a heart specialist who treated both de Varga and the Prince was arrested and charged with destroying evidence. She claimed that de Varga's lawyer had asked her to fake an alibi for his client. The lawyer was then arrested too. De Broglie's company which dealt in arms had gone bust and its managing director was found shot dead in a forest.

In 1981 the defendants are still in jail and investigations have produced nothing but innumerable theories. The three examining magistrates working on the case have not had much luck, and have met with obstruction after obstruction. It was said that this was partly deliberate and that the French Government would cook up masses of red tape to keep the whole case under wraps until after the elections in the spring of 1981. Nobody knows for sure why de Broglie was murdered, but the politician who held forty-two directorships certainly made more than that number of enemies.

MARKED 'SCANDAL'

A Fishy Business

'MAYBE some people might regard my coming at them from out of the sea as being the act of a comedian, but I am deadly serious ... you need to be a good PR man.' This is what Jeremy Thorpe told *Daily Mail* reporters during his 1974 election campaign. But Thorpe's policy of treating people like friends was to cost him his political life; in May 1976 he resigned the leadership of the Liberal Party after what he called 'a sustained witch-hunt'.

The scandal was first mentioned in the national press on 29 January 1976, when Norman Scott, a former male model and stable-person, blurted out the seventeen words that were to start the ball rolling: 'I am being hounded by people all the time because of my sexual relationship with Jeremy Thorpe.'

MALE MODEL AND A £2,500 PRESENT

Scott then moved to centre stage and issued a series of highly inflammatory statements. On 3 February 1976 he alleged that he was given money on the day of the 1974 general election. It was payment for letters and papers belonging to him.

This was not the first time that Scott had been involved in a front-page story. The year before, Scott's dog Rinka had been shot for no apparent reason. Airline pilot Andrew 'Gino' Newton was to appear in court. His trial opened on 16 March 1976, and resulted in his being sentenced to two years' imprisonment.

PRIVATE EYE

No. 369
Friday
Feb.6 '76

15p

THAT ALLEGATION

THORPE'S REPLY

My members are right behind me

Speak for yourself, ducky

A dog is shot dead —and scandal looms

In April 1977 Newton was released from jail. In October he sold his story and said, 'I was hired to kill Scott'. Then Bessell started shooting his mouth off. He claimed that a leading Liberal supporter was present when a group of them discussed getting rid of Scott. It was the same man who Andrew Newton said had hired him to shoot Scott. The Director of Public Prosecutions ordered inquiries into the allegations.

Rumours were flying thick and fast, and on the evening of 27 October 1977 Thorpe held a press conference. He described his relationship with Scott as 'affection and nothing else'. He said he did not intend to resign as an MP, and there 'was not a scrap of evidence' to link him with the contract that Newton was talking about.

JEREMY THORPE CHARGED

Nevertheless, in August 1978 Thorpe was charged with conspiring to murder Scott. Charged with him were David Holmes, John Le Mesurier and George Deakin. On top of the conspiracy charge, Thorpe alone was charged with incitement to murder. According to the prosecution, he wanted Scott killed because 'he was a continuing danger'. Andrew Newton was alleged to have been hired for £10,000 under Holmes's orders, but he had used a gun that jammed at the vital moment so that only Scott's dog was shot. Scott's statement was sensational. The four men were committed for trial at the Old Bailey.

The prosecution set out to prove that Thorpe had had a homosexual relationship with Scott; that he tried to hush it up after it had ended; that he somehow incited Holmes to arrange to have Scott murdered; and that, when this had failed, he set about arranging a conspiracy to murder Scott.

The prosecution described the night of 8 November 1962, when Thorpe took Scott to spend the night at his mother's house. He brought a copy of the book *Giovanni's Room* to Scott's room, pointing out to him a chapter in which two men make love. Later he came back into the room with a tube of vaseline, put some on his penis, and made love to Scott. Scott said, 'I just bit the pillow . . . I was afraid of waking Mrs Thorpe.' After they had made love twice, Thorpe left the room. When he returned in the morning, Scott feared it would happen again, but Jeremy just asked him how he wanted his eggs done.

Old Bailey sensation—trial cut short as only one of accused decides to give evidence

THORPE STAYS SILENT

The defence attempted to discredit the three main prosecution witnesses, Bessell, Scott and Newton. Deakin appeared in the witness box, but on 3 June Thorpe and the other two men decided to stay silent.

A PARASITE!

And also WHINER, SPONGER, CROOK AND LIAR

One fatal defect, says QC

THORPE: 'A GREEK TRAGEDY'

The affair was described in the summing-up as 'a Greek tragedy' and Thorpe a man with one defect. The judge was vicious in his assessment of Scott, describing him to the jury as a 'hysterically warped personality', and said that Thorpe's silence did not mean that he was guilty. On Friday 22 June the verdict was given as not guilty.

Thorpe headed home after two days in jail to a champagne party and an old Thorpe-style victory wave from his balcony. The votes of the jury were called the twelve most precious ones of his life. Two Sundays after the verdict there was a service of thanksgiving in a church near Thorpe's country home. The church was far from full – a sad reflection of his now dwindling support.

THORPE CLEARED

Thorpe heads for champagne party and a holiday as jury clears him of death plot

FREEDOM

RONNIE BUGGED AT BLAIR?

A Bug in 'The Ear'

ON 5 OCTOBER 1981 the *Washington Post* printed the second of their new gossip columns, headed 'The Ear', which they had taken over after the *Washington Star* had closed. Written by Diana McClellan, a small item was buried away among all the chit-chat which was a potential bombshell. It claimed that a close friend of Rosalynn Carter had said that Blair House (used by visiting heads of state and foreign dignitaries when visiting the White House) was bugged during the periods when it was occupied by President-elect Reagan and his wife on their pre-Inaugural trips to town. According to Ms McClellan, 'at least one tattler in the Carter tribe' had listened to the tape – and was talking about it.

Surprise was expressed by many observers that, if this item was true, it had not been the subject of an extended piece of investigative journalism – which after all was the *Post*'s style – and placed on the front page. If Reagan had been bugged, had important visitors suffered the same fate? Was Watergate looming all over again?

Jimmy Carter's former Press Secretary, Jody Powell, immediately declared that the story was totally untrue and demanded a retraction. Carter's lawyer, Terrence Adamson, wrote to the *Post* and told them it was libellous, and, even if they did decide to apologize, his clients would be suing the paper for $1 million in damages. By now the offending story had spread all over the US media and was the hot gossip of the moment. Executive Editor Ben Bradlee claimed at least twenty people had known of the story before it was printed, and he wasn't going to write a retraction. A

few days later, however, the paper printed a most bizarre editorial, which said it was impossible to believe the rumour but it was hoped that people who had read the paper were able to sort out fact from fiction. The article said that 'The Ear' did not accuse the Carters of placing the bugs in Blair House themselves, and admitted that the story was untrue. No one was sure whether this was a retraction or an apology, especially when the *Post* still claimed the bugging story had been circulating among very highly placed public figures in Washington.

Jimmy Carter still intended to sue, he said, and added, 'As a former President I don't have much money, just some privacy and my reputation.' He was said to be 'really hurt' by the intimation that he 'would stoop so low' as to bug his successor. But lawyers pointed out that to win a libel case he would have a tough fight on his hands: it was necessary to prove that 'The Ear' story was untrue and that the paper had displayed 'actual malice' in repeating it.

Finally the *Post* climbed down, and on 23 October they printed an apology on the front page, saying that although their story had come from a 'reliable source' they now accepted that it was false. The next day Carter issued a statement saying he had dropped his case.

A few months later *Time* magazine carried a story about what Carter was up to now that he was out in the political wilderness. It seemed that he was shunned by the Democratic Party, and that candidates never called him up or asked for his help. He was seen as an embarrassment, and one of his aides said, 'They are treating him like a leper.' Meanwhile Carter was finishing his book about his term of office, although his friends thought he was being too kind towards people in his administration.

Auntie and the Jaeger Suit

IN THE AUTUMN OF 1962 an Admiralty clerk, John Vassall, who earned just £18 a week, was secretly followed by detectives. They noted that in fifteen days he wore fifteen different suits, and indeed extended his wardrobe during the period, by walking into a branch of Jaeger and paying cash for a forty-six guinea number. He was arrested as he left work on 12 September and when detectives accompanied him back to his flat in Dolphin Square, they found two cameras and 140 photographs of seventeen top-secret Admiralty documents. He appeared at Bow Street a few weeks later charged with two offences under the Official Secrets Act.

JUNIOR ATTACHÉ

Vassall was born in London in 1924. His parents were not happily married and John grew up very close to his mother, who was a nurse. At boarding school he had his first homosexual relationships. He joined the RAF in 1943 and trained as a photographer. While awaiting call-up he had a temporary job as a clerk in the Admiralty and after the war he applied for a clerical position overseas, looking forward to travelling as much as possible. His first posting abroad was in the British Embassy in Moscow where he was a lowly naval attaché's clerk. He had 'junior attaché' printed on his cards. The law at this time made homosexuals very vulnerable and Vassall attacks the security forces in his autobiography for not realizing that he was a potential blackmail target – they didn't seem to have realized he was gay.

BLACKMAIL

Through the Russian interpreter at the Embassy, Mikhailsky, he was introduced to a group of people who took him to dinner in a private room in a restaurant. Mikhailsky was in the KGB, and after Vassall had been got thoroughly drunk and drugged, an all-male orgy was staged and incriminating photographs of Vassall were taken. These were then used to blackmail the terrified clerk into supplying the Russians with naval secrets. He was paid in cash and spent the money on holidays; nobody at the Embassy questioned the lavish life-style of their clerk.

In 1956 Vassall returned to the Admiralty in London but the KGB retained his services. He claimed he tried to commit suicide at one stage – he was so fed up with spying – but KGB agents stopped him from jumping out of a window. Before he left Moscow he met the man who was to be his spy-master in London, Nikolai Korovin, whom he knew as Gregory.

HOW I WA CAUGHT IN THE KGB SEX TRAP

When Vassall appeared in court in 1962 he pleaded guilty to the charges and was sent for trial at the Old Bailey.

At the trial it was said that Vassall was part of a spy ring which was run by Korovin and which included Gordon Lonsdale, George Blake, Harry Houghton and Ethel Gee. Lonsdale had been sentenced to twenty-five years in 1961, Houghton and Gee had got fifteen years each and Blake had been given forty-two years. A film found on Lonsdale could not have been taken by either him, Houghton or Gee, and the Secret Service eventually traced it to the Admiralty. Activities quietened down for fourteen months, until after the Blake case, but Vassall had resumed his spying in March 1962. Another lead came from the Soviet defector Anatoli Dolnytsin who gave MI5 the code name of someone working in the Admiralty. On 22 October 1962, Vassall was sentenced to eighteen years.

As Vassall swapped his made-to-measure suits for some shapeless prison clothes, all hell broke loose in Parliament about the Government's handling of the situation. Lord Carrington, first Lord of the Admiralty, said he would assume full responsibility if there had been any security slackness at his Ministry. Patrick Gordon Walker, MP, claimed that Vassall was only able to spy because he was continually picked out for tasks above his status and salary and was given free access to secret documents. The Civil Lord of the Admiralty from January 1957 to October 1959 had been Thomas Galbraith, and Vassall had worked for him from June 1957 until he left. Galbraith told a reporter on 23 October 1962 that he thought Vassall 'had a screw loose' but didn't suspect him of being a spy.

To stop all the rumours, Macmillan set up the Radcliffe Tribunal to look into the whole affair. They caused a sensation by releasing letters from Galbraith and his wife to Vassall, which were printed in all the papers on 7 November. The three civil servants heading the inquiry said that they did not think that the letters revealed any security leaks. Nevertheless, they did show that a top man was very friendly with his humble clerk. One letter described how Vassall was getting his boss's office redecorated while he was away. It was said that Galbraith had tried to help Vassall to get a job as a courier. Vassall was hoping for a job in the Cabinet Offices or at 10 Downing Street. The next day, to cheers in the House, Galbraith resigned his post in the Scottish Office. The Radcliffe Tribunal had the power to subpoena witnesses, including MPs and journalists, and Macmillan demanded they get to the bottom of rumours about the relationship between Vassall and Galbraith.

CONVERSATION TAPED

Vassall's cleaning lady had told a journalist from the *Daily Express* that she had seen Galbraith come to Vassall's flat and go into the bedroom with him for about fifteen minutes. Her conversation had been secretly tape-recorded, and when it was played back to her at the inquiry she said she had been lying – she knew the man was not Galbraith. Galbraith admitted

he had been to Vassall's flat on one occasion and denied he knew that the office called Vassall 'Auntie'. Vassall told the Tribunal he owned fifteen to twenty suits, and the expensive furniture in his flat had come from friends. He denied an improper relationship with Galbraith, but admitted he had bought women's clothes by mail order. He said he only wore them in his flat and had never done so in the West End.

Reginald Foster of the *Daily Sketch* and Brendan Mulholland of the *Daily Mail* were sent to prison for refusing to name the source of their information. There was a terrific row about it in the Commons and they were eventually released. From then on Fleet Street was at war with the Government and had its revenge with its coverage of the Profumo affair, later in 1963. The Radcliffe Report was thought to be a whitewash job. When it was published the *Sunday Mirror* reassumed their crusade against gays, and published an outrageous article entitled HOW TO SPOT A POSSIBLE HOMO. It went on, 'The Admiralty, the Foreign Office and MI5 don't seem to know', and offered advice. A picture of Vassall was captioned 'Vassall – a spy and homo. A gilt-edged specimen of his type.' It quoted the Radcliffe Report on why Vassall hadn't been spotted: 'So far as we can see, nothing short of active police detective work would have offered any clue to the fact he was a practising homosexual.' The *Sunday Mirror* listed types of 'homos', including 'the fussy dresser', the 'over-clean man', the 'toucher', the man 'adored by older women' and 'the man who drinks alone'. It was called 'a short course in how to pick a pervert'.

Vassall was released from Maidstone prison in October 1972, having served ten years of his sentence. He had been a model prisoner, working in the canteen and the library. He spent a period in a Catholic monastery, where he wrote his autobiography. A television play was made about his period in Moscow and the trial; when he saw a preview, he wept.

MAC ORDERS PROBE AS SPY IS JAILED

Farewell to a Traitor

ON 3 FEBRUARY 1950 a civil servant called Dr Klaus Fuchs was charged at Bow Street magistrates court with passing secret information to the Russians. The FBI claimed that the charges had been brought as a result of information they gave Britain. Fuchs had been working on atomic research at Harwell.

As Fuchs's background emerged, it seemed quite incredible that no one had realized earlier that he might be a security risk. He had been born in Frankfurt, Germany, in 1911. When Hitler was rising to power in 1932, he joined the German Communist Party, and shortly afterwards he joined their underground branch. When the Nazis started to persecute the Jews, he fled to France and on the invasion of France he again fled, this time to England, declaring himself to be violently anti-Nazi. He started a promising academic career, continuing his scientific studies at Bristol University, and then at Edinburgh, where he was made a Doctor of Science. In 1940, when England was in danger of invasion, he and other Germans in his category were interned and sent to Canada. He returned when the danger had passed and went to work at Glasgow University. In June 1942 he joined the team at Birmingham University doing research into atomic power. The next year he became a British citizen and continued his work at Harwell. From 1943 he informed the Russians of his work, and received expenses in return.

For a period of eighteen months, starting in 1946, Fuchs worked in America. It was thought that he had continued to pass information to the Russians throughout this time. The Americans were said to be keen to try him, and there was talk of extradition proceedings.

SUSPECTED LEAK

The American Atomic Energy Authority had suspected a leak from Harwell for some time, but they were unable to persuade the British authorities that this was true. In September 1949, however, the Americans finally convinced the British that there had been leakages from the Harwell team during the eighteen months they had spent in America. British counter-espionage called the FBI, without telling the American Atomic Energy people, and FBI agents came to Britain without informing President Truman. When agents watching Fuchs discovered that one of his acquaintances was someone they had suspected as a Russian agent, they pounced. Fuchs was arrested in Shell Mex House in London.

Newspapers described him as a 'Jekyll and Hyde'

PA-Reuter Photo

character, and the unsmiling Dr Fuchs was sent for trial at the Old Bailey, accused of passing information on four specific occasions: once in Britain in 1943, twice in America in 1944 and the last time in Britain in 1947. These were said to be just specimen charges, relating to a period of almost seven years, right up to March 1949, during which he had passed secrets to the enemy.

Time magazine said that one of Klaus's sisters, a painter, was once an active anti-Nazi worker. She had helped her husband to escape from Germany, but had committed suicide by jumping under a train after the persecution of the Jews had unbalanced her mind. Their father, a pacifist, was now working as a college professor in East Germany. *Time* alleged that although Fuchs had joined the British Communist Party, no one had subsequently stopped him from having access to top secret files. He had stayed away from Party meetings and had not associated with known Communists. (Other newspapers later disagreed as to whether Fuchs had in fact ever joined the Communist Party in Britain.)

TRIAL

Fuchs's trial opened in March 1950. He explained in a statement how he was able to lead a normal life and at the same time pass complex secrets to the Russians. The prosecution said he had never stopped being a Communist, and when he started to work on atomic research he naturally thought the Russians should have the information. They said, 'He became a kind of controlled schizophrenic – the dominant part of his mind allowing him to do things which the other part of his mind clearly recognized were wrong.' At first he had merely informed the Russians that work was being undertaken on a new kind of bomb, but they pressed him to supply more and more details. He had met agents every two or three months and had visited the Russian Embassy in London on one occasion. On his return from America he had been paid about £100 by the Russians to cover his expenses. When the investigation started into the leaks from Harwell, he had already decided that he wanted to leave, and, when confronted with the evidence, he admitted that he had been spying.

Fuchs pleaded guilty to the charges and received a fourteen-year sentence. The trial was a short one, and so attention on what he had actually done was minimized. As a result of his evidence four other spies were convicted in America, and Fuchs's role gradually became clearer. Fuchs had told the British judge that, although he hadn't joined the British Communist Party, most of his friends in Britain were left-wing. In America he had handed over his secrets to an agent in a ring headed by the notorious Anatoli Yakovlev, the Vice-consul at the Russian Embassy in New York.

'BETRAYED BY THE RUSSIANS'

Fuchs and co-spy Dr Nunn May, who was sentenced to ten years in 1956, were later thought to have been betrayed by the Russians because they refused to continue to collaborate in passing over secrets. Fuchs certainly hinted in his statement that he had rather revised his opinion of the Russians since he started giving them secrets in 1943. He had doubts about their post-war foreign policy as it became more evident that the Russians would try to expand their influence over Europe. Harry Gold, who had been Fuchs's courier in America, was sentenced to thirty years. It was rumoured that while in jail Fuchs was allowed to continue his work on the bomb, as the authorities were anxious to use his brilliant mind.

In May 1959 newspapers reported that Fuchs had played a much larger part in the development of the Hydrogen bomb than had at first been revealed. The Chairman of the American Congressional Committee on Atomic Energy disclosed that it was largely the work of Fuchs and his collaborator, mathematician Dr John von Neumann. They had filed a 'disclosure of invention' in America in May 1946, four years before America announced that they were making the bomb and six years before they conducted the first test. America had decided to go ahead and develop the bomb because they feared that Fuchs had given the Russians not only details of atomic energy research, but also information about the new weapon. American scientists were surprised by the news, because they had thought the bomb was the work of Dr Edward Teller. The British Atomic Energy Authority said that Fuchs was only part of a team and that the major problems relating to the bomb were solved after he was jailed. Many people did not believe this whitewash.

On 23 June 1959, Fuchs was driven from Wakefield jail – he was said to have read the whole of the prison library – to Heathrow airport, where he boarded a Polish plane to East Berlin. He wore an old-fashioned suit and looked the typical boffin, with his pens stuck in his jacket pocket. On the plane reporters sat all around him, and he was photographed eating his in-flight lunch. The *Mirror* captioned it 'Exit a traitor'.

On his arrival in East Berlin he was taken to meet his sick father in a summer chalet outside the city. Before being driven off in a limo he told reporters on the plane, 'I bear no resentment against Britain or any of the Western countries for what has happened.' Before his release it had been rumoured that he had hoped to be able to stay in England.

Politics

The Company You Keep

'Company', when applied to politicians, generally means that of the female variety. Rita Jenrette told the story of her not so wonderful marriage in Washington, and everyone rushed out and bought the paper to see if they got a mention. Politicians sometimes choose strange friends, but none more so than technocrat Giscard d'Estaing when he picked the 'Emperor' Bokassa, whose country provided him with such wonderful hunting trips. Too bad if, while he was out shooting gazelles, his host was chewing human flesh.

The Girl Who Kept Rocky Happy

ON 26 JANUARY 1979 millionaire art-collector and ex-Vice-President Nelson Rockefeller died of a massive heart attack. One of America's senior politicians and four times Governor of New York State, he was a well-known philanthropist and respected statesman. The death was the subject of an immediate cover-up by his family. But thanks to their crude handling of the situation, it escalated from the sad loss of a public figure to a sexy scandal that figured on every major television news programme and on the front page of all American newspapers.

The first statement said that Rockefeller had died at 10.15 p.m. in his main office in the Rockefeller Center with his security aide/chauffeur present. He had had dinner with his wife Happy and two of their six children, and had gone to work to do some research for a book about his extensive art collection. The family refused a post-mortem and the body was cremated almost immediately.

After the funeral, a family spokesman stated that Rockefeller had in fact died one hour later, at 11.15, in a town house on 54th Street which he used for meetings and meals. He had been with his researcher, 31-year-old Megan Marshack (other sources were to claim she was only 25), discussing the art book. The discrepancy in the reported time of death was put down to the fact that Ms Marshack had been 'confused and recalled it incorrectly'. Meg, not the security aide, had called for the ambulance, and the police had a tape of the call. When assistance arrived, she was giving Rockefeller mouth-to-mouth resuscitation – but he was dead.

Reporters couldn't interview Ms Marshack as she had gone into hiding. It was revealed that she had met Nelson when he was Vice-President and she was working in Washington as a radio reporter for Associated Press. In 1976 she went to work for him as a junior press aide, and when he left office in January 1977, she moved to New York and continued to be employed as a research assistant on projects concerning his art collection. She lived in a luxury apartment just a few doors from his town-house office on 54th Street.

Five days later it transpired that Rockefeller had had his heart attack at 10.15 and an hour had elapsed before the police were called. Megan's first reaction had been to ring her friend, TV personality Ponchitta Pierce (who subsequently went into hiding too), and she sent round the doorman of the apartment building where she and Meg lived to see what he could do. When Rocky's will was read out, Meg was named as a

Two girls in riddle of tycoon Rocky's death

The smokescreen and the scandal

ROCKY 'DIED AS HE MADE LOVE'

'surprise beneficiary'. He relieved her of the obligation of repaying the £22,500 he had lent her to buy an apartment. The *New York Post* reported a 'gathering storm' as the Rockefeller family split into two camps. One wanted to tell all, and the other favoured total silence; but everyone seemed to agree that Rockefeller would have stood a good chance of living if the ambulance had been called promptly.

The tabloids were really getting their teeth into the affair as rumour and counter-rumour grew. It was said that the body was 'partly clothed' and that Meg had been alone with Rockefeller, wearing a 'long black evening dress' or a 'dressing gown'. Another rumour said that Ms Pierce had been present when he died. Finally Ms Pierce issued a statement saying that she

had arrived at the house, seen what was happening, and made the call for help. The ambulance men said that they noticed the remains of a meal and a partly drunk bottle of wine in the room. They did not see any signs of books or research papers.

Some digging around in Meg's past showed that Rockefeller had paid her a salary of £30,000 a year, five times what she was earning before. She had few friends, and had no life apart from her duties for Rockefeller. Her ex-boyfriend was on the Rockefeller payroll as a photographer. Other staff talked of her total devotion to her boss, and verified rumours that he provided her with lavish expenses and open credit cards. Nevertheless, she had confided to some people that the demands of being 'on call' twenty-four hours a day to the 70-year-old millionaire were getting her down. It was noted that the pair had spent many hours together cataloguing works of art in spite of Rocky's poor health.

The District Attorney's office eventually declared the matter closed. The Chief Coroner of New York was fired after making remarks which implied that the old man and the pretty girl were making love when he died. Such statements were said to be 'improper behaviour' on the part of the official. Finally, when Rockefeller's young grandson met Megan months later, he was reported to have said to her, 'I hope you made my grandfather happy.'

Rockefeller son wants death mystery cleared

THE CAPITOL very scandals in the corridors of power

Congressmen fear the Washington 'lovers lis

Nothing to lose: Rita Jenrette

'Diary of a Mad

Rita, Paula, and Ms Brandy Tell All

THE FIRST three months of 1981 were not enjoyed by many Congressmen in Washington. Apart from the trauma of the attempted assassination of the President, they had other, more embarrassing, affairs on their minds. By April no less than three ladies had announced that they were writing books which would blow the lid off the seamy side of politics in America. All three claimed that their experiences were based on information gathered from the most respectable quarters: the nation's most staid politicians.

Rita Jenrette, the ex-wife of Democratic Congressman John Jenrette, sold her memoirs of life in Washington to *Playboy*, and they appeared in two issues entitled 'Diary of a Mad Congresswife'. While her husband was being convicted for his part in the ABSCAM affair, Rita was preparing to take off her clothes for Hugh Hefner's magazine. In return Hef gave her a diamond embedded in her fingernail. Rita had met her husband in 1975. His first wife had cited twenty-three co-respondents when they divorced, but that didn't seem to deter Rita. Still, she realized the honeymoon was over when she found him in bed with a woman old enough to be his mother. Rita also revealed that she and her husband had made love on the steps of the

Woman's talk . . .

Capitol while an important debate was going on inside. She talked of frolicking in jacuzzi pools with all the top people in town and stated that top Congressmen used illegal drugs and frequented massage parlours. She was expected to make over $100,000 from the magazine story with more on top for her book; she also went to Hollywood to discuss a film based on her unusual marriage. By the time she separated from her husband, she had caught him with fifteen different women. While Rita took her cheque

Lovely Rita's acts of congress give Washington the shudders

148

and went to look for a flat in New York, away from
the fleshpots of Washington, Congressmen's wives
appeared on television and radio shows all over
America to defend their image. 'She's no more
feminine than us because she appeared in *Playboy*,'
said one.

ongresswife'

THE SCARLET LADIES OF CAPITOL HILL

Close on Rita's tales came those of Paula Parkinson, a
30-year-old blonde who, like Rita, had appeared
starkers in *Playboy*. She worked as a professional
lobbyist in Washington; her job was to persuade
Congressmen to support the cause of the pressure
group who employed her. One such cause concerned
legislation relating to farmers' crop insurance, but no
one was talking much about crops when in March
1981 top columnist Jack Anderson said on television
that Paula had videotapes of the most respectable
politicians, including several eminent Republicans, in
compromising situations with her. It seemed she had
top names on her lovers' list. Paula had meanwhile
retreated to Texas to write a book based on her exotic
experiences. The Justice Department investigated
charges that she had swapped sex for votes, but she
denied the allegations.

It was revealed that Paula had spent a 'golfing'
weekend with three Republican Congressmen, one of
them a leading Reagan supporter, and they had a cosy
time in a cottage in Florida. Within a few days
newspapers had printed the men's names. They denied

REVEALING : Former beauty queen Rita Jenrette

The X-plosive
secret life of
playgirl Paula

New sex scandals rock Washington

that any sexual activity had taken place, and one said, 'It was lights out at 10.30.' Another said of Paula, 'She wasn't much good at lobbying – she was never too sure what side of the issue she was on.' Rumour had it that one of Paula's tapes featured sex on a trampoline. The leading sex magazines and book publishers were reluctant to touch her story, and it was whispered that one or two possible victims had threatened her with legal action if their names were disclosed. In April she denied owning tapes of seventeen different sessions, saying she had one tape and 'a short list' of lovers. She wouldn't dream of blackmailing the men, she protested, claiming the men themselves 'had let the cat out of the bag'. 'I didn't get votes for sex,' said lobby-person Paula.

At the same time as Paula was trying to sell her memoirs, a retired San Francisco madam who had run the city's most exclusive brothel for ten years was just completing her life story. Brandy Baldwin exposed what goes on at the summer-camp gatherings of one

public. Brandy Baldwin said that every year she rented a cottage nearby and installed herself with her top prostitutes. They put on erotic shows for the Bohemians, and there was an exciting competition in which the winner was 'jumped on' by four girls. It was very popular, she said. Obviously American politicians like to spend their holidays in very much the same way as they spend their time in Washington.

Madam's parties for top people

of America's most exclusive organizations – the all-male Bohemian Club. Its 900 members include Gerald Ford, Nixon, Reagan, and Vice-President George Bush, and Prince Charles has visited its headquarters outside San Francisco for lunch. Every summer about 2,000 members and guests congregate for what President Hoover called 'the greatest men's party on earth'. Top politicians and businessmen all gather on a 3,000-acre estate and split into small camps. The Club put on theatrical events; one top lawyer had dressed in tights and wings as a wood nymph, and Richard Nixon had once played a spear-carrier. Members drank, enjoyed themselves, and urinated on trees in

GISCARD: A TALE OF TWO PRESIDENTS

Bokassa's Empire was £13 million in debt, and the average annual income was just £71 per capita. So why were France and President Giscard d'Estaing propping up such an ill-run country? One reason was the fear that the Russians might gain control, which would not only have been worrying politically, but would also have removed from French influence a country with uranium deposits valued at over £70 million as well as ivory and diamonds. Nevertheless, the French were criticized over their involvement with the coronation (which cost the country £200 per member of the population) and many countries refused to attend. Giscard and Bokassa were regularly photographed embracing each other at airports, and the French President awarded Bokassa the Légion d'Honneur. Giscard was also said to have installed his relatives (including his brother Jacques) in key jobs and to own business and property interests there.

In May 1979 it was discovered that Bokassa had ordered the killing of about 100 (later estimates put it as high as 200) schoolchildren, because their parents were too poor to be able to afford the compulsory school uniform. The clothes were available only from a shop owned by one of Bokassa's three wives. When the children demonstrated in protest, they were rounded up and herded into prison. Then they were clubbed or stabbed to death, and their bodies were buried in mass graves or dumped in the river. An eyewitness claimed that he saw Bokassa personally kill thirty-nine of the children. It was said that some had been suffocated in airless cells and others clubbed to

The Jam Jar of Diamonds and the French President

WHEN THE President of the Central African Republic, Jean-Bedel Bokassa, fancied a spot of promotion, he decided to install himself as Emperor. The French Government footed a large part of the £10 million bill for the farcical ceremony, which took place in one of the twenty poorest countries in the world.

BOKASSA: TYRANT RIDICULED BY THE WORLD

The 'emperor' who dressed to kill...
and massacred children

death with nail-studded weapons. Bokassa's Prime Minister denied the atrocity, but it was confirmed by Amnesty International. Up to this point France had unswervingly supported Bokassa's régime. The Emperor, whose name unfortunately translates as 'butcher's boy', denied the killings and said that the trouble had been caused by Marxist students inspired by a foreign power. In June he set up a 'Year of the Child' and declared that he would fine or imprison anyone who arrested a child or a student for any reason other than 'common law' crimes. Although publicly the French Government denounced the massacre, they still supported the country with financial aid, anxious not to lose sight of all that uranium. A five-nation inquiry team which looked into the allegations relating to the massacre reported in August 1979 that Bokassa was personally

Price of silence on Giscard gems

responsible. He contested the verdict. France was forced to announce that it was cutting its aid to the Central African Empire, although it would continue to supply assistance with health, education, and food. Bokassa proceeded to have forty subjects who had testified against him at the inquiry assassinated.

In September 1979 Bokassa was toppled in a bloodless coup and replaced by his moderate nephew Davic Dacko. France sent out troops at his request, and there was much speculation as to the extent of their involvement in the coup. As far as France was concerned, it had safeguarded the country against a possible Soviet bid for power. Bokassa had fled to Libya, and from there he flew to France. As news reached the outside world that he had left behind mutilated bodies in his refrigerator and was possibly a cannibal, President Giscard refused to let him into France and Bokassa's plane remained on the runway before flying off the Ivory Coast. It was discovered that before he left home he had emptied the Imperial coffers, getting away with about £500 million. As

Bokassa started life in exile, revolting stories about his behaviour filtered out of Africa. Forty bodies were found in the palace crocodile pond, and it was said that at his coronation guests were served human flesh. He kept a jam jar of diamonds in his study and offered them to favoured guests, and it was alleged in October 1979 that Giscard had received gems worth over £100,000.

Giscard d'Estaing publicly owned up to receiving the diamonds for the first time on French television during the Presidential election campaign in March 1981. He called them 'normal gifts between heads of states'.

According to the *Sunday Times*, French voters' general reaction when asked whether the diamonds would influence their votes was 'I'd do just the same'. Nevertheless, opponents of Giscard toured the country sticking giant paper diamonds over his eyes in the 1981 election posters, and the affair must surely have contributed to Giscard's serious defeat in the election.

MR MILLS THE SEX BOMB!

G-string Hillbilly and Wild Old Wilbur

CONGRESSMAN Wilbur Mills was a man feared by generations of American Presidents. He had been called 'a thorn in the side of Johnson', 'tough with Nixon', and 'one of the most powerful figures in Congress'; he even seemed to scare Jack Kennedy. A tough legislator, he had enormous influence on which way the American Government allocated its spending, and was once quoted as saying, 'I will always do what I think is right, and nothing will stop me.'

These were prophetic words in the light of events which followed a row in a car one night in October 1974. Mrs Annabella Battista, aged thirty-eight, threw herself from Wilbur Mills's car and into the Washington Basin in an apparent suicide bid. This exciting event took place at 2 a.m. when the car was spotted travelling fast without any lights on. Annabella was said to be a go-go dancer and another occupant of the vehicle a masseuse. A third passenger was later identified as Wilbur Mills, although he originally denied he had been in the car at the time.

Then the fascinating saga of the secret double-life of Wilbur Mills emerged. Mills, the virtual dictator of American financial policy and a devout churchgoer had met Annabella (stage name Fanne Foxe) the year, before. Two striptease artistes said that on the night Fanne and Wilbur met in the Silver Slipper Club, he spent £680 on whisky and champagne. He then tried to buy the club where she appeared, but the deal was dropped when his lawyers discovered that it had once been closed for prostitution.

Stripper Fanne Fox tells of love in a tub

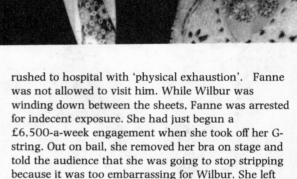

While investigations into his finances got underway (for it appeared that he was splashing about more money than he earned), Wilbur Mills lay low. His whole family seemed to have succumbed to a 'bug'. Fanne told the press, 'I didn't jump into the Basin, I fell in. I got hysterical because the police officer was drowning me. I didn't need his help. I am an expert swimmer.'

A week later Wilbur emerged from his house, and it was announced that Fanne's marriage had broken up. Her husband said that Wilbur paid her £10,500 a year as his 'personal assistant'. Since the incident she had dropped her title of the Argentinian Bombshell and re-christened herself the Tidal Basin Bombshell, and her earnings as a stripper had leapt from £300 to £1,500 a week. Despite the scandal Wilbur Mills was re-elected, and in December he stunned his political friends by appearing on stage with Fanne in a burlesque house in Boston. Wilbur referred to her as his 'G-string hillbilly' and, indeed, she stood beside him starkers except for a G-string. Later he told journalists, 'She has a wonderful act and I can get her into the movies if she wants.'

'PHYSICAL EXHAUSTION'

A couple of days later the Democratic caucus stripped him of his powers. When he was told he had lost his job, he said that it was just fine, he never liked it that much anyway. He didn't appear to understand what was going on, and it wasn't surprising that he was rushed to hospital with 'physical exhaustion'. Fanne was not allowed to visit him. While Wilbur was winding down between the sheets, Fanne was arrested for indecent exposure. She had just begun a £6,500-a-week engagement when she took off her G-string. Out on bail, she removed her bra on stage and told the audience that she was going to stop stripping because it was too embarrassing for Wilbur. She left the stage in tears to a standing ovation.

Mills at last admitted he was an alcoholic and said he had given up drink. He refused to resign his seat in the House of Representatives and entered a clinic for a 'cure'. The next month he was out. He gave Fanne a Cadillac, but the affair was doomed. Fanne wrote her autobiography, *The Congressman and the Stripper*, and said that he had made her pregnant. She had an abortion because she was frightened the baby might be deformed as a result of his alcoholism. She also told how his wife had once found them naked in the bath together.

HELPING ALCOHOLICS

By November 1975 Wilbur Mills had withdrawn from political life; instead he devoted much of his time to helping alcoholics. He had been drunk during top White House talks and couldn't remember what was said for days on end. He said he had enjoyed the last year of his life – which he had spent without a drink – better than any that went before.

WHO'S COUNTING? NOT EVANGELINE!

'Those Little White Lies'

THE NEW YORK NEWSPAPERS had a field day in the spring of 1981 when what had been billed as one of the 'weddings of the year' became the focus of much amusement. It was discovered that the bride had not entirely told the truth about her rather exotic past. The groom was none other than the Governor of New York, Hugh Carey, a highly respectable figure whose first wife had produced thirteen children before dying of cancer. At Reagan's inauguration Carey met Evangeline Gouletas, a wealthy Greek, who informed the Governor that she had only been married once before. They embarked on a whirlwind courtship, and

How many husbands?

it was noted in the gossip columns that 62-year-old Carey had dyed his grey hair to a more youthful shade as he pursued the 44-year-old woman of his dreams.

'Engie' was a rags-to-riches success story, a lady who had worked her way up as co-founder of American Invesco, the country's largest converters of apartments. The company was said to be worth at least a billion dollars, and uncharitable souls thought her affair with Carey revealed that it was really political power which she was after. At the time of their courtship, the company was under investigation because of the hard-sell tactics they employed, the low quality of the renovations they carried out, and the mistreatment of tenants. Nevertheless, Carey proposed within five weeks of their meeting. Gossips thought that the swiftness of his offer was because he was on the rebound – just three weeks before he had met Engie, Carey's previous girlfriend, Henry Ford's daughter, Anne Ford Vzielli, had told him that she certainly didn't want to marry him.

Undeterred by the gossip, Engie sent out hundreds of invitations. By the time of the wedding she'd owned up to another ex-husband, and the marriage certificate recorded that her two previous attempts to

tie the knot had taken place in 1955 and 1958. Engie said she thought that her second husband was dead – but he turned up to open a new restaurant in California. Still, the wedding was really lavish – 500 guests went to the church and 700 frolicked at the reception – and newspapers described the event as HUGH CAREY WEDS THE EMPRESS OF MONDO CONDO and NOT SO SWEET EVANGELINE.

Hugh's status with his Roman Catholic voters was already suffering badly, but it was dealt a body-blow by further revelations about Engie in the *Chicago Tribune*. The *Tribune* disclosed that a third marriage existed in Engie's life, from 1958 to 1963. Then Carey issued a statement saying: 'I'm certain in my own mind that I possess all the relevant facts about the marriages . . .' However, some wits thought that Carey might demand a recount. One explanation for Evangeline's behaviour was she didn't want to admit

Gov's coy Bride

that, although she had been a success in the world of business, she was something of a failure at marriage.

It was decided not to prosecute the Governor's wife for lying on her wedding certificate, and Mr Carey probably wisely anticipated the effect which all this hanky-panky would have on his constituents when he announced that he would not be standing for re-election.

LBJ PROTEGE CAUGHT IN SCANDAL!

Bobby Baker and the Quorum Club

BOBBY BAKER was a protégé of President Lyndon Johnson. He had worked his way up from the humble post of pageboy in the Senate at the age of fourteen to that of Majority Leader (a position similar to Chief Whip) by the time he was thirty-seven. Bobby, a good-living fellow, seemed to know just as much about his fellow politicians' sexual and drinking habits as he did about their voting patterns. He was a founder member and part owner of the Quorum club in Washington, a place where 'tired' government officials were served drinks by scantily clad lovelies and the walls were covered with paintings of female nudes. It was a place frequented by political lobbyists, whose job was made easier by girls like Ellen Rometsch, a German ex-model who acted as a hostess there.

In October 1963 she was thrown out of America because of her amorous activities with men in power. It was feared by politicians (and hoped by journalists) that the story would turn out to be as exciting as the Profumo affair they had just witnessed in England. Ellen's husband had been working in the military department of the German Embassy in Washington, and on their return home he started divorce proceedings. The couple were investigated by the German Government, who found no evidence of espionage. Ellen's friend Ingrid, who shared a flat with her in Washington, said, 'You would never suspect her of being a party girl.' She added that she had left the flat, however, because she disapproved of what Ellen was willing to do for money.

157

A closer look at who belonged to the Quorum club (motto: 'Happy is he who keepeth the law') revealed that the members included four Senators, two Representatives, two Vice-Presidential aides and five lobbyists. A Senate committee started to look into whether Bobby Baker had used his job at the Senate to help him in business deals.

The Senate examined his finances and found that on a salary of £7,000 a year he had amassed a fortune of £714,300, owned two houses, one of which was in Washington and said to be the location of wild parties. The house also boasted wall-to-wall lavender carpet and his secretary Carole in the spare bedroom. The committee decided that Baker had used his inside knowledge to float companies, buy property, tip off businessmen about forthcoming legislation and government policy, and make a fortune. Some of the cash was rumoured to have found its way back to the pockets of LBJ himself. It was discovered that Baker was running a vice ring, was a contact for an abortion racket, owned slot machines, and was a moneylender and land speculator. He had given Johnson an expensive hi-fi set as a present. It was estimated that altogether he had made $2½ million in two years.

While Carole was refusing to answer any questions put by the investigating committee, another deal involving Baker and Johnson emerged. Baker got a friend to sell Lyndon Johnson and his wife some expensive life insurance, and in return the friend bought advertising time on Mrs Johnson's Texas radio station. The deal was set up by another Johnson aide called Walter Jenkins. Then Jenkins resigned when he was arrested near the men's lavatory at the YMCA on a charge of disorderly conduct involving 'indecent gestures'. The secret services had failed to uncover the fact that Jenkins had also been arrested in 1959 on a charge of 'disorderly conduct (pervert)' – whatever that might have involved!

Senator Goldwater said that the Johnson administration was 'dark with scandal'. Bobby Baker was found guilty of acting 'unethically' and of feathering his own nest. He was sentenced to between one and three years' jail for tax evasion, larceny, and conspiracy.

Baker provided 'extras' for Quorum members

THOSE KENNEDY BOYS DO LIKE GIRLS

Joe, John and Bob, and a Lot of Ladies

PRESIDENT KENNEDY'S AFFAIRS are quite well recorded, but those of his father haven't received much attention, perhaps out of deference to his mother. In March 1981 film star Gloria Swanson published her autobiography, and in it she detailed her affair with Kennedy Senior, whom she met in 1927 when she approached him to invest in *Sadie Thompson*, a film she wished to make. At that time Joe and Rose Kennedy had eight children, and he was a banker who wanted to make money in the movies. Gloria was twenty-seven and extremely beautiful, had two children and was married to her third husband. She got the backing she wanted and began an affair with Joe.

At Joe's suggestion she made *Queen Kelly* with Eric von Stroheim as the director. It was a disaster and Joe was furious, partly because his money was being wasted by the director over-shooting to an incredible degree. He then proposed a trip to Europe, where Gloria was to attend the première of one of her films. To her amazement he brought Rose along too, saying that his wife had always wanted to meet her. Swanson took a girlfriend and the odd party all sailed to Europe together, with Mrs Kennedy acting as chaperone to the two girls. If she knew of the affair, she certainly didn't let on. However, Henri, Gloria's husband, had definitely picked up on what was going on, and he asked for a separation.

ACCOUNTING ERROR

Joe desperately wanted his name as producer on the credits of a smash-hit film, but the next script he commissioned for her was terrible. It flopped. He was cross that *Sadie Thompson*, which had been her idea, was doing well. When Gloria found out that Joe had given someone a car for dreaming up the title of his latest flop, and then charged it to her account, she was furious. When she confronted him with it, he dashed back east, and it was soon announced that he had decided to concentrate his efforts on politics in the future. Gloria and her husband were divorced, and she discovered when she went through her accounts that Joe had charged her for a fur coat which he had given her as a present. She returned to work to try to gather some money together – the last few years had left her relatively broke.

THE SLAP AND TICKLE SECRETS OF JFK AND MARILYN

Secret Loves Of The Kennedys
Bob Kennedy's Friendship With Marilyn Monroe
—Did He Call Her Just Before She Died?

Part Three

Perhaps Gloria's memoirs make the behaviour of Bob and John easier to understand. Both led double lives: to their voters they presented the image of happily married family men, and yet neither seemed to be able to resist a pretty girl. But John certainly treated his lovers as non-emotional relaxation from the cares of office; he didn't want to get really involved. At the time of Marilyn Monroe's death in August 1962, it was rumoured that she was having an affair with a prominent man. In the following year various writers have claimed that it was John F. Kennedy, his brother Bobby, or both. Tapes were said to exist of Marilyn on

Jackie Oh!

the telephone to Bobby, and she was extremely flattered when asked to sing at the President's inaugural ball. Kitty Kelley's book *Jackie Oh* revealed that before John was elected at the end of 1959 the couple were having marital problems, and that Joe had persuaded Jackie to remain with John although she had threatened divorce. John allegedly had affairs with White House secretaries, film stars, lift operators, journalists and socialites. On the night of his inaugural ball Jackie went home early and he ended up having a quickie with a girl who'd been waiting for him at a friend's house. Most of his affairs were

conducted while Jackie was out of Washington. He'd have nude bathing parties in the White House pool, and girls would streak naked through the corridors of power before being dragged into the presidential bed. One long affair was with artist and socialite Mrs Mary Meyer. After Kennedy had been assassinated she was found dead by the Potomac river with a bullet through her head. The suspect was released and the murder was never really solved.

MAFIA LINK

The liaison of John's which caused the most comment was his romance – if it can be called that – with Judith Campbell Exner. This emerged when a Senate committee under Frank Church investigated the nation's intelligence agencies in 1975. When they interviewed Judith, to their horror they discovered that at the same time as dating Kennedy she had been seeing Sam Giancana, a leading member of the Mafia. It was said that Frank Sinatra had introduced Judith to Kennedy at a party in Las Vegas. Their affair started seven months before he was elected President. A Kennedy aide told the committee he could not remember Judith 'because there were about thirty girls around at any one time'. The Senate were convinced that Judith had nothing to do with Kennedy's assassination, but it was disclosed that the affair had

The President, The Lady and The Godfather

Judith Campbell's two lovers: a Mafia double-cross

come to the attention of the FBI when Bobby Kennedy, then Attorney General, had ordered the tapping of the telephones of two Mafia chieftains. He was conducting a vigorous anti-Mafia campaign at the time, and to his embarrassment he was challenged with the information about his brother's relationship by J. Edgar Hoover, the FBI Director. Hoover said that in a period of fifty-four weeks the couple had spoken to each other seventy times, and some of Judith's calls to the White House were made from Giancana's home. An hour after being told this, John Kennedy called Judith for the last time. Then it was alleged that Hoover used this information to persuade Kennedy to let him harass, investigate and tap the phone of Martin Luther King, the civil rights leader. Giancana had been subpoenaed to give evidence to Church's committee, but he had been mysteriously murdered two days before he was due to testify. Sinatra's involvement in the affair was discussed, and it was said that after Kennedy discovered the singer's friendship with certain shady figures he dropped Sinatra from his circle of friends.

NEW REVELATIONS

In 1976 Judith Exner published her autobiography, in which she made some interesting revelations. She told how Ted, John's younger brother, had tried to get a date with her and she had turned him down. He behaved in a petulant manner. John Kennedy had told her his marriage was on the rocks, but that he and Jackie weren't going to get divorced because it would harm his career. She rated Giancana a 'slightly better' lover than Kennedy. According to Judith, the President made love to the music of the Broadway show *Camelot* on their first meeting, and once made her furious with a three-in-a-bed proposal. On another occasion he burst into her room and left after twenty minutes to return to his work. She claimed she had sex with Kennedy in the White House on at least twenty occasions. By the time their affair ended, however, he wasn't a very good lover – back pains meant that he relied on her totally to give him a good time, and she resented that!

Politics

Bribery

The House of Commons keeps a register of British MPs' interests and Members are *requested* to submit details of their income outside their salaries. But the register does not cover income from share-holdings or the occasional 'gift'. Although our men and women in power like to say that the giving of gifts is 'as old as time' (or some other dreary phrase), I prefer to reply with Mencken's famous riposte: 'There is no such thing as a free lunch.' And as you'll see from the following examples, free lunches were pretty low on the bribery scale: land, rugs (which turned out to be expensive carpets), holiday trips, and horses are much more desirable. Another surefire way of ensuring things are run the way *you* want when bribes may fail is a spot of ballot-rigging.

Fake Sheikhs and Hidden Cameras

AT THE BEGINNING of February 1980 the FBI announced that they had started investigations into six (later to become eight) Congressmen on suspicion of accepting bribes from Arab agents. A few days later the story of the fake sheikhs emerged: they were in fact upright members of the FBI under their flowing robes, beards, and sunglasses. Code named ABSCAM, it was the biggest and most complex entrapment scheme yet dreamt up by the FBI. They set up a fake company, Abdul Enterprises, with luxury offices in Washington. Dressed as Arabs, they used foreign currency and private planes, and bought a luxury house in Florida which they fitted up with bugging devices and hidden video cameras. They also purchased a glamorous yacht for entertaining their clients. Into the trap walked seven Congressmen and an eminent Senator. All were leading politicians seeking to make a dollar or few on the side. Once the word was out in Washington that Abdul Enterprises needed political friends, people started rushing through the door to offer their services – always at the right price. Although many politicians expressed doubts as to the ethics of the operation once it was made public, the tapes that the FBI produced were damning evidence.

One of the first to be convicted was Democrat John Jenrette. A videotape showed Jenrette accepting a £20,000 bribe from a bogus Arab sheikh representing a fake company. His wife Rita found $25,000 hidden in one of his shoes and handed the cash to the lawyers. In return for the money Jenrette had promised the 'Arab' that he would introduce new immigration legislation.

Stung Again
Another Abscam conviction

The sixth conviction in the operation came in February 1981 as Richard Kelly became the first Republican to face the court. While Kelly pleaded that he took the money as part of his personal probe into corruption in Congress, the FBI showed a damning film of him telling an FBI 'Arab' that he would help two fake 'sheikhs' emigrate to America. As he stuffed the $25,000 bribe in his pocket, he declared to the 'Arab', 'If I told you how poor I am, you would cry.' A Florida businessman and an accountant were convicted with him, and the three faced up to twenty-five years in jail and fines up to $40,000. The judge said he found 'ABSCAM has an odour to it that is absolutely repulsive'. Hearings were taking place in New York to try to establish whether the FBI had gone over the top in persuading politicians to commit illegal acts. Nevertheless, the Justice Department was convinced that the convictions they had obtained would not be overturned on appeal.

A Wolf in Sheik's Clothing

Abscam's biggest TV special debuts in a Brooklyn court

Senator Harrison Williams with FBI agent Richard Farhart, a.k.a. Yassir Habib

In April 1981 the trial of the most senior man accused, New Jersey Senator Harrison Williams Jnr, started. He had served in the Senate for twenty-two years and had just been declared 'the most popular politician' in his own State. In the recordings and videotapes Williams was seen talking to a bogus Arab millionaire, 'Sheikh Yassir Habib'. Williams said he would try to persuade the President to award a Government contract for the construction of a titanium mine in Virginia to Abdul Enterprises. In return he would get part ownership of the mine and a cool $12.6 million. He also said he 'would do everything in his power' to help the sheikh get permanent residency in the US. He was seen boasting of his influential connections, and his lawyer was filmed telling Habib how Williams was 'happy as a lark' about the mining deal. Williams claimed in his defence that he was a victim of entrapment, but he was found guilty.

OH, BROTHER!

Silly Billy

IN THE SUMMER of 1980, when Jimmy Carter was facing a tough fight ahead in the American Presidential elections, he was dealt a real below-the-belt swipe by his brother Billy. Billy, an alcoholic, had made a fortune out of ridiculous publicity appearances since his brother's election, but this paled in comparison with the events that unfolded during July and August. It was tolerable that the President's brother acted the buffoon in public, but what many Americans found worrying was the implication that he might have influenced US foreign policy in any way.

The story broke in July when, much against his will, Billy Carter was forced by the American Department of Justice to register as a Libyan agent and to admit that he had received $220,000 from the Libyan Government, which he said was a 'loan'. Jimmy Carter denied knowing that Billy had received cash from the Libyans until, on 14 July, he said that he found the arrangement 'inappropriate'. A week later Billy was getting into deeper water: the *Evening News* headlined their story BILLY LIAR SINKS CARTER'S HOPES as they told how a spokesman from the Department of Justice had said that Billy Carter could be prosecuted if it was proved he had made false statements about his relationship with the Libyans. It seemed that already on two separate occasions Billy had boobed: in January 1980 he had denied getting any money from the Libyans, and in June he had not told the truth about when he received the money and its purpose. He claimed at first that he had only received £130 and presents including a saddle and a scimitar. Jimmy Carter agreed that he had shown brother Billy classified State Department cables about

his first trip to Libya in September 1978; this was most unusual behaviour. Now the polls showed that only twenty-two per cent of the electorate approved of Carter's performance (during Watergate Nixon had convinced twenty-five per cent of the population that he was doing a good job). On 1 August, the *Daily Mail* printed 'the picture that could cost Carter the White House' – a picture of Billy, coke can in hand, sitting with Libyans in seats reserved for the PLO, next to the arms supplier who dealt with the organization. The *Mail* commented that Billy's open friendship with the Libyan régime was likely to lose Jimmy the votes of the influential Jews who had helped him into office. When asked about the damage the picture might do his brother, Billy replied, 'Jewish critics can kiss my

ass.' It was thought that Jimmy might decide to kick Billy's instead.

It seemed that investigations would be opened into the money that Billy received from the Libyans. He had pocketed £8,400 in December 1979, but failed to disclose this when questioned by the Justice Department. He now admitted accepting a £100,000 loan.

'A GOOD JOB'

The cables which Jimmy Carter had shown to Billy were then discussed in the press. One had a note attached to it: 'You did a good job under the "dry" circumstances – Jimmy', obviously alluding to the fact that alcohol was not permitted in Libya. Jody Powell, the White House spokesman, said that the cables did

Witness tells – Billy's drunken antics in Libya

not amount to a 'hill of beans'. On 4 August Carter made an hour-long television appearance to explain his part in the rapidly growing scandal. He said that he had repeatedly told Billy not to go to Libya in 1980, and that when Billy was drying out in an alcoholics' ward in Georgia, he sent someone to dissuade him from a trip he was planning in March. The *Sun* carried a report on Billy's reaction to his brother's TV press conference under the headline NUTS TO YOU. Billy told reporters, 'He has no influence on me; I still have some friends that are Libyans.' Although Jimmy said he loved his brother, they were only talking to each other through lawyers.

Meanwhile, at the Senate committee hearing national security adviser Brzezinski said that he had discovered that Billy was trying to get oil from Libya for an American company, and when he had warned Billy that this was potentially embarrassing for his brother, Billy replied that he was entitled to his privacy and had a 'right to make a living'.

On 21 August Billy gave an emotional performance in front of the committee. He said, 'Billy Carter is not a buffoon, a boob or a whacko ... I am a common

citizen with uncommon financial and family problems . . . I would never do anything to hurt America because I love my country.' The Justice Department alleged that Billy had received $20,000 after arranging for a top Libyan official to see Brzezinski in November 1979. They contended that the balance of the money he had received from Libya was a payment for lobbying on the country's behalf, whereas Billy contended it was a 'loan'. Unfortunately for Billy, no papers had ever been signed or repayment plan committed to paper, so he had a hard time proving his point.

NEW REVELATIONS

Just as President Carter might have thought the worst was over, the *New York Post* printed a picture of Billy with ex-CIA agent and arms dealer Frank Terpil. Frank boasted of 'his powerful ally'. On 14 September Jimmy got another body blow: Mario Leanza, a real-estate man who had accompanied Billy to Libya on the 1978 trip and had given the evidence about the planes deal to the Senate committee, gave a detailed interview to the *Chicago Tribune*. Billy had told the Senate he hardly knew Leanza and Leanza was anxious to set the record straight. Mario said that on their trip to Libya Billy was drunk a lot of the time,

wore the same shirt for five days in temperatures around 100 degrees, drunkenly impersonated his brother, demanded $50,000 in advance from Libya before he went on the trip, made wild promises about securing the Libyans the planes they needed, and was involved in sexy scenes on the plane trip with a lady who kissed and cuddled all the men in his party, and who some of them thought was a CIA agent. On his return to America, Leanza said, Billy had donned a Palestinian Liberation Army uniform and attended a reception with Libyan diplomats in a mosque in Atlanta. He also alleged that Miss Lillian, Billy's mother, had received a gift from their Libyan hosts at a US Embassy party in Rome. In the *Sunday Times* issue of 14 September, Billy admitted he had discussed arms deals with Frank Terpil. By this time Terpil had jumped bail in America and was believed to be in Libya.

At the end of September 1980 the Senate report cleared Billy of any violation of the law, although it criticized him strongly, and the press generally thought that his brother had bungled his handling of the affair. Jimmy Carter subsequently met with a crushing defeat in the Presidential election.

Billy Liar sinks Carter's hopes

Sherman Adams
and the 'Carpet Bribe'

SHERMAN ADAMS had been assistant to President Eisenhower for over five years when he was accused of taking bribes in June 1958. Adams was not only a close friend of Ike, who described him as 'an invaluable public servant doing a difficult job efficiently, honestly, and tirelessly', but he had the ear of his boss to such an extent that he was known as the 'acting' President. The scandal broke when his opponents accused him of using his influence to help a friend, the rich industrialist and textile manufacturer Bernard Goldfine, who was in trouble with a Government department. Goldfine was alleged to have paid a $2,000 hotel bill for Adams. Eisenhower immediately affirmed his confidence in his aide, who denied the allegations.

A few days later Adams admitted that he had received 'a couple of mats, some fabric, and other small items', but described the exchange of gifts between families and individuals as being 'as old as civilization'. To others the taking of bribes seemed to go that far back too, but it was difficult to equate these accusations against Adams with his straight-as-a-die reputation (he had even been known to use his own stamps to stick on letters he sent from the White House in order to save the Government money).

Resignation demands continued to grow, however, but Eisenhower refused, saying simply, 'I need him.' An investigation by the head of the Securities and Exchange Commission announced that he could find no evidence that Adams sought favours. The press recalled that President Truman had had similar trouble with his military aide, General Vaughan, and the so-called 'deep freezer scandal'. But Adams's enemies continued to declare that he had accepted bribes, and at the end of June 1958 they said they totalled over $1 million and included a tractor, fifty-five cattle, trees, a miniature golf course, an all-electric kitchen, horses, and lengths of vicuna cloth. A Boston financier said that Mr Goldfine had claimed 'Adams was taking care' of him, and that in return he bought the Presidential aide a home and sent his children to expensive private schools. Cartoons of a wonderful $700 vicuna coat which Adams had received featured in many American newspapers. The rug which Adams said was 'loaned' to him turned out to be worth $2,400.

Adams was known as a stern moralist who decried the 'influence peddling' of the previous Truman régime, and yet as the scandal unfolded it transpired that he

had smoothed things over for Goldfine when he had been accused by a Government department of describing the content of his fabrics incorrectly. He said that the coats contained ninety per cent wool and ten per cent vicuna, when in fact they contained nylon. Goldfine was also accused by his shareholders of fiddling his books, and a suit was brought against him by an economist who had invested in his company.

VICTIM

Adams resigned on 22 September 1958. The President accepted his aide's departure, but said, 'I deeply deplore the circumstances which have forced him to resign', and described Adams's five years at the White House as 'brilliant'. Adams's last words on the matter were that he was the victim of a 'vilification drive'.

SHERMAN ADAMS RESIGNS
SEES 'VILIFICATION' DRIVE
PRESIDENT VOICES SADNES

REAGAN'S FIRST SCANDAL

Say "Goodnight"

Mr Allen and the 'Forgotten' Cash

IN NOVEMBER 1981, a Japanese newspaper reported that Richard Allen, President Reagan's National Security Adviser, had taken a $1,000 bribe in return for arranging an interview between Japanese journalists from a woman's magazine and Nancy Reagan. The interview was said to have taken place the day after the inauguration in January 1981. This was potentially highly embarrassing to the administration, because the law restricts the size of any gifts which officials can receive while in office, and it also reflected badly on Mrs Reagan if, as the Japanese newspaper implied, she gave interviews when cash had changed hands.

The moment the story broke, official inquiries were launched in all directions. The Justice Department launched one to see if Allen was guilty of breaking the law, and the FBI started investigating the gift of two Seiko watches which Allen was alleged to have received, as well as an inaccurate statement that he was said to have made about the selling of his company, a consulting firm. It appeared that Allen's date of sale did not quite match up with everyone else's! He was also said to be in trouble with the White House lawyers because he didn't list other sources of income – apart from his official salary – on his financial disclosure forms.

MEDIA BLITZ

Within weeks Allen decided to take leave from his job to mount a media blitz to try to counter all the rumours surrounding him. At the end of November he appeared on 'Meet the Press' and announced his leave of absence. He then popped up on all the three major networks' morning news programmes in just five days to put his point of view. He announced that he would be starting legal action against those who had started the 'false' stories about him. All this, of course, was said to have embarrassed President Reagan enormously. Allen's claim was that he took an envelope containing $1,000 as it was being handed to Nancy Reagan and put it in the office safe, and then forgot about it for eight months. By now it was rumoured that Reagan was hoping Allen would

resign, although Edwin Meese, his boss at the White House, was sticking by him. In the midst of the media blitz the Justice Department announced that they could not find Allen guilty of any criminal charges. It was said that the long-forgotten envelope actually had '$10,000' written on the outside, but only 1,000 actually remained in it. It seemed possible that the three Japanese journalists involved had received $10,000 from their magazine as expenses for the trip, of which 1,000 was allocated for the Nancy Reagan interview. Payment or gifts in return for such an interview was regarded as traditional practice in Japan, and Allen claimed he planned to turn the money over to the authorities. According to him, the two Seiko watches which he was also accused of receiving while in office had been given him before he was sworn in as National Security Adviser. However, a Japanese journalist declared that Allen had taken a watch after the interview with Mrs Reagan had taken place. After interviewing thirty-six people in the US and Japan (but not Nancy Reagan), the Justice Department obviously believed Allen's version of events.

'FORGOTTEN' INCOME

Things still didn't look so hot for him on the business front, however. Although Allen had filled in forms declaring that he sold his company in January 1978, in fact the sale actually took place in January 1981 – three years later – and in the meantime he'd been receiving a salary from it. He had also 'forgotten' to list for tax purposes $5,000 which the company had been paying him in consultancy fees.

As the scandal grew, Reagan acted behind the scenes to try to limit the amount of embarrassment. Edwin Meese announced that an 'appraisal' of the entire National Security Council had been ordered. The pressure on Allen to resign was mounting. On 1 January, when reporters telephoned Allen and said that they'd heard Reagan was planning to replace him, Allen declared, 'I'm unaware of such plans.' But by 4 January he'd been persuaded to toe the line, and duly resigned, much to everyone's relief. Reagan then announced that the job was being upgraded, and that Allen's successor, William P. Clark, would be reporting directly to the President, bypassing Meese. Allen admitted he had not wanted to resign – he'd asked for reinstatement after his leave, but had been told it was

Richard

just not possible. He was given a new job as a consultant on the President's Foreign Intelligence Advisory Board, somewhat of a downgrading in responsibility. According to Allen, the upgrading of his former job did not mean that Meese had fallen from favour. Although the White House internal review said that Allen was clear of any wrong-doing over the affair, as the first senior White House official to resign since Reagan took office he was somewhat in disgrace in Washington. The internal inquiry had discovered that Allen had met with former clients of his company and dined with them in the White House, but it stated that he did not behave improperly in doing so.

Newspapers said that two of Reagan's advisers, James A. Baker and Michael Deaver, had been pushing strongly for Allen to go since the beginning of

December, but they could not win over Meese until the end of the month. Finally, it was thought that Allen had been a bit of a misfit at the White House anyway – he just wasn't their style. Apart from offending Nancy by even taking the envelope containing the money (no matter what he planned to do with it), it was said that his laugh-a-minute impersonations of politicians, including Nixon, hadn't gone down too well with the more pompous of his fellow workers. He'd never managed to build up a good rapport with the President, and it was further said that he didn't get on too well with Secretary of State Haig. After his resignation Allen said he'd been hounded by the press – even though a month earlier he'd been only too keen to use the same journalists to put across his version of events.

Hijinks

High Life and Low Life

The stories included in this section cover ladies from all walks of life. What they have in common is that, for various reasons, they all made front-page news. Some achieved a greater degree of notoriety than others, but in their own way each was found irresistible in the eyes of the press – especially if the stories also had a humorous aspect, as in the case of Joyce McKinney, for instance. If influential politicians or show-business personalities are involved, so much the better; but in the end it all boils down to the fact that, to a journalist, a good story is a good story.

BRITON DENIES U.N. SEX RACKET

Sex at the United Nations

and

Twenty Years on the Run

A SMALL ITEM in the Sunday papers on 5 March 1961 mentioned that Harry Alan Towers, described as a British TV producer, had been arrested in New York and accused of running a call-girl racket from his swanky apartment on W 55th Street. The girl charged with him was called Mariella Novotny, aged nineteen. Mariella was accused of prostitution offences and Towers was charged with importing her into America for immoral purposes. A 'little black book' had been found at Towers's flat and was now in the hands of the police. It was said to contain the names of 'theatre celebrities'. Mariella told the police she had up to three men a day and gave Towers the money. A man called Ronald Chapman also appeared in court; he said that he was her husband but that they did not live together. Towers's lawyer said the charges were 'incomprehensible' and that his client was 'a man of substance', who knew prominent people on both sides of the Atlantic.

Towers was released on bail and promptly disappeared. Mariella was said to have been deported

as a 'wayward minor', although she later claimed the police were holding her passport when she booked a cabin on the Queen Mary in an assumed name and sailed off back to England, telling the ship's purser that she had lost her passport.

In 1960 Mariella had married Horace Dibben, an antique dealer, at Caxton Hall, so who 'Chapman' in New York was is anyone's guess. Mariella was born Stella Marie Capes. After her marriage she changed her name from Dibben to Novotny. She had a daughter, called October Henrietta, and wrote a best-selling book *King's Road*.

Harry Alan Towers had been in the RAF and began his show-business career as a script writer. He started a company which sold radio recordings all round the world and many famous people worked for him. By

STAR-STUDDED LIFE OF A 'VICE KING'

the late fifties he had moved into television as a producer, and was said to have made – and then lost – £350,000. At the time of his arrest in New York he was described as a 'bankrupt'.

Two months after his disappearance, Towers told friends that he would eventually give reasons for his behaviour. He said, 'I am not a man on the run.' At the time that the New York police were claiming that he managed a call-girl racket involving fifteen girls from the United Nations building, Towers emerged in Moscow, where he got VIP treatment. Rumours spread that his girls were involved with the KGB and that the operation was an attempt to discredit certain politicians. From Russia he went to Denmark, China, Czechoslovakia, and Ireland. He lived in London, but disappeared again in 1973 when American Express served a bankruptcy order on him for over £700 worth of unpaid airline tickets.

Top Hollywood names played in his movies

In 1980, almost twenty years after his sudden exit from America, he re-surfaced in Canada, where he had been working as an executive producer on a number of feature films. He was a legal immigrant, and none of his colleagues knew of his past. A New York newspaper reported in November 1980 that he was willing to come back to America to face the 1961 charges if his lawyer could work out a deal with the district attorney. Towers had always maintained his innocence.

He told the press, 'It never occurred to me that anyone would make a political connection', referring to his trip to Russia. He said that Mariella claimed she had dated Jack Kennedy and had embroidered the story by saying that he had introduced them. He accepted that the little black book which had lain in police files for twenty years was his, but said it contained the names of work contacts – people in the film industry. However, a policeman in New York told reporters, 'At the time the people involved with this case were young politicians, lawyers and diplomats. Now they're famous. This is dynamite.' Nobody, it seemed, wanted the names to come out in court if a deal could be done. It was rumoured that some of them were men now serving in the Reagan administration. If the case came to court, then the little black book would be used as evidence.

VICE CHARGES DROPPED

Eventually it was announced that Towers had returned to New York and the vice charges had been dropped. He would face only the lesser charge of jumping bail. Horace Dibben, Mariella's husband, told journalists that even if the little black book – which Mariella claimed was her diary – stayed locked up, she had a 'fabulous memory' and lots of other notes and letters. The *Sunday People* rose to the bait and printed her story (certainly not the first paper to do so in twenty years). She claimed, sure enough, that Towers had introduced her to Jack Kennedy and she had had sex with both Bobby and Jack, at the United Nations building. She claimed that no money ever changed hands and that she had been introduced to Kennedy to discredit him politically. The FBI and the CIA, she said, both showed her pictures they had taken with secret cameras of her afternoon sex sessions. According to Mariella, the stories of her charging $500 a time just weren't true. Meanwhile a whole bunch of top US politicians breathed a sigh of relief, as the little black book – address book or diary – stayed firmly locked up, and Mariella pocketed a few quid for her well-worn 'memoirs'.

'THREE DAYS OF FUN, FOOD AND SEX'

Joyce was discovered in Devon, trying to avoid the police by wearing different-coloured wigs. As she was driven to face charges, she held up a sign in the window of the police van which read, I AM INNOCENT. PLEASE HELP ME. She was charged with kidnapping Kirk and possessing a toy gun with intent to commit an offence. On 7 October the *Daily Mirror* printed another wonderful picture of Joyce, this time fighting with the police and holding up another note for photographers which read, PLEASE, PLEASE TELL THE TRUTH, MY REPUTATION IS AT STAKE. Joyce herself didn't tell the truth that often, but she certainly knew how to get on the front page of a newspaper.

Lovesick actress went after her man with shackles and chloroform, court story

At the committal hearings, it was said that she had used chloroform and shackles to capture Kirk, and it also emerged that she had entered Britain on a false passport. She and her companion, Mr Keith May, were seen kissing and cuddling in the courtroom. Joyce took the stand and said that she and Kirk had once been lovers and he feared excommunication from the Mormon Church because as a missionary he had taken a vow of celibacy. The headline writers couldn't believe their luck when she came out with the immortal words, 'For the love of Kirk I'd have skied down Everest in the nude (with a carnation up my nose).' Pictures of the bespectacled, clean-cut Kirk made such exotic claims hard to understand. It turned out that Joyce had set the scene for love-making at the cottage by playing their favourite sexy music from two

Love in Chains

JOYCE MCKINNEY, a 27-year-old busty blonde from Carolina, burst into the headlines on 19 September 1977. It was reported that the police were watching ports and airports for a couple they wanted to question over the kidnapping of a Mormon missionary, Kirk Anderson. Twenty-one-year-old Kirk had been found at the weekend after having been held prisoner for three days in a cottage in Devon. He had been snatched from his church in Ewell, Surrey. Kirk said that he had come to England from America to escape the unwelcome attentions of his former girlfriend Joyce, who had made his life a misery after he ended their relationship. Her friend Keith May was thought to have posed as a potential Mormon convert to entice Kirk into the getaway car.

'For Kirk, I would have skied down in the nude with a carnation up my nose . . .'

years before. She tore off his pyjamas and his Mormon 'chastity' garment (afterwards he burnt this piece of clothing because he felt it had been desecrated). Kirk claimed that during the time in the cottage he was chained to the bed, and Joyce forced him to make love to her. He said that intercourse took place on three occasions, and that the second and third times he did not object as much as the first.

Joyce claimed that the bondage routine was to help Kirk with his sex problems. She said it was three days of fun, food, and sex, and that Kirk liked being tied up. She alleged that in America he had told his mother he had been raped by Joyce, and when she was ostracized she had to leave town. She also claimed he had made her pregnant and she had had an abortion. This time she had kidnapped him because she wanted him to make her pregnant – and then he could go free. Her lawyer said that Joyce wasn't overstating her case, but of Kirk he remarked, 'Methinks the Mormon doth protest too much.' Joyce cried in court as her lawyer talked of her deep-seated, sincere love for the missionary, but the judge was not impressed and committed her for trial at the Old Bailey. Joyce was released on bail.

In February 1978 Joyce was refused permission to return home to America for her granny's funeral, and she was pictured sobbing as her mother left. The curfew that had been imposed on the bubbly blonde was lifted by a judge, however, and soon she was seen at premières, discos, and nightclubs. On 11 April she attended the première of *The Stud* with Peter Tory, the editor of the William Hickey column in the *Daily Express*, but the following day she went missing. It turned out that a van driver had been hired to take Joyce and Keith May from their flat to Paddington the morning after the première. They had already reported in to the police station, a condition of their bail. Heavily disguised, they took a taxi from Paddington to Heathrow, wearing badges saying, 'I am a deaf mute. Can you help me?' They had passports in the name of dead children. They were carrying sixty pounds of excess baggage, but they passed a note to the official on the check-out desk saying it was full of costumes for a mime show, and out of sympathy for their plight they were not charged. Before boarding the plane, they went to a photo booth and posed for pictures in their disguise and sent them to a national newspaper.

Peter Tory and a *Daily Express* photographer turned up in Atlanta and met the runaways. Joyce and Keith were disguised as Indians. Another of her disguises on the run had been a nun's outfit. She claimed she had sold her story to *Penthouse*, and said she wasn't coming back to England because she wouldn't get a fair trial.

NOT SO DUMB!

'This is not a case of the lady doth protest too much. Methinks the Mormon doth protest too much'

Then the *Daily Mirror* printed a story called 'The Real McKinney'. Joyce seemed to have left quite a lot of gaps in previous versions of her story of love among the Mormons. According to the *Mirror*, she was born in 1950 and grew up in North Carolina. In 1973 she had gone to Provo, Utah, where she was remembered as a pushy young lady who behaved extremely badly when she didn't get her way. After twice failing to win a local beauty contest, she fiddled her way into becoming Miss Utah. Then she hung around the Osmonds, and their mother later said 'she was something of a problem'. She used to cruise round town in her car, looking for promising men. In July 1975 she met Kirk; after he dumped her and went to California, she followed him. She then spent eighteen months on the vice circuit as a sex hostess. She took ads in the local papers advertising her services, offering clients a bathe, a blow-dry, and a massage on her fur-covered water-bed. She always stopped short of intercourse, according to Steve, her former flat-mate: she was 'saving herself' for Kirk, hoping to win back his affections. She even went to porno movies to learn how to improve her techniques in order to impress him. Using a variety of false names like Misty and Kathy Vaughan-Bare, she managed to save £25,000.

She met Keith May through one of her ads, and he really fell for her.

When in September 1976 Kirk got the Mormon Church to send him to England, she planned her revenge. She recruited a bodyguard and flew with him and Keith to London, taking masses of disguises and using a fake passport. The bodyguard panicked and turned back. She also lined up the pilot of a private plane to whisk Kirk off to the Continent, but he too vanished. So she ended up in the Devon cottage with her dream-boat chained to the mattress. One of her friends said Joyce was so fascinated by Kirk because he was the only man who did not want to go to bed with her.

In July 1979 Joyce and Keith were arrested in North Carolina just as she was finishing a photo session for a girlie magazine. They were charged with making false statements in order to obtain passports. They were freed on bail and told they would not be extradited to the UK. Later that year they split up over a book they were writing. Joyce said it would be the book with everything, particularly sex and religion. She phoned Peter Tory at the *Daily Express* in London. He hung up on her.

The <u>Real</u> McKinney

J
Job Wanted

Gorgeous Former
"MISS USA"
Contestant Desires Work!
Beauty Brains and Talent!—
THE BEST GAL IN THE
FREEP!
(PhD in Drama/Film, former
model, actress & state beauty
queen 38-24-36 a slim, sweet
Southern Blonde)— How
would you like HER to leisurely
bathe you, lovingly blow-
dry/style your hair, then give
you a delicious nude massage
on her fur-covered waterbed?
($100)—or try her "Fantasy
Room"—(Your fantasy is her
specialty! ___ B&D, escort
service.

Funny how the very word 'eloped' has a dated feel about it. Young people rarely elope these days. For a start they can get married younger; and secondly, perhaps parents have accepted that by sixteen their offspring are adult enough to make up their own minds about the future. Or is it that we all accept the concept of divorce more readily in the 1980s? In California, you don't need to be married to get involved in the problems of 'divorce'. Under its laws, a couple who have lived together may be deemed to have entered into the same contract as those who took marriage vows. In the Lee Marvin hearings, however, they washed their dirty linen in public just as in the divorce cases of twenty years ago.

Dr. Sam: Murderer or Victim?

Trial by Jury, Convicted by the Press

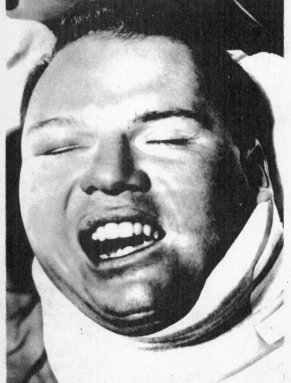

DOCTOR SAM SHEPPARD was an affluent osteopath who worked at his family-owned clinic in Cleveland, Ohio. He was married to Marilyn, his childhood sweetheart, and they were expecting their second child. They seemed the perfect society couple, enjoying sport, living in a lakeside house, and owning three cars and a boat. But Sheppard's cosy life was shattered by the events of 4 July 1954.

The previous day Sheppard, Marilyn and their son Chip had been for a picnic, and in the evening they entertained friends to dinner. Sam had fallen asleep on the couch while the others watched television before leaving. On waking he thought he heard a cry from his wife; he found her in the bedroom, savagely beaten about the head. He telephoned his neighbour, Mayor J. Spencer Houk, and said, 'I think they've killed Marilyn.'

Houk came over, and from the moment the police arrived on the scene Sheppard's life was never to be the same. For the next twenty-two years he was to unceasingly protest his innocence and undergo a series of courtroom battles that made his case a milestone in American legal history. Sheppard told the police that when he heard the cry from his wife he ran upstairs to her room, where he was hit on the head from behind with a heavy object. When he came to, he chased 'a burly intruder' down to the lake, where he was knocked out again. He staggered back to the house and telephoned his friend the Mayor.

The police were suspicious of Sheppard's story right from the start. His son Chip and their dog had slept undisturbed through the attack, there were no fingerprints and no murder weapon. Marilyn had died from twenty-seven savage blows to her skull with an instrument which the coroner described as being of a surgical type, and the police estimated that it would have taken forty seconds to inflict her injuries but only six seconds for Sheppard to have run up the stairs.

The police told Sheppard bluntly that he was the prime suspect but his friend Mayor Houk would not order his arrest. Meanwhile the local newspapers conducted a vicious campaign to get Sheppard behind bars, with headlines like WHY ISN'T SAM SHEPPARD IN JAIL – QUIT STALLING, BRING HIM IN; another article was entitled GETTING AWAY WITH MURDER. After the attack Sheppard had been admitted to hospital with a black eye, cuts around the mouth, and what his brothers claimed was a broken neck, but disbelievers said it was a mere spinal injury. Either way, he wore a neck brace in public for some time.

SOCIETY DOC ARRESTED

Although Sheppard said that his 31-year-old wife had been the only woman he'd ever loved, and offered a $10,000 reward to try and help solve the crime, his case wasn't helped by Susan Hayes, a laboratory technician, who said she had been romantically involved with Sheppard the previous March. Other women told journalists and the police that Sheppard was a womanizer and a flirt. It was said that family correspondence showed his marriage had been in some trouble for four years. Sheppard's refusal to take either a truth drug or a lie-detector test just added fuel to the growing fire of innuendo that was sweeping Cleveland.

GUILTY VERDICT

Sheppard was finally arrested on 30 July and was questioned by detectives for five days. After being released on bail, he was then rearrested at his father's house and charged with his wife's murder. Their house had become a tourist attraction, and the case filled both the local and the national newspapers. Thirty-year-old Sheppard was found guilty of second-degree murder and was sentenced to life imprisonment. The court had a 'carnival atmosphere' according to one judge.

During the years spent in jail, Sheppard never wavered from his version of events and continued to fight for a retrial. In 1959 a German divorcee called Ariane wrote to his parents telling them of her concern that an innocent man should remain in jail. Her sister had been married to Josef Goebbels, Hitler's propaganda chief. In 1961 Ariane received her first letter from Sam, and they became pen-pals. In 1963 the blonde German was allowed to visit him in jail, and declared: 'I felt as if we had known each other all our lives.' They announced their engagement and she conducted a press and television campaign protesting his innocence. This was at a time when Sheppard had appealed for clemency to the state Pardon and Parole Commission, who not only turned him down but (perhaps because of Ariane's connection with Goebbels) moved Sheppard to a maximum-security jail and refused his fiancée further visits and a marriage by proxy. By Christmas 1963 she was exhausted and suffered a nervous breakdown.

In July 1964 Sheppard was freed when Judge Weinman ruled that the original trial had been 'a mockery of justice'. He declared that the jury could not have been impartial because of the extensive press coverage of the case, and that some of the jurors had heard quotes from Sheppard's alleged mistresses on the radio during the hearing. The original judge had also acted improperly in not acceding to Sheppard's pleas that the trial be held in another location. Sheppard left jail and went to a local hotel to await the arrival of Ariane and his son Chip. He planned to marry 35-year-old Ariane that very evening, with Chip as best man. Later in the day his hopes were dashed when he was told that the judge's order had been blocked and there was a chance he might have to go straight back to jail. Ariane heard the bad news on the car radio while driving to meet her fiancé for only the second time. Luckily there was enough legal stalling to allow Sheppard to remain free, and they were married in Chicago the next weekend.

While Sheppard remained free on bail, Judge Weinman's decision to allow a retrial was overturned in May 1965 by a 2 to 1 decision in the Court of Appeals in Cincinnati. They said that although newspaper coverage of the original trial had been 'shabby', it had not prejudiced the jurors. Sheppard's lawyers continued to battle on, and in June 1966 the US Supreme Court annulled the original trial verdict and allowed a fresh trial to go ahead. But frankly, most Cleveland citizens had now lost interest in the case – after all, they felt that, after spending nearly ten years in jail, Sheppard had served his time. Meanwhile Ariane had returned to Germany, and there were rumours that the marriage was going through a shaky patch. Sheppard had returned to his practice and was once again living the affluent life.

When the second trial opened in November 1966, the scene couldn't have been more different from the hysteria of 1954. With Ariane by his side, Sheppard had a brilliant defence attorney, Lee Bailey. This time television equipment was not allowed in court, and

GUILTY!

SMUGGLED DIARIES

A week later his book, *Endure and Conquer: My Story*, was on the stands. Critics found that it had a 'ghost-written flavour' and that the only interesting part of it was the original material based on his diaries and letters smuggled out of jail. Sheppard had rebuffed homosexual advances from other prisoners, who thought he was 'square' and 'a loner'. Many books and millions of words had been written about the case – Ariane had sold a six-part syndicated story of the pen-pal romance to a newspaper chain. An experiment at a Dutch university department of parapsychology had been carried out into the case, and the results had indicated Sheppard's innocence.

Sheppard's story was described as 'an American tragedy'. In the years between the two trials his mother and Marilyn's father had both committed suicide. Not surprisingly, his book was bogged down with all the legal minutiae of the case, and one critic thought that the 'epic' book about him had yet to be written. Sheppard's case certainly brought about a change in the way that newspapers and television could comment on murder trials – he was just lucky that he came from an affluent family who could afford a protracted and expensive battle to establish his innocence.

there were few seats for the press. No one involved in the trial was allowed to make statements about it outside the courtroom. Everyone wondered if Sheppard would take the stand (a retrial usually benefits the defence unless the defendant takes the stand and the prosecutor can trap him into changing his story so that it does not match the original). In the event neither Sheppard nor his ex-mistress Susan gave evidence. The defence case was that Marilyn was killed by the jealous wife of an unnamed neighbour who may have had an affair with her. A biochemist testified that a blood spot in Marilyn's bedroom came from neither Sheppard nor his wife, but from a third adult. He also concluded that the murderer was left-handed (Sheppard was left-handed). He thought that possibly two intruders committed the crime – one a woman who killed Marilyn, the other a man who knocked Sheppard on the back of the head. A delivery man testified that he once saw Marilyn give a key to a man with whom she was having coffee. Sheppard's old friend, ex-Mayor Spencer Houk (now divorced), denied that he had ever received a key to the house. A doctor also testified that Sheppard's injuries could not have been self-inflicted since he had indeed suffered a spinal fracture. The original murder weapon had never been found, nor was any surgical instrument like it on sale. After the jury had been out just one day, Sheppard was finally acquitted. He leapt to his feet with joy and burst into tears.

Liz and Richard and Ann and Liz and Henry, Not to Mention Suzy . . .

ALTHOUGH *Cleopatra* caused Twentieth Century-Fox enormous financial problems and made them sell precious land to complete it, the film launched Burton and Taylor as the King and Queen of Movies. *Cleopatra* may have been a turgid epic, but it established Richard and Liz as a top box-office draw. They went on to make a couple of terrific films together – *The Taming of the Shrew* and *Who's Afraid of Virginia Woolf?* – but then proceeded to make some pretty serious flops. Their private life followed a similar pattern. Happily married in 1964, Burton was telling journalists in 1967: 'She wears me out with her impossible demands . . . She talks too much and too loud, she swears like a sailor, she doesn't know when to stop drinking, and she never slows down.'

Liz Will Drive Me To An Early Grave Declares Richard Burton

Burton Talks About...

LIZ
- Her Sex Problems
- Filthy Language
- Wild Booze Bouts

By 1973 they were going their separate ways, Liz in turn having tired of Burton's heavy boozing. She was pictured with Henry Wynberg, a new act in the Liz/Richard circus routine. Wynberg was born in Holland, where he trained as a bellboy and carried luggage – a useful training for one of Liz's boyfriends. He had worked as a waiter and then as a used-car salesman. He and Liz met at a party and dated a few times. When he read that she and Burton had really split, he called her in Rome to offer her a shoulder to cry on, and they spent five months together in Europe. When Liz returned to Los Angeles for an operation, Henry visited her in hospital, but Burton was next in the queue and before long Wynberg was back to selling cars. Wynberg then claimed that he and Liz had been together only to make Richard jealous, and that he was secretly engaged the whole time. True or not, reporters spotted Wynberg 'openly weeping' now that Liz and Richard were again 'an item'. In April 1974 Liz returned to Wynberg which prompted Richard to remark, 'I wouldn't buy a second-hand car off him.'

'BURTON STOLE MY WIFE'

Richard had not been idle, either. After a little scene with a waitress called Kim, he met Ann de Angelo while shooting *The Klansman*. His affair with Ann continued, and when he was taken to hosital in Los Angeles with bronchitis (some newspapers unkindly thought this might be a euphemism for a large consumption of liquid refreshment) she sped to his bedside. Newspapers declared BURTON'S LADY ANN SUED FOR DIVORCE as her husband Tony, a janitor, had plainly had enough. He then sold the story of 'How Burton Stole My Wife' to the English papers. But although work had started on sorting out a Burton/Taylor divorce, a few weeks later Lady Ann returned home to Tony in sleepy Oroville, California. The divorce came through in June 1974.

SHARK ATTACK

In October Henry turned up again, this time in court, accused of altering the milometer readings in the cars he was selling. He was fined £110, and rumoured to owe £4,000 spent on his trip to Europe to be with Liz. He made the headlines again the next January, when he was reported to have saved Liz from a shark attack while swimming. Meanwhile Burton had gone from his Lady Ann to a real member of the aristocracy, Princess Elizabeth of Yugoslavia, who had been a good friend of 'Queen' Elizabeth Taylor. Their affair had started in October 1974, when Richard had wooed and won her in a single day, saying 'We are going to be married as soon as possible.' She had taken him to see her cousin, Princess Alexandra. By November she was crowing: WE ARE IN LOVE SAYS LIZ THE SECOND, but a couple of weeks later, after barely eight weeks

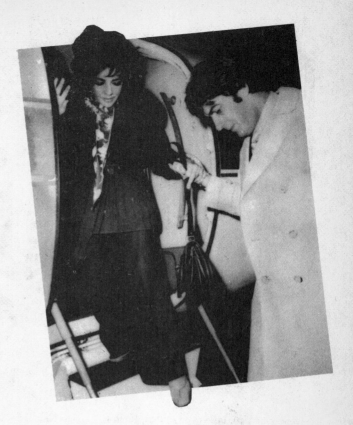

together, their affair had come to an end. But by now another lady had appeared on the scene, black model Jean Bell. Princess Elizabeth returned to England, telling Richard (via the newspapers of course), 'Darling, you are killing yourself with drink.' Jean had appeared nude in the centre spread of *Playboy*, and first met Burton on the set of *The Klansman*. Rumour had it that Burton was really covering up for her true love, a top Hollywood executive who was married. By August Jean was photographed leaving Switzerland, saying, 'It is all over between me and Richard, Elizabeth Taylor wants me out of his home.'

REMARRIAGE

When Taylor and Burton remarried later that month in Botswana, Jean revealed that it was she who had brought them back together again and had got Richard off the booze. Liz sent a limo to pick her up on her arrival back in California and Burton paid for her son to go to an expensive private school. As for Henry Wynberg, Burton claimed that 'there was never anything more than friendship between Liz and Henry'. In Hollywood, where the used-car dealer had a considerable reputation as a stud, this was thought to be unlikely, to say the least.

SUZY JOINS THE BURTON SHOW

Hunt's wife sees actor as Liz flies to Mum

After their marriage in the bush, Burton went to New York to rehearse *Equus*, and there he met 26-year-old Suzy Hunt, who had just separated from her husband, racing driver James. Liz meanwhile had an eight-day fling with a Maltese advertising man she had met in Switzerland. When she arrived in New York, Elizabeth and Burton shared the same hotel suite, but at the opening of *Equus* there was an astonishing photograph taken of Burton kissing Suzy while Liz looked on. Next day Liz was packing her bags to go home to mum, while Richard went back on the booze. Richard and Suzy became inseparable, and James Hunt flew to New York to try, unsuccessfully, to sort his marriage out. Liz and Richard were divorced, and she later married husband number seven, American politician John Warner, while Richard married Suzy Hunt.

In 1982 Richard and Suzy separated, as did Liz and her husband. When Liz came to London to star in a play in the spring, Richard turned up and they were seen out on the town together. But he returned to the filming of *Wagner* and later flew to a clinic in Los Angeles with his latest girlfriend, whom he had met on the film set. Liz was now dating a dentist, and it was firmly rumoured that she and Burton would be reunited – but only for a film.

'Nothing about him frightens me—even his rages. I have to laugh and when he runs out of gas, he laughs too'

Both S...
and Act...
Pleased

Lee, the Man Who Brought the World 'Palimony'

IN JANUARY 1979 legal history was made in America when singer and actress Michelle Triola sued actor Lee Marvin for an estimated half of his income during the six years of their affair. The affair had come to an abrupt end in May 1970 when he suddenly married his childhood sweetheart, Pamela. In November 1971 Michelle failed to receive her monthly cheque from Lee, and she decided to take him to court. When she tried to telephone Lee, Pamela (according to Michelle) told her to 'get lost' and 'find a new boyfriend'.

DRINKING

Michelle engaged the celebrated show-business lawyer Marvin Mitchelson to fight her case for the sum of £500,000 in alimony, or, as it quickly became known, 'palimony'. Michelle had changed her surname to Marvin four days before they split up, but denied that this was to gain any financial advantage. She produced letters from Marvin which showed that he accepted responsibility for looking after her. She claimed that during the six years they were together she gave up her career to look after him. The court was told of Lee's drinking: he had once dangled a young girl out of a hotel window by her foot in Las Vegas after a binge; and when Michelle tried to work as a nightclub singer, she lost her job because he turned up drunk all the time. She said that because Lee didn't want any more children she had had two abortions and one miscarriage; as a result she was unable to have children.

According to Lee, when he told Michelle he loved her, he was just making 'idle male promises'; this incensed Michelle, who then tried to claim an extra half-million pounds because he had lied to her, but the judge said that she couldn't change her plea. (Lee's first wife told newspapers that he was fighting for a cause close to his heart – male chauvinism.)

After a case lasting nearly twelve weeks, Michelle was awarded £52,000 – not quite what she had expected. She already owed a third of that amount to her

lawyer, and the judge phrased the award so that it was not an alimony payment, but rather money for her to rehabilitate herself. He said he hoped she could use it to learn new skills or to polish old ones. Michelle's reaction was mixed. It was a lot less money than she had hoped for, but she hailed it as a victory for all women, saying it paved the way for other people in similar situations. She said that men and women would have to work out an agreement in writing before they lived together, and declared, 'If a man wants to leave his toothbrush in my house, he can bloody well marry me.' Lee also claimed the verdict was a success. He described it as 'sensational ... we won on all counts'. He said it was clear that the payment was not alimony. Perhaps the person who did best out of the case was Marvin Mitchelson. He portrayed the battle as 'marriage on trial', and took on the cases of the common-law wives of actor Nick Nolte and rock star Alice Cooper. Homosexuals also hoped that they would benefit from the case, since it seemed to establish that marriage was not the only basis for claiming compensation when a relationship ended.

CHANGED MAN

Donald Zec wrote a piece about Marvin the hell-raiser, and recounted how the actor had once drunk seventeen Martinis with Richard Burton during a lunch break. In September 1980, however, Lee arrived in London with Pam and announced, 'I'm a changed man ... the older you get, the worse the hangovers become.'

THE NEW MILD MARVIN

A 'lonely hearts' advert in The Times ... that's how it all began for Christabel

How the Ad in 'The Times' Led to the Virgin Birth

CHRISTABEL RUSSELL was born in 1895, the daughter of a soldier. She was a beautiful, strong-willed girl, who was crazy about hunting and loved parties, when she answered an ad in *The Times* placed by three lonely young sailors seeking young ladies who would write to them. They met Christabel when they came home on leave, and all three immediately fell for her. After being fêted and whisked around town, she became engaged to one of them, but in the event she married another, John Russell, in 1918.

There is no doubt that Christabel was somewhat ignorant of the facts of life, and she decided that she didn't want marriage to change her hectic social life one bit. So her husband agreed that they would not have children for a few years – and to Christabel that meant no sex life. His parents, Lord and Lady Ampthill, disapproved of the marriage, and were further enraged when Christabel opened a dress shop in Mayfair. This was thought to be very *infra dig*, and she finally blotted her copybook by refusing to wear her wedding ring. Nevertheless, the unconventional marriage seemed to work, with her retiring husband staying at home while she toured the hot spots of Europe and wrote him letters about her prowess at the tango. Their sex life was non-existent except for what Christabel called 'Hunnish scenes', in which her husband walked in his sleep from his bedroom to hers and then threatened to shoot himself if she did not allow him to get into her bed. They were spending a few days at his parents' house in December 1920, when one of these distressing scenes took place. To her horror Christabel later found she was pregnant, even though full intercourse had not taken place. Her son Geoffrey was born in October 1921, but by then her husband had started divorce proceedings.

FIVE HEARINGS

The ensuing court drama was to last until 1935 and cost over £40,000, a ruinous sum of money for those days. Even then the battle wasn't over, and two branches of the Russell family found themselves locked in legal dispute in court in 1976, when the case was finally resolved after fifty-five years and five hearings. In the first divorce hearing John Russell petitioned on the grounds of Christabel's adultery with Edgar Mayer and an unnamed man, said to be the father of her son Geoffrey. Lord and Lady Ampthill were the chief witnesses. They said their son was flabbergasted when Christabel announced she was pregnant, because she had always denied him his rights as a husband. They could see no similarity between the baby and their son when he was the same age. The baby was brought into court and inspected by the jury. Christabel agreed that she had denied her husband full intercourse, and medical evidence said that she was still a virgin when pregnant. Conception had taken place without full penetration – such instances are more fully documented nowadays, but in the 1920s the case was sensational. Her defence was accepted and Russell lost the case.

MRS. RUSSELL WINS FINAL APPEAL.

MAJORITY VERDICT IN HOUSE OF LORDS.

£40,000 COSTS.

HUSBAND GIVEN LEAVE TO APPLY FOR NEW TRIAL.

WHICH BABY IS THE BARON?

Rival barons in 'virgin birth' battle look the other way

There was another trial in 1922, however, and fashionable society queued round the block for seats for a re-run of the 'virgin birth' case as it had come to be known. This time the jury found that she had had intercourse with an unknown man, and the baby was declared illegitimate. Russell was granted a divorce. She lost her appeal, but won in the House of Lords. Two years later, as guardian of her son, she brought an action to establish his legitimacy and his right to the baronetcy. In 1926 Geoffrey Russell was declared the rightful heir. The marriage was finally dissolved in 1937, when Christabel divorced her husband. She lived off the income from her dress shop and an allowance from her ex-husband, and she and Geoffrey had a wonderful time together travelling all over the world. She was totally devoted to her son, who grew up to be a theatrical impresario.

CASE RE-OPENED

John Russell inherited the title of Ampthill on the death of his father. Before his death in 1973 he had remarried twice, but Geoffrey, his ignored son, expected to inherit the title. Indeed, he was named as heir in all the obituaries. He wrote to the House of Lords requesting to take his seat, but was told that his half-brother John Russell (by Ampthill's third marriage) had already applied for it. And so the legal wrangle over whether Geoffrey was the legitimate heir to the title was re-opened. This time it was heard by a committee of the House of Lords.

The hearings deeply distressed Christabel. She thought the matter had been closed years before, but it just shows how bitter Russell's family had been over the original marriage. When the case opened in February 1976, the House of Lords committee heard much of the same evidence that had been used in the 1926 illegitimacy dispute. John Russell offered to withdraw if Geoffrey would take a blood test. In April the House of Lords gave the title to Geoffrey. He said he had contested the case to preserve his mother's honour. She died before the decision was announced, and his family were said to be very bitter at the young John Russell for raising the issue all over again.

Hijinks Affairs

When a public figure has an affair, it rarely gets written about until some event forces it on the public's attention. In Billie Jean King's case, a disgruntled ex-hairdresser with a penchant for suicide bids let the press say openly what they had been hinting at for years. Jean Harris fits the bill of the lover as 'victim'. She had been replaced by a younger woman and became a human doormat. Onassis couldn't keep his affairs private, since they involved such well-known personalities.

'Integrity Jean'
and the Casanova Diet King

ONE MARCH EVENING in 1980 Jean Harris, a highly respectable headmistress of a girls' school in Virginia, drove up to New York State to spend the weekend with her lover, Dr Herman (Hi to his pals) Tarnower, co-author of the best-selling *Complete Scarsdale Medical Diet*. Tarnower, aged sixty-nine, lived in a lavish mansion in one of the most expensive areas in the world. It was a life-style he could well afford – it was estimated he had made about £6 million on the diet book, which he and his co-author prefaced with generous thanks to Mrs Harris for 'her splendid assistance'. But Jean was more than Herman's helper; she was also his lover, and had been so for fourteen years. She had tolerated the thirty or so affairs the ageing doctor had had with other women during that time, because she believed that ultimately it was her he really cared about. He had won her with roses and holidays abroad, and she spent her weekends in his company. Seven years before, however, Tarnower had engaged a new administrative assistant, 38-year-old Lynne Tryforos. The younger woman became the doctor's lover too, and Jean Harris felt a growing sense of rejection.

Two days before the weekend in question, Jean wrote to Herman after she discovered that he was planning to take Lynne to a dinner being held in honour of his achievements. The 'Scarsdale letter' was an eight-page outpouring of bitterness, and in it she called Lynne a 'dishonest adultress . . . a slut and a psychotic whore'.

Head guilty

Jean thought that Herman should stop seeing Mrs Tryforos because she felt there was no room for anything second-rate in his life. She even talked of considering plastic surgery to make herself young again to rekindle his love for her. Tarnower never received the letter. Jean drove up to the house, and on entering the bedroom saw a nightie and a set of hair curlers that did not belong to her. There was an argument and she produced a gun. Shots were fired, and Tarnower was hit three times. He later died. The maid called the police and they arrested Jean as she was about to drive away from the house. She was charged with murder and released on bail.

At the trial in February 1981 Jean claimed that she killed her lover by accident while he struggled to stop her from killing herself. The prosecution alleged that she deliberately shot him because she was jealous about Mrs Tryforos replacing her in his affections.

CLOTHES SWITCHED

American papers described it as 'the trial with everything' – sex, money, murder, and snobbery. The court heard stories of holidays in Greece and on the French Riviera, of dinner parties in Paris, and of Jean finding notes from other lovers pushed under the door of their hotel room. Another girlfriend sent Herman a loving message through the columns of the local paper where he was staying. It transpired that Herman's housekeeper was instructed to remove all traces of one woman's stay before the other came to visit; clothes were switched from wardrobes and cosmetics removed from the bathroom. Jean Harris was visibly

with Mrs Harris. As far as they were concerned, she was a woman who had been wronged by her lover, and he had got what he deserved. She said that Herman had once proposed and then cancelled the wedding. Lynne had been his lover for at least five years, and when Jean received a copy of Herman's will sent through the post anonymously, she found her name scratched out and Lynne's inked in. At the time of the murder, Jean was under a lot of pressure at school: she had had to expel four girls for drugs and the governors were giving her a tough time. It turned out that she was more or less addicted to tranquillizers and amphetamines, which were given to her by Herman. On one visit to his house, she found her clothes slashed with a razor. By now five people in the court were writing instant books on the subject.

But Jean Harris didn't arouse much sympathy amongst younger women. She was headlined as THE ULTIMATE UNLIBERATED WOMAN – the sort that would do anything, no matter how degrading, to keep a man. It was felt that she was doing her best to seduce the jury of eight women and four men, but after eight days of deliberation, they reached a verdict of guilty. Jean told her lawyer, 'I can't sit in jail', and she became hysterical. It was revealed that Tarnower had left Jean £96,000 in his will which she would lose if the conviction was upheld.

Jean, who had been nicknamed 'Integrity Harris' by her pupils because it was a word she used so often, spent her first nights in jail since the actual arrest. She began a partial hunger strike and said she would not live like an animal in a cage. During the trial she had told friends that she would not spend one night in jail, but one month later she was sentenced to at least

f murdering her lover

embarrassed when her underwear was produced in court. One of the most intriguing aspects of the saga was how bespectacled, ageing Tarnower, the man whose book promised that you could lose from fourteen to twenty pounds in weight in fourteen days, obviously kept his weight down with a sex life that was, to put it crudely, rampant.

When Jean finished her evidence, there wasn't a dry eye in the house. Members of the public cheered and broke into spontaneous applause. The case was described as a 'woman's trial': the gallery was full of 35- to 55-year-old matrons who strongly sympathized

fifteen years, the minimum the judge could impose after the jury had found her guilty of second-degree murder. The judge said, 'I wish the events of 10 March had never taken place and that you'd never left Virginia. I found you to be a brilliant woman. But the best I can say to you is "Best of luck".' Jean called the sentence 'a travesty'. Mrs Tryforos remained silent, as she had done since the killing.

In May NBC-TV transmitted a three-hour dramatization of her trial, and the reviewers thought it was 'excellent' television. A woman spectator outside the court told a journalist, 'Men are all the same ... they say they love you, say they'll be yours for ever, and then some piece of skirt comes along and they're off with the speed of light.'

The Unhappy Trio:
Maria, Ari, and Jackie

MARIA CALLAS, star of the operatic world, and Aristotle Onassis, one of the world's richest men, met at a ball in Venice in 1957. Onassis attended with his wife Tina and Maria was accompanied by her husband Meneghini. It was noted that Ari definitely noticed Maria. In December 1958 Ari sent her roses when she appeared at a charity gala in Paris. This time her husband definitely did notice. When they met Ari the following spring and he invited them to go on his yacht, the *Christina*, Maria demurred because she had to sing at Covent Garden. Ari told her he would be there. This time his wife noticed, for he had never shown any interest whatsoever in the opera.
On 21 June he and Tina saw the performance, and afterwards he threw a party for Maria at the

Dorchester. In July Maria and her husband went on a cruise on the *Christina*, and by the end of it their marriage was over – Maria had fallen for Ari. Onassis told Meneghini he loved Maria, and while Meneghini filed for a legal separation Maria and Onassis flew together from Nice to Milan and then to Rome. She made a public statement about the end of her marriage, but denied a romance with Ari. Tina filed for divorce in New York, naming not Maria but an old school friend. Onassis tried to persuade his wife not to divorce him – he was reluctant to marry Maria and preferred the idea of a famous lover. When Maria hinted publicly that she would like to marry him, he just ignored it. The pattern of their relationship was set: it appears that although they had a terrific sex life, he couldn't cope with a woman so talented and successful in her own right. This is why he ultimately married Jackie Kennedy, who was as famous as Maria, who could also deal easily with great wealth and the jet-set life he loved, but who was a woman with absolutely no career of her own. Maria was too like a man for Ari, and his ego couldn't stand it.

The effect of their relationship on Maria's singing became increasingly apparent. She reduced the number of performances she gave and eventually had to take pills to sleep, pills to go on stage, and injections to calm her nerves. Every summer Maria and Onassis would go on a long cruise, and all the problems would be forgotten; she would stop rehearsing and just relax.

JACKIE FLIES TO MARRY ONASSIS

JACKIE IS FRIGID

JACKIE'S HONEYMOON WAS A FLOP
...She Locked Onassis Out Of Her Bedroom

They did this in 1961 and 1962, when Maria sang at President Kennedy's birthday party in America. Ari had become very friendly with Jackie's sister Lee, and scandal sheets thought they were having an affair. In 1963 Jackie gave birth to a son who died the next day, and Ari offered her his yacht for a cruise to cheer her up. Jack Kennedy was most unenthusiastic about the arrangement. Like Meneghini, who had also hated the prospect of a trip on the *Christina*, Jack seemed to sense what might happen. In the event, in spite of him saying it looked bad politically, Jackie went. She took her sister and another couple as chaperones, and Maria stayed at home in Paris. The press went wild about it. When the trip ended, Ari gave Jackie and Lee expensive jewellery as presents. The day after Kennedy's funeral, Ari attended a dinner at the White House – he had already become that close to Jackie.

WEDDING

For the next few years he see-sawed between the two women. Although Maria knew about his affairs, she deeply resented being supplanted by Jackie. The next summer, the summer of 1967, friends noticed that she and Onassis were not getting on so well. By the autumn Jackie and Onassis were being photographed together in nightclubs. He was definitely wooing her, and in January 1968 Ari's name was added to the list of her potential husbands. Finally it was announced that Ari and Jackie were to marry. The wedding took place three days later, on 20 October 1968, on Ari's private island of Skorpios. The same day, Maria was photographed attending a film première in Paris and a party at Maxim's, and Onassis was reported to have sent her a diamond-studded belt as a parting gift. A few weeks later the gossip columnists were hinting that the honeymoon was a flop as Ari discovered that Jackie was stand-offish and not as liberated about sex as he was. There were even stories that she locked him out of their room on the wedding night. Whatever the truth, he did spent part of their honeymoon doing business, and she soon flew back to New York. Ari then started trying to see Maria all over again, and they had dinner together.

By the end of 1969 Jackie had spent over $1½ million, and Ari was reported to be fed up. As Onassis and Jackie spent more and more time apart, the press began to hint that there was something seriously wrong with the marriage. Divorce was hinted at in July 1969, less than a year after they had tied the knot. Their sexual incompatibility was the source of much speculation, and when letters Jackie had written to her old friend Roswell Kilpatric were published in February 1970, Ari hit the roof. One, written while she was on her honeymoon, said, 'I hope you know all you were and are and will be to me.' Onassis was then seen out on the town in Paris with Maria, and Kilpatric's wife sued for divorce. Jackie arrived in Paris and insisted on eating at the same table in the same restaurant as Ari had taken Maria to. In order to taunt Jackie, Ari visited Maria again, knowing that the photographs would end up in the press. The meeting took place on a Greek island on Maria's patron saint's day, and he presented her with jewellery. The photo of them kissing appeared around the world. However, their relationship subsequently cooled again, and Maria had an affair with the singer Pippo di Stefano.

WILL REWRITTEN

In January 1974 Onassis and Jackie flew to Acapulco (where she had spent her honeymoon with Jack), and while they argued he rewrote his will on the plane, making his daughter Christina the chief beneficiary. He finally decided to divorce Jackie, having started proceedings in 1972. But early in 1975, Onassis fell gravely ill, and during his hospitalization Jackie was shunned by his family and aides. After his death she didn't observe a period of mourning. When the will was revealed, she found she had been left only a bit more than the faithful servants, although she was also given an allowance for her children and a share in the island and the yacht. As Christina was barely speaking to her, negotiations started to try to buy Jackie out so that they need never have to meet again, and in November 1976 it was announced that Christina had paid Jackie about £5 million for her shares in Skorpios and the yacht, on agreement that she broke all ties with the family and abandoned all claims on the estate. Jackie ended up with double her original provision under the terms of the will and about seven times what Ari had been planning to offer her if they divorced. As a widow she was better off than ever. In contrast, Maria became a virtual recluse; she died in September 1977 of a heart attack in her flat in Paris.

Yes, she emerged richer as a widow than she had ever been as a wife...

Billie Jean King confesses affair with woman and her husband says: It makes no difference

YES, WE WERE LOVERS

Love-All
and Billie Jean Loses Out

AT THE END OF April 1981 a scandal rocked America, which was just settling in under its arch-conservative President, Ronald Reagan. The man who was once reported to be upset that his son had chosen a career as a ballet dancer because it did not seem terribly masculine, could not have been too happy with the revelation that Billie Jean King, one of the country's top sportswomen, was accused by a former secretary of having a lesbian affair with her that had lasted seven years.

The story emerged when 32-year-old Marilyn Barnett filed a court action in Los Angeles under the California 'palimony' laws, demanding financial support for life and a house in Malibu worth around £350,000. (In 1977 the California Supreme Court had decided that unmarried couples could draw up contracts for division of property and money in the event of their relationship coming to an end. The most famous test case had been that of Michelle Triola and actor Lee Marvin, where she had been awarded £52,000 'rehabilitation' money.) In this action, Marilyn was also setting a precedent: it was the first time that a well-known person had been the subject of a 'palimony' case involving a relationship with a member of their own sex. Marilyn said that she had met six-times Wimbledon singles champion Billie Jean in 1972. She gave up her job as a hairdresser to

concentrate full-time on being Billie Jean's personal assistant. After six months they had moved on to a sexual relationship, and Marilyn claimed that Billie Jean told her, 'Go buy yourself a house.' They lived together in the house in Malibu, sharing the mortgage payments, and spent time in New York together at Billie Jean's flat there. Marilyn claimed that after her affair with the tennis star ended in 1979, Billie Jean and her husband Larry, whom she had married in 1965, asked her to move out of the house so that they could sell it. She demanded compensation from Mr King for his part in the eviction demands, and said that the property was in her name as well as Billie Jean's.

The country was astounded by these revelations, and Billie Jean issued a statement saying she was 'shocked and disappointed' by Ms Barnett's action. She also said the allegations about her sex life were 'untrue and unfounded'. Her friends said that her marriage was sound and there was no hint of any problems. On 1 May, however, Billie Jean changed her tune and decided to come clean. She admitted that she and Marilyn had been lovers and said their affair had been over for some time. At a news conference attended by her parents and her husband, she leant her head on his shoulder and declared, 'I've decided to talk with you as I've always talked – from the heart.' She thanked Larry and said he had been her lover and her best friend for nineteen years. She called the affair a 'mistake' and said that she would assume responsibility for it.

Billie Jean is sued by 'woman lover'

Another thing to emerge was that Billie Jean had known for some time that Marilyn would sue her. It turned out that since their relationship had ended, the former hairdresser had tried to kill herself on two occasions: the first time, she had thrown herself off the balcony of the Malibu house and broken her back – she was now confined to a wheelchair – and the second time, she took an overdose.

TIP OF THE ICEBERG

Billie Jean said publicly that she felt her behaviour had 'stained' the sport, and offered to resign as the President of the Women's Tennis Association. She received many letters of support and her friends rallied round her. While some tennis stars like Wendy Turnbull and Pam Shriver spoke out to defend Billie Jean, other people claimed that lesbians on the tennis circuit were now 'scared to death' and were 'closing ranks'. According to the American press, Billie Jean's story was just the tip of the iceberg. The *New York Daily News* said at least six other top players had had

lesbian affairs, and named Martina Navratilova as one of them. She lived with lesbian rights campaigner Rita Mae Brown, but denied that they were lovers. An Italian tennis star said that affairs between the top players were common. It emerged that when Tracy Austin was fourteen she had been propositioned in the locker rooms, after which the family supplied a female bodyguard until her mother took over as chaperone. Australian player Michele Tyler said that lesbianism was 'rife' on the world circuit and it was one of the reasons why she had given up professional tennis three years before.

Billie Jean's husband: It's all my fault

In spite of all these declarations, many people thought that Billie Jean's private life should remain private. Nevertheless, she gave a television interview in which she said she had offered her husband a divorce. He admitted he felt 'a twinge of jealousy' when he found out about the affair, but said that at the time he was partly to blame because he was so wrapped up in his considerable business interests that he hadn't devoted enough care and attention to his wife. Larry declared he would have felt more 'threatened' if her lover had been a man. It looked as if whichever way the court case went, Billie Jean would be the loser: she managed to get an injunction preventing publication of her letters to Marilyn – who had been offered over £12,000 by a newspaper for them – but she faced the withdrawal of valuable sponsors and product endorsements. It seemed that the advertisers of America could not handle a lesbian affair quite as well as Billie Jean and her understanding Larry.

The stars rally to Billie Jean

MELANIE'S MR. GOODBAR

Buddy and Melanie

HOWARD 'BUDDY' JACOBSEN has been described as 'the greatest American social-climber since Jay Gatsby'. Certainly he was a compulsive liar – he claimed to be half Indian and half Italian when in fact he was Jewish, and his model girlfriend thought he was thirty-three when in reality he was forty-nine. Buddy was a highly successful horse-trainer by the mid 1960s, and he was the first to give a woman jockey a ride in New York State, But Buddy was obsessed by two things – power and girls. Even though he was earning around $100,000 a year, he kept ending up broke, and he felt that his comfortable life in Queens with a wife and two sons just wasn't his style. So Buddy started out to change his life. He became a landlord to would-be fashion models with a house on 84th Street on Manhattan's East Side, but what the girls attracted by low rents didn't know was that their friendly landlord had bugged their rooms and was tapping their phones! Buddy was by now investing in real estate and building a glamorous circle of friends around him.

The saga that ended with Buddy behind bars for second-degree murder started the day that he met model Melanie Cain. She had come from the Mid-West in July 1973 at the age of seventeen to be a model, and was immediately accepted by the prestigious Ford Agency in New York. She was successful right from the start, landing her first job in the VO5 hair-conditioner ad. One day a model friend invited Melanie back to her apartment, which happened to be in Buddy's building. Later, on a modelling assignment by the pool in the building, she met Jacobsen, and within a few weeks she had moved into one of the

He wanted to own her

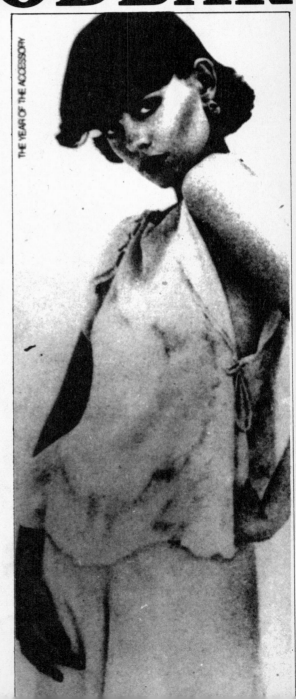

THE YEAR OF THE ACCESSORY

Trouble in singles world

apartments. He pursued her avidly, inviting her out to dinner (which she at first refused), sending her flowers and sleeping outside her door. Buddy had style – he had led a whole bunch of his friends away from oh-so-trendy Elaine's to another restaurant, Nicola's, and in 1969 he had taken part in a racing strike that had cost him his trainer's licence and the New York Racing Association several million dollars in revenues. So Buddy was famous for getting his way, and by December 1973 Melanie gave in to him and their affair started.

As Melanie became more and more successful, she grew dissatisfied with the Ford Agency, and Buddy suggested that she should start her own. So the My Fair Lady Agency was born, with Buddy naturally 'taking care' of the legal and business side of things while for some months Melanie, a highly sought-after model, was the only girl on the books, and in their bid to expand the business the couple started touring the country looking for new talent to sign up. Buddy liked them as young as possible, and while Melanie was on the road he was impressing the nubile young recruits, often between the sheets. One day Melanie returned to find him in bed with another girl and walked out in tears. In fact Melanie was to leave Buddy seven times

altogether, including the final break. She just kept going back. But she was beginning to have serious doubts about his age, and went to the New York public library, where, after digging in the files, she discovered her lover was not in his thirties as he had claimed, but almost fifty. He had tried to pass himself off as thirty-four with fake ID cards, and it later turned out that the boys he said were his brothers were really his sons. Melanie met again a man whom she had met with Buddy a couple of years before. His name was Jack Tupper, and he was co-owner of a bar. They had dinner. This time she told Buddy she was leaving for good, and that she was in love with Jack. Jack Tupper then disappeared and his charred body was found in the Bronx with multiple stab wounds and lacerations.

Nearly two years later, after the longest trial in the history of the Bronx, involving seventy-nine witnesses, Buddy Jacobsen was convicted of second-degree murder. After a month of his sentence, during which he spent the time wheeling and dealing from his prison cell, Buddy managed to walk out. After forty days he was recaptured in California, where he was discovered learning to roller-skate and thinking of starting up in business again by buying a local rink.

Hijinks

Unique People

Ever since the first sex-change operations were discussed in the press in the 1950s the public's curiosity about them has continued. Trans-sexualism is now more openly discussed, but this doesn't mean that the general attitude is any more sympathetic. After the first wave of interest in sex-change operations, attention focused on how these people were managing to carry on their lives. There were divorces, marriages, and sad stories about their children. As more people underwent this kind of surgery, new ethical and moral questions were raised. But as long as the media turn the spotlight on these people they will find it difficult to fit into society.

Christine Jorgensen – the GI Who Became the 'Woman of the Year'

CHRISTINE JORGENSEN created an international sensation in 1952 when it was discovered that the blond, blue-eyed GI George, who had left New York in 1949 to see Europe and have fun, had been transformed into a 26-year-old glamour girl. Christine, who had been a male transvestite, had had a sex-change operation in Copenhagen and was now said (by reporters) to be 'more attractive than the average woman' – whatever that might mean. Christine was trying to work as a photographer and wasn't too pleased when the news leaked out about her former existence. She didn't think it would help her in her career. She'd made a film and was planning to take it on a lecture tour, but feared this would be impossible because of her notoriety. It was reported that William Calhoun, a 24-year-old GI, had been granted leave because of the way his friends had pulled his leg after they discovered that his girlfriend, whose picture was pinned up above his bunk, was Christine. On 7 December 1952 the *Mirror* told readers that Bill was writing to tell Christine that the news about her operation did not affect their relationship. He always thought she was a proper woman and now he saluted her courage. It was disclosed that Christine had had a long series of operations – and not just the one everyone had thought – as well as a rumoured 2,000 injections. When she returned home from hospital reporters asked her ridiculous questions like 'Do you

I WAS A MAN

THE FRANKEST STORY FOR YEARS

wear pyjamas or a nightie? Do you shave? Will you have children?' and perhaps most ludicrous of all, 'Do you like ball games or needlework?'

DETAILS REVEALED

In February 1953 her story appeared in the *Sunday Pictorial*, and the public, unused to such operations, waited eagerly for more details. A Scandinavian doctor testified that Christine was now a woman; the American Ambassador in Denmark signed a certificate saying that Christine was legally a woman. Christine told *Sunday Pictorial* readers that as a child she had wanted dollies and not a toy train. She had not liked the rough fabric that boys' clothes were made of or the ordeal of going to summer camp. Her long eyelashes had been much admired by little girls. She declared that she was selling her story to help others

like her who had not yet had the operations necessary, and said 'isolation bore down heavily on me'.

To get over his feeling of being different from everyone else, George decided to develop an interesting career. After taking a course in photography, he had taken a job with Pathé News, but was then called up. He had fallen in love with an older boy, but became very worried about the relationship, and never let him find out he was a transvestite. After his discharge from the army he had been unable to get his old job back at Pathé, so he had gone to Hollywood and ended up filling shelves in a supermarket. Then he had gone to a school for medical technicians in New York to learn about hormones and to see if he could become a woman. A doctor had told him it was impossible, but he had secretly got hold of female hormones and started to take them. As his body began to change, he had read that Scandinavian doctors might be able to help, and went to Copenhagen, resolving that 'George' would not be coming back.

GUINEA PIG

He met Dr Hamburger and underwent a series of operations, for which he was not charged a fee by the surgeons, as he was a guinea-pig case. After the first operation, when his testicles were removed, he got a female passport. He then underwent the final plastic surgery.

Christine was awarded the Scandinavian 'Woman of the Year' award, in 1953. The operation was attacked by critics for turning her into a sexless being, a 'demasculinized' person. Because it was illegal for the sex glands to be removed in the United States it was thought that perhaps Christine was the first American sex-change. Some prisons in America had experimented with voluntary emasculation for sex-offenders, as an alternative to a long sentence. When the *Mirror* reporter asked her if she liked being a woman better than a GI Christine told him, 'Don't be insulting.' She said she had received many moving letters from trans-sexuals and this encouraged her to tell her story.

By November 1953 she was making a lot of money as a cabaret artiste and nightclub singer. She became engaged to an artist, but the engagement came to nothing. In April 1959 she wanted to marry a certain Howard Knox, but she was refused a marriage licence because her birth certificate said she was male. A film, *The Christine Jorgensen Story*, was made. She cut a glamorous figure in a skin-tight satin shorts suit (aged fifty-five) as she re-launched her nightclub act in 1981, in New York, but she had never married.

"Perfect" Manservant

MASQUERADE OF HARD-WORKING WOMAN

Detective Recalls "Marriage" To A Girl And Old Bailey Case

THEFT CHARGE : £1 FINE

Woman's Pose As Knight, Soldier, Chef, Actor And Cricketer

The Woman Who was a Cricketer, 'Colonel', Actor, and the Perfect Manservant

YOU CAN'T BE SENT to jail for dressing up as a member of the opposite sex. But in the 1920s a cruel judge made 'Colonel Barker' a laughing-stock by declaring that because she turned out to be a woman, and hadn't revealed this when marrying another lady in 1923, she had 'outraged the decencies of nature and profaned the house of God'. The judge gave her a nine-months' sentence, and from then on Colonel Barker changed employment all the time, used different names, and finally managed to die in anonymity. She was a curiosity because her pose was so studied. Not content with wearing a suit, she invented a wonderful *alter ego* for herself, and slapped a few medals in with it.

During the trial on the charge of making a false entry in a marriage register, the full story of Colonel Barker

emerged. She had been born Lilias Irma Valerie, in Jersey, the daughter of a sportsman who had desperately wanted a son. He taught her to box, fence, and play cricket, and she was educated at a convent in Brussels. In 1918 Lilias married an Australian, Harold Arkell-Smith, but it didn't take long for the marriage to flop, and she went off to run a tea-shop in Warminster with a girlfriend. Then she met another Australian, Pearce Crouch, and they lived together.

BACHELOR

She had two children, a boy and a girl. By 1923 she dressed as a man and changed her name to Captain Barker. In November of that year she 'married' a chemist's daughter in a church in Brighton, and gave her marital status as 'bachelor'. She told her 'wife' she couldn't consummate the marriage because of war wounds, and then promoted herself to Colonel and added a DSO for good measure.

SHE POSED AS A 'HUSBAND' FOR 30 YEARS

"COL. BARKER" ACQUITTED

REVELATIONS AT TRIAL FOR THEFT

Fear Of "Many Things Which Might Be Discovered"

COURT TANGLE OF "HE" & "SHE"

"Col. Barker's Secret"

As the Colonel, she toured Britain acting with a repertory company playing male roles. She ran an antique shop, went hunting and even joined a cricket club. Her real sex was never guessed. She helped to run a farm, and joined the Fascist movement.

RAID

In 1927, after a raid on their headquarters, she made her first appearance in court, charged in the name of Colonel Barker and accused of keeping a gun without a licence. She was led into court by a friend, wearing bandages over her eyes, and claimed to be blind from a war wound. She was acquitted. In 1928 she lived with an actress in Mayfair as man and wife, but the following year was declared bankrupt. When she failed to turn up for the hearing, a warrant was issued for her arrest. In March she was taken to jail, where it was discovered she was a woman. After being remanded on bail, she was later charged with making a false entry in a marriage register. From that moment on, Colonel Barker was front-page news.

In 1934 she was arrested in the name of John Hill while working as a kennel hand, charged with stealing a lady's handbag. Again her secret was revealed in court. She was acquitted, and moved on to another job and another name. In 1937 she was working as a butler to a lady in London when she was arrested on the charge of stealing £5 from her employer, who described her as 'the perfect manservant'. Everyone had been convinced she was a man. Colonel Barker was fined £1 with £5 costs. During the Second World War her son (then in the RAF) wrote to her, convinced she was his father. He never discovered the truth, and was killed on a bombing raid. Colonel Barker served in the Home Guard and lived in a Suffolk village with her 'wife' Eva, who died in 1957. She was known now as Geoffrey Norton.

When she died in 1960 it was some time before the national press found out, for she had specifically requested that she was to be buried with no publicity. Everyone in the village was astounded at the news. Except the vicar – he had already guessed.

The press loves them when they're good, but loves them better when they're bad. The rest of us watch on as though their lives are the stuff of the silver screen. They inhabit that heady realm where the air is thin, the music is loud, the money and the champagne flow freely. They're mean and wild and (they sometimes feel) beyond reproach. And we watch on in rapturous fascination at their antics – be they family feuds, affairs, or murders.

Sunny's kids tell on Step–Dad Claus

As Sunny Sleeps, Claus is Convicted

IT WAS A TRIAL tailor-made for the press. It had all the ingredients of the Scarsdale murder case just a few months before, and more: money, power, drugs, sex, and, as a special attraction, the beautiful victim lay in an irreversible coma in a New York hospital.

The Sleeping Beauty trial, as it was nicknamed, featured balding yet charming Claus Von Bulow, accused of administering deadly insulin shots to his wife, Sunny (proper name, Martha Crawford Von Anersperg Von Bulow), with the ultimate intention (according to the prosecution) of killing her and

inheriting her wealth so that he could marry his glamorous actress mistress, Alexandra Isles. The case divided not only the family – Sunny's children by her previous marriage and the staff at the family home all came out against Claus – but also New York and Newport society. Claus had made plenty of friends among America's rich and powerful, and many ladies rushed to his defence; against them were ranged the cynics who regarded him as a fortune-seeker who had married old money to better himself.